Irish Politics and Social Conflict
in The Age of
The American Revolution

CURRAGH CO. KILDARE

DUF
6 MTS
OUT 2 WEEKS
BACK IN FOR
14 DAYS. haha
90/91

IRA

OUT SOON

CROW ATHY
CO KILDARE
18 MTS
90/91

Irish Politics and Social Conflict in the Age of the American Revolution

by

Maurice R. O'Connell

Assistant-Professor in History
Fordham University

Philadelphia
University of Pennsylvania Press

7462
Printed in the United States of America

To My Wife

Preface

Despite the appearance of some books and articles on specialized topics, there has been no general study of Irish history at the time of the American Revolution since Lecky's *A History of Ireland in the Eighteenth Century.* This remarkable work, written about 1880 as part of his English history, is now long out of date. As was the fashion in Lecky's day, Irish historians have until recent times tended to emphasize the purely political aspects of the national story. The availability of much new material and the heightened interest in social developments call for a new and more comprehensive study of this important period. The present work deals with Ireland for the nine years, 1775 to 1783, from just before the outbreak of the American Revolutionary War until about a year after its conclusion.

For valuable guidance and advice I am deeply grateful to Professor Holden Furber of the University of Pennsylvania and to Professor R. Dudley Edwards of University College, Dublin. I am much in debt to Ashley Powell, B.A., of the Irish Bar whose advice on Irish land tenure saved me from serious error. My gratitude is also due to Professor Leonidas Dodson of the University of Pennsylvania; Professor Robert E. Burns of the University of Notre Dame, who enabled me to examine valuable material; Brigadier Maurice D. Jephson, C.B.E., for placing important family documents at my disposal; Eric J. McAuliffe, who investigated several points on my behalf; Basil O'Connell, K.M., whose knowledge and understanding have been very important to my work; and Eoin O'Mahony, K.M., whose insight into the Irish past has been of great value.

I should also like to record my appreciation of the assistance of Miss Josephine O'Conor, Max Neville of the Irish Bar, Liam O'Brien, Sean O'Reilly, Maurice Twomey, Thomas J. O'Neill of the Irish National Library, and the Hon. Desmond Guinness.

I am indebted to the University of Pennsylvania and to the University of Portland for aiding me financially in carrying out my research. The Director and Staff of the National Library of Ireland very graciously gave me every possible assistance. I should like to thank also the officials of both the London Public Record Office and the Manuscript Department of the British Museum.

Maurice R. O'Connell

Contents

List of Illustrations

Irish Politics and Social Conflict
in The Age of
The American Revolution

I

Introduction

By the middle of the eighteenth century Ireland had begun to experience a considerable increase in wealth and population. Dublin and many provincial towns were growing in size and architectural significance; the erection of elegant town houses and classical public buildings, and the inauguration of a town planning which today we recognize as distinctively Georgian, reflected this increase in prosperity. Agricultural development provided the landowning classes with higher rents which in turn led to the building of mansions, great and small, to an extent which has induced observers in the twentieth century to regard the typical "gentleman's residence" as a Georgian house dating from the second half of the eighteenth century. The most celebrated account of this economic and cultural progress comes from Arthur Young who travelled through Ireland in the late seventeen-seventies:

Ireland has been absolutely new-built within these twenty years . . . cities, towns, and country seats . . . the roads . . . are now in a state that do honour to the kingdom . . . the rents of land have at least doubled in twenty-five years, which is a most unerring proof of a great prosperity.

And he concludes with the assertion that

upon the whole, we may safely determine that, judging by those appearances and circumstances, which have been generally agreed to mark the prosperity or declension of a country, Ireland has since the year 1748 made as great advances as could possibly be expected, perhaps greater than any other country in Europe.[1]

This conclusion is borne out by the Irish Revenue Commissioners in 1779 when they refer to the "great increase of building in the towns and universal rise of rents and price of land."[2]

This fair picture told only part of the story for the land was deeply divided along religious, racial, and economic lines. These divisions were rooted in the past among a people who, even as early as Norman times, had shown little aptitude for assimilation. The large majority, probably more than two-thirds of the population, were Catholics; the remainder were divided into Anglicans (members of the Church of Ireland) and Presbyterians. The Anglicans included perhaps 90 per cent of the landowning classes, practically the entire body of lawyers, officers in the army and navy, and holders of political and administrative positions. In addition, they held what amounted to a monopoly of parliamentary seats: Catholics were *legally* excluded, and Presbyterians, owing to the Test Act, which debarred them from membership of corporations, and because they formed no appreciable part of the landowning classes, were *virtually* excluded. The latter lived almost entirely in the northern counties where, together with an indefinable number of Anglicans, they were descendants of the settlers planted during the reign of James I in what is called the Ulster Plantation. Because they composed middle and lower classes, the Presbyterians were more securely based than the Anglicans, who were throughout most of the country a tiny ruling minority. There also existed in the northern counties a Catholic population; and relations between Presbyterians and Catholics had been traditionally hostile. Thus, no part of the Protestant population, Anglican or Dissenter, can be regarded as having felt entirely secure.

Constitutionally, Ireland was an independent kingdom governed by King, Lords, and Commons. But as the king was the King of Great Britain, and virtually all the more important political and judicial offices lay in his nomination on the advice of the British Cabinet, Ireland was less independent than most of the American colonies. Its parliament, of medieval origin and possessing two chambers —Lords and Commons—had nearly all the pomp and ceremony of its English elder sister, but less real freedom than some of the American assemblies. The House of Lords, composed of bishops of the Church of Ireland appointed by the British government, and a large number of temporal peers enjoying governmental favors of one kind or another, performed a function usually subservient to the Administration. The House of Commons consisted of three hundred members, of whom sixty-four represented the thirty-two counties, two sat for Dublin University, and the remainder represented boroughs—a term which, for convenience, can be used to include cities, towns, manors, and the election districts officially entitled boroughs. The majority of the boroughs were little more than villages and were normally under the control of patrons who were usually landed aristocrats. Most of these patrons were committed to the support of the Government in return for favors of one kind or another. Thus, the Irish Parliament was a docile institution except when public opinion had been thoroughly roused or the members themselves felt so indignant as to oppose the Administration on particular issues. On such occasions, the British Cabinet was nearly always forced to temporize or even to abandon a measure completely. The docility of the Irish legislature must not be exaggerated, since the London government took great pains to ensure the passage or rejection of particular measures and was wary of offending sentiment in Ireland whether inside or outside parliament.

Constitutionally, the Irish Parliament was restricted by two enactments, one passed by itself and the other by the Parliament of Great Britain. The former was the act of 1494, called Poyning's Law, which with subsequent modifications stipulated that the Irish legislature could not meet or initiate bills without the prior approval of the English Privy Council, that is, for all practical purposes, the British Cabinet. The latter was the British Declaratory Act of 1719 which stated that Ireland was subject to the legislation of the British Parliament. This meant, of course, that the Irish Parliament was to some extent a subordinate body. Similarly, though not directly as a result of this act, appellate jurisdiction of the Irish House of Lords was subject to that of the English House.

Poyning's Law would have rendered the working of the Irish Parliament extremely cumbersome if a practical device had not been found. This device consisted in the passing through either house of a draft bill, known as the "heads of a bill," which would then be sent to the Lord-Lieutenant for consideration by the Irish Privy Council. That body could reject, pass, or amend the heads, but if not rejected, they were then transmitted to the English Privy Council which, similarly, had the power to reject, pass, or amend. Provided it was not rejected, the measure was sent back to Ireland and introduced to the Parliament as a proper bill, but it could not then be amended: it could be only passed or rejected. The Irish House of Commons stood much on its dignity so that if the heads of a bill were one of finance and if they were altered by the English Privy Council, the Irish Commons would reject them on their return from London on the grounds that a money measure must take its rise in that house. Immediately, it would introduce a new heads, identical with that sent back by the English Privy Council, and honor would be satisfied.

For many decades prior to the accession of George III, the British Government had controlled the Irish Parliament by granting to a small number of borough-owning aristocrats, called undertakers, the greater part of the political patronage of the country in return for their support in procuring and maintaining a pro-government majority. Such a system was obviously not to the taste of the young king, and it is not surprising that in 1767 a new lord lieutenant, Viscount Townshend, was sent to Dublin for the purpose of breaking the power of the undertakers and bringing the Irish legislature under a more direct supervision. He accomplished his mission by residing continually in Ireland (unlike former viceroys), by a lavish increase of pensions, places, and peerages (this particular example of alliteration is almost a stock phrase in eighteenth-century government), and by placating public opinion and the opponents of the undertakers with an octennial act. This measure was designed to curb aristocratic control of the Commons by making it necessary to hold a general election at least once every eight years. Townshend also succeeded in having the Parliament increase the standing army on the Irish Establishment (i.e. on the Irish Revenue) from 12,000 to some 15,000, the extra 3,000 men being intended for service in the empire at large. For most practical purposes, the new system did not depart too much from that of the undertakers, since many of the latter, particularly the Earl of Shannon, made their peace with the government and, by giving parliamentary support, were able to retain a substantial part of their former patronage, but governmental favors now flowed more directly from London and Dublin Castle (the seat of administration in Ireland) and the circle of beneficiaries was widened.

As one might expect in this period of increasing affluence, there arose among the Protestants, especially among the Anglican ruling classes, a more vigorous sense of national identity and independence than had formerly been the case. The spokesmen of this sentiment came to form a vaguely defined group in the Irish Parliament called Patriots. Their aim was to render the Irish legislature more independent of the British government and more responsive to Irish political opinion. They did not seek separation from Britain but, on the contrary, saw the British connection and the monarchy as necessary and desirable. They were regarded as a parliamentary opposition by the British Cabinet, which in its conduct of Irish affairs relied mainly on patronage and "arrangements" with borough-owning aristocrats. It was not surprising that the Patriots should soon become critical of this position and be accorded support by large sections of the mercantile, professional, and middle classes.

The Patriot group included peers such as Lord Charlemont and the Duke of Leinster, as well as commoners who owned large estates, such as Thomas Conolly, Denis Daly,

and William Brownlow. Others were Edmund Sexton
Pery, Henry Flood, Walter Hussey Burgh, Gervais P.
Bushe, and Barry Yelverton. The most famous of them,
Henry Grattan, entered the Commons in 1775, and by the
end of 1779 had become their leader. Occasionally, one or
the other entered government service and, as a result,
usually lost much of his popularity, since he was then considered as having abandoned something of his political
integrity in favor of personal advancement. Pery obtained
the office of Speaker of the House of Commons, Henry
Flood became one of the Vice-Treasurers, and Hussey
Burgh accepted the Prime Serjeantship. The patronage
and influence which attachment to the administration
might confer could render a member of parliament very
useful to his constituents and thus strengthen his following. Such was the case with Pery and John Hely Hutchinson who represented the important cities of Limerick and
Cork. It was this parliamentary opposition to British control which is generally regarded by Irish historians as the
embryo of Irish nationalism.

For reasons of convenience and clarity, the term "Patriot," which has been used by historians and was employed by contemporaries, will continue to serve as a
description of this group. The use of the term will not
denote any necessary connection between it and patriotism
whether one defines patriotism as love of one's country or,
as Samuel Johnson would have it, "the last refuge of a
scoundrel."

Like all groups or parties in the eighteenth-century
politics of England and Ireland, the Patriots were not a
compact body acting in unison. They frequently differed
from each other even on important issues, since their activities were based on similarity of opinion and sentiment
rather than on any definite agreement to support clearly

defined policies. They were regarded in England, and regarded themselves, as Whigs—as the Irish equivalent of the opposition in the British Parliament to George III's cabinets.

During the American War, and beginning with the formation of the Volunteers and the nation-wide agitation for Free Trade, there occurred a new development in Irish life. This was the political awakening of the middle classes. Awareness had existed, but only among very limited groups, whereas now it was diffused throughout the whole country. As will be shown in Chapter III, the Volunteers, these semi-military associations, were middle-class in membership though nearly always commanded by men of landlord rank. The sense of corporate power acquired in the Volunteers' successful agitation for Free Trade was to have a lasting effect and was to teach the middle classes that they had a strength hitherto not realized. The ultimate aim was a reform of parliament so as to gain for the middle classes a real share in political power which previously had been centered in the aristocracy and gentry.

And who were the middle classes? To this question there is no precise answer except as regards the larger towns where the middle classes are easily identified as merchants, manufacturers, and members of the professions. The very names of many of the Volunteers corps in Dublin are self-explanatory—Merchants, Goldsmiths, Lawyers, Attorneys. But what of the rural areas? Therein lies the difficulty. All legal historians and contemporary observers agree that the Irish system of land tenure was chaotic, so that the legal status of a landholder did not necessarily indicate his social and economic position. In Chapter IX, for example, it is shown that a certain type of leaseholder could be anything from a modest farmer to a landed aristocrat. The easily identified yeomen in England had only a very limited number of Irish equivalents. In Ireland, on the other hand, there existed an extensive group called "middling-men" or middle-men who were practically unknown in England. These men were of varying social and economic position who rented, usually on lease, substantial acreages from more substantial middlemen or from landlords, and who, in turn, rented out their holding in small farms. Very often, the term "landlord" must be understood in a social and economic sense rather than a legal one, because many landlords held long leases and were thus merely tenants if we wish to describe them in a legally correct, but totally unrealistic way.

It is much wiser to link the middle classes to the Volunteers. Since the latter consisted of 25,000 men in 1779 (a conservative estimate), and in later years of, perhaps, double that number, it is obvious that their membership permeated the middle classes throughout the country. The function of the Volunteers—to preserve law and order in town and country, as shown in Chapter III—justifies their being called defenders of property. Furthermore, the various contemporary descriptions establish them as men of substance. Their campaign for parliamentary reform enables us to see them much more clearly as those socio-economic strata between landlords and peasantry. That is the definition of middle classes which will be used in this study.

The task of arriving at a precise definition is rendered all the more difficult because the term "class," as used in its modern sense to denote a socio-economic stratum, occurs first about the beginning of the nineteenth century. Even today the word is seldom precise, but its equivalent in the eighteenth century was either too vague or too confined, taking such forms as "order," "degree," "interest" or "estate." [3] It may be said that the word should not be used for the eighteenth century and that it is an urban and not a rural term. In answer to these objections it can be held that the only convenient term to describe these strata is middle classes; any other term would be cumbersome and, at best, no more realistic. At the risk of appearing dogmatic it can be argued that a nineteenth-century or urban term can legitimately be employed to describe a mainly rural section of the population in the eighteenth century, if "the cap fits." To cast aside an apt and convenient term simply because it has not been hallowed by historical usage, seems but an addiction to convention.

NOTES FOR CHAPTER I

1 *Arthur Young's Tour in Ireland, 1776–1779,* A. W. Hutton, ed. (London, 1892), II, 253–54, 258.

2 George O'Brien, "The Irish Free Trade Agitation of 1779," *English Historical Review,* XXXVIII (October, 1923), 576–81.

3 Asa Briggs, "The Language of 'Class' in Early Nineteenth-Century England," *Essays in Labour History: in Memory of G. D. H. Cole,* Asa Briggs and John Saville, eds. (New York, 1960), pp. 43–73.

II

Irish Opinion on the American Revolution

In 1772 Townshend was replaced as viceroy by Lord Harcourt who held the position until the end of 1776. The latter's principal achievement lay in inducing the Irish Parliament to support the British government in attempting to suppress the American Revolution. It was a foregone conclusion that the Patriots would see the colonists' cause with sympathy and as resembling their own. This identity of interest had been pointed up by no less a person than the redoubtable Benjamin Franklin on a visit to Ireland in 1771. Dublin had proved as hospitable to him as Paris, and he was entertained by "both parties, the courtiers and the patriots." [1] The Irish House of Commons paid him the honor of admitting him to sit with the members, and he was favorably impressed with his reception. Of the leading members of the Patriot group he wrote:

I found them disposed to be friends of America, in which I endeavoured to confirm them, with the expectation that our growing weight might in time be thrown into their scale, and, by joining our interests with others, a more equitable treatment from this nation [the English] might be obtained for them as well as for us.[2]

At the opening of the parliamentary session of 1775–1776 Harcourt succeeded in having each house include in its customary address of loyalty to the king a passage asserting that

. . . whilst your Government is disturbed by a Rebellion existing in a part of your American Dominions, which we hear with abhorrence and feel with indignation, we shall be ever ready to show our most devoted and inviolable Attachment to your Majesty's sacred Person and Government, in the assertion of your just Rights, and in the support of your legal Authority.[3]

This condemnation of the colonists was subjected in both chambers to determined though unsuccessful opposition. In the Lords an amendment was proposed expressing concern with "the unhappy differences which now subsist between the Parliament of *Great Britain* and your *American Colonies*", and the hope that they might be terminated "without further Effusion of Blood." The amendment clearly implied that the struggle was a quarrel and not a rebellion, and that greater efforts should be made by the British Government to procure peace. Despite the efforts of the Opposition, the address was passed by an overwhelming majority (the normal procedure on government-sponsored measures in the Irish House of Lords), the minority consisting of Charlemont, Irnham, Leinster, Meath, and Powerscourt.[4]

In the Commons the address to the king was voted by a majority of 36, 90 in favor and 54 against. The Administration argued that it was important to persuade the

Americans of their rebelliousness and to give them no countenance. The Patriots saw the Americans as merely defending their rights, their action no more a rebellion than the Glorious Revolution. One of their number, George Ogle, summed up their view with the rhetorical question: "If you vote the Americans to be rebels, for resisting a taxation where they are not represented, what can you say when the English will tax you." [5] The fact that 28 of the 37 county members who voted on the address cast their vote against it is an indication that those who could be described as more representative of the landowners of the country were favorable to the American cause.

In the following month—November, 1775—the Irish Parliament agreed, in spite of the most determined opposition of the Patriots, to send 4,000 troops overseas for imperial service, it being understood that the British government would pay for their maintenance. In the Lords a protest against this measure was entered by six peers— Charlemont, Leinster, Meath, Powerscourt, Irnham, and Wandesford—on the grounds that the war was unjust, the Americans had the right to resist arbitrary taxation, and the Glorious Revolution had demonstrated that resistance to the Crown was not necessarily rebellion. Their protest included the assertion:

That at present we must conceive, that the object of this War was the establishment of the power of the British Parliament to tax America; a power which, we know, is not inherent in the general Constitution of the British Empire . . . the arbitrary levying of money is contrary to all Freedom, and particularly to all English Ideas of Freedom, we are not surprised to hear, that such attempt has been resisted by a Nation born of Britain, warmed by her Principles, and taught by her Example. [6]

That sympathy with the Americans was widespread among the Anglican ruling classes is further borne out by the relief expressed by the Lord-Lieutenant when the address to the king in October had been passed:

I saw the moment approaching when this important question would have been pressed upon me by the Opposition . . . who were daily gaining strength upon this ground. . . . I have never passed moments so happy as those have been since the question was determined.[7]

Among the Presbyterians it was obvious that sentiment would be pro-American. Throughout the eighteenth century there had been a steady stream of emigration of Protestants from the north of Ireland to America, most of whom were Presbyterians, known in America as Scotch-Irish. These Protestants in the years immediately preceding the Revolution constituted the largest racial group of immigrants.[8] One Presbyterian minister in Ireland commented that "there is scarcely a Protestant family of the middle classes amongst us, who does not reckon kindred with the inhabitants of that extensive continent." [9] In his reports to London, Harcourt described the Presbyterians as Americans "in their hearts" and "talking in all companies in such a way that if they are not rebels, it is hard to find a name for them." [10]

Dr. R. B. McDowell had shown that in newspapers, pamphlets, public meetings and addresses, and other expressions of opinions, there was widespread sympathy for the colonists, and the minute examination of newspapers undertaken by me merely confirms his findings. Yet he is careful to add the caution (with which I fully agree) that such sentiments were expressed mainly by individuals and groups under no obligation to take immediate action or accept responsibility in political affairs. Thus, their pro-American enthusiasm must not be accepted too readily at its face value.[11] Throughout the war the British army recruited large numbers in Ireland, and there is no evidence that this activity was obstructed by persons or groups however pro-American their sympathies may have been.

Running through opinion generally in Ireland was a strong streak of admiration for the colonists which expressed itself very often in colorful but, none the less, genuine ways.

While some officers of the Police were employed in that . . . necessary employment of pig-hunting, one of the swine . . . did not appear so amenable to order as he ought. . . . He thought it an infringement of his liberty to obey the hand of power . . . but with a truly American spirit exerted himself to rise up against . . . oppression. He turned against one of the halbertmen, and . . . fairly threw his opponent in a heap of mud. Though this could not be called a clean fall, it procured the swine's freedom, for, while the droll figure of the halbertier excited the mirth of the bystanders the formidable grunter took to his feet, and . . . escaped to safety.

Towards the end of the Revolutionary War, Irish opinion began to realize that something entirely new was being achieved in the American colonies. On January 31, 1782, a letter to the *Freeman's Journal* said of America: "Liberty has there erected her throne, and reigns uncontrolled in civil and religious matters." A year later, a Volunteer corps called for a free constitution:

At this *great crisis*, when the Western World, laying the foundations of a rising empire, temptingly holds out a system of equal liberty to mankind, and waits with open arms to receive the emigrants from surrounding nations.[12]

In the campaign for parliamentary reform the *Dublin Evening Post* of August 9, 1783 welcomed the independent spirit of electors in dealing with imperious landlords:

Tenantry should recollect that America stands with outstretched arms ready to receive the injured and oppressed Sons of Liberty, where industry will meet a sure and abundant reward.

Political opinion in Ireland on the American issues has been studied by an American scholar, Raymond J. Barrett, in a doctoral dissertation entitled. "A Comparative Study of Imperial Constitutional Theory in Ireland and America in the Age of the American Revolution." [13] Dr. Barrett considers that concern with money matters "inclined the Irish to view control of finance as the foremost question in the American dispute. 'No taxation without representation' was a maxim that caught the imagination of Irishmen." He maintains that American constitutional developments had little effect on Ireland, that

the similarity of the relationship of the two countries to the British Parliament is obvious enough, but may, perhaps, have exerted an undue fascination for historians. . . . It might not be fair to assert that constitutional theory occupied a completely subsidiary place with Irishmen, but it is safe to say that it did not overshadow other considerations as it did in American thought.[14]

As an additional explanation of the comparative lack of concern in Ireland about imperial relationships, the author states:

The first and inescapable problem for the Irish was to win control of their parliament. The subject of imperial representation and the relationship of Ireland's domestic legislature to the empire was secondary. . . . [The Americans] found themselves impelled into the field of imperial relationships by their desire to preserve the power already acquired by their local representative bodies.[15]

While I have not attempted any special examination of the theoretical aspects of Ireland's connection with the British Empire, I find Dr. Barrett's conclusions entirely reasonable. From innumerable sympathetic references to the American colonists, one gets the impression that many Irish politicians were more interested in embarrassing Dublin Castle and the British Government than in giving moral support to the Americans. Anti-government newspapers constantly harped on the theme, and again one discerns a venting of spleen rather than a constructive interest in imperial affairs. A picturesque example of this rather doubtful concern for the colonists can be seen in the radical opposition newspaper, the *Freeman's Journal,* when Free Trade was conceded at the end of 1779. Editorial denunciations of the tyranny of George III suddenly gave way to rejoicing over the news of British victories in America and the West Indies.

As will be shown in the appropriate passages, the Thirteen Colonies were regarded as a haven to which discontented Presbyterians, and even Anglicans and Catholics, might emigrate, yet references to America were often quite disconcerting. Some prisoners captured on privateers were held at Kinsale, Co. Cork, and so many died as to cause public uneasiness. The agent in charge of them defended himself with the statement that "thirty-five only have died, most of them by the small-pox, a disorder, as I am informed, commonly fatal to Americans." [16]

A very unflattering opinion of religion in America was quoted by a traveller:

The people of New England and the Northern Provinces, are in general formalists and fanatics, hypocritical Sabbath-day Saints, who think religion consists in a mechanical attendance upon sermons. From New York to the extent of the Middle Provinces they are less rigid, and more liberal. In Philadelphia, there is much decency and appearance of Religion, and from thence to the extremities of Florida, no religion at all.[17]

Unquestionably, there were some men prominent in politics who genuinely sympathized with the colonists. Outstanding among these was Lord Charlemont whose correspondence and memoirs leave no doubt as to his sentiments. Another was Sir Edward Newenham, M.P. for Co. Dublin, who dedicated to Washington a gothic tower which he erected in 1778 in the grounds of his Georgian mansion, Belcamp, Raheney, Co. Dublin. Part of the inscription on the tower ran: "Oh, ill-fated Britain! The folly of Lexington and Concord will rend asunder, and forever disjoin America from thy empire."[18] In February, 1778, some American prisoners were being held in Ireland, and the Duke of Leinster, then a pro-American Patriot, subscribed the generous sum of £100 to their relief.

These expressions of sympathy, whether genuine, sentimental, or merely expedient, were voiced by Anglicans and Presbyterians. With the Catholics, things were entirely different. They were seeking the most elementary civil rights and, consequently, were unlikely to lose their night's sleep if American Protestants were taxed without representation. What the vast majority of them thought about current political matters is impossible to say. In all probability they were too sunk in illiteracy and poverty to know or care very much about the issues absorbing the attention of the upper and middle classes. Their leaders in September, 1775, presented a petition of loyalty to the Government expressing their "abhorrence of the unnatural rebellion which has lately broken out among some of his Majesty's American subjects." As evidence of their allegiance they offered

two millions of loyal, faithful, and affectionate hearts and hands, unarmed indeed, but zealous, ready and desirous to exert themselves strenuously in defence of his Majesty's most sacred person and Government.[19]

Individual Catholics gave bounties in support of recruiting drives to an extent which induced Harcourt to welcome such a bounty from a Protestant peer partly because of "any clamours that might prevail if none but the Roman Catholics had shown a zeal and readiness to forward the service at this juncture." [20] The British government had decided to recruit Irish Catholics into the rank and file of the army, as shown by a letter of Lord George Germain, Secretary of State for the American Colonies, to Sir John Irvine (sometimes spelled Irwin), Commander-in-Chief of the army in Ireland:

I find from [Lieutenant-General] Cuninghame that the Roman Catholics do not enlist for America with the zeal that was expected. If that humor continues, you will do well to explain that circumstance fully to the directors of the Military Department here, that they may adopt some surer method of completing the troops in America before it be too late, for they will listen to no project of new corps as long as they flatter themselves with being able to recruit the regiments from Irish Roman Catholics, etc.[21]

Protests were made in the Irish House of Commons by individual members because of the report that the Government intended to recruit Catholics "to fill the regiments going to America." Major (later Sir) Boyle Roche replied by saying he had been recruiting and his instructions were to recruit Protestants. In the recent (Seven Years) war, he added, Catholics had been enlisted for service in America and had fought loyally. The Chief Secretary, John Blaquiere, denied that the instructions concerning recruiting received by Dublin Castle from London contained any provision about Catholics. The Solicitor-General considered the whole discussion unnecessary since "by the laws now in being, whatever a man's religion might be before enlisting, he is by them, and by the Articles of War, obliged to be a Protestant." [22] The defense put up by the Administration is not very convincing. Since it was illegal to arm Catholics, official instructions from London would obviously have contained no explicit reference to such recruits; any order to enlist Catholics would have been implied or given verbally. During the war, correspondence between London and Dublin was regularly interspersed with instructions to grant permission to British officers to recruit in Ireland. That Catholics were being recruited, and in large numbers, (despite the forebodings of Germain) is shown by the attempt of the Lord-Lieutenant (the Earl of Carlisle) in 1781 to have the Catholic bishops issue exhortations to deserters to return to their regiments. [23]

The recruiting of Catholics for service in America infuriated many Protestants. The newspapers in 1775 were full of editorials, letters, and reports of meetings denouncing this practice, and warning or advising Catholics to desist from entering military service. A correspondent styling himself "Hampden" (the nom-de-plume is in itself revealing) reported that the King "intends to call upon his Roman Catholic subjects . . . for their personal assistance against his Protestant subjects in America." Let Irish Catholics beware, he added, because they are in the power of the Protestants: "A petit Constable enforcing the law has more authority than a monarch invading the law." [24]

Lord Kenmare, the wealthiest of the Catholic landlords, arranged for the raising of a regiment by Major Boyle Roche, and gave a bounty to each recruit. The result was a spate of letters, one of which ran:

a Popish lord openly invites his faithful followers to take up arms, and Government countenances the act. Irish Papists . . . [are being permitted] to murder American Protestants.[25]

In the north of Ireland "A Whig," in attacking the corruption of the Government, poured gall on his argument with the assertion:

Popery has been established in the vast and unbounded province of Quebeck, with the unlimited power vested in a military government, thereby, when fit occasion offered, to intimidate and awe the Protestant colonies into subjection.[26]

An editorial in the *Freeman's Journal* of August 8, 1775, maintained:

It is but a few years since pensioner [Dr. Samuel] Johnson and the Scotch had the most *cordial contempt* for each other. They are now seemingly united under the present ministry, and enemies to American resistance.

NOTES FOR CHAPTER II

1 Benjamin Franklin to William Franklin, January 30, 1772, *Works of Benjamin Franklin,* ed. John Bigelow (New York, 1887), IV, 453.

2 *Ibid.,* IV, 445, Franklin to Thomas Cushing, January 13, 1772.

3 *Irish Lords Journal,* IV, 790 *et seq.;* *Irish Commons Journal,* IX, 170 *et seq.*

4 *Ibid.*

5 HJ, October 11, 13, 1775; FJ, October 12, 1775.

6 HJ, December 1, 1775; *Irish Lords Journal,* IV, 803–804.

7 Harcourt to Lord Rochford, Secretary of State for the Southern Department, October 11, 1775, W. E. H. Lecky, *A History of Ireland in the Eighteenth Century* (London, 1892), II, 163.

8 W. F. Dunaway, *The Scotch-Irish of Colonial Pennsylvania* (Chapel Hill, University of North Carolina Press, 1944); p. 39.

9 R. B. McDowell, *Irish Public Opinion, 1750–1800* (London, 1944), p. 44.

10 Lecky, *History,* II, 163 *et seq.*

11 McDowell, *op. cit.,* p. 48.

12 DEP, January 16, 1783.

13 Raymond J. Barrett, "A Comparative Study of Imperial Constitutional Theory . . ." Ph.D. dissertation, Department of History and Political Science, Dublin University, 1958).

14 *Ibid.,* pp. 23–26.

15 *Ibid.,* p. 117.

16 HC, March 4, 1782.

17 FDJ, August 18, 1781.

18 Richard Lewis, *The Dublin Guide,* (Dublin, 1787), p. 59. The house is now occupied by the Oblate Fathers, and the tower still stands.

19 Lecky, *History,* II, 165.

20 *Ibid.,* p. 161n.

21 HMC, Stopford-Sackville Papers, Sept. 13, 1775, I, 136–3'.

22 HJ, October 30, November 10, 1775.

23 A. Cogan *Diocese of Meath, Ancient and Modern* (Dublin, 1862–1870), III, 56–58. Judging by the reaction of the (Catholic) Archbishop of Cashel, it seems likely that Carlisle's proposal was rejected by the Catholic prelates.

24 HJ, September 29, 1775.

25 HJ, September 4, 1775.

26 FJ, March 30, 1775.

III

The Origins of the Free Trade Crisis

Towards the end of 1777 an economic depression settled on Great Britain and became acute as a result of the French entry into the war in March, 1778. There was a consequent difficulty in borrowing, and the number of bankruptcies rose in the succeeding twelve months.[1] No doubt the Irish economy was affected by the situation in Britain, but the main cause of the depression in Ireland was the American Revolutionary War. It practically destroyed her considerable contraband trade with North America, while the wartime conditions it imposed injured her equally illegal commerce with France.

The Irish depression was rendered worse or, at least, more productive of discontent by the laying of an embargo on the export of provisions. The situation might not have been so disastrous for the government had it not been for the fact that for many years expenditure had been greater than revenue, and loans had been resorted to on an unprecedented scale.[2] Any serious reduction in income, or increase in spending, was likely to have a crippling effect on the ability of the administration to meet its commitments. Disaster came with the need to organize a militia for the defense of the country after France's entry into the war. The Government was unable, because of lack of money, to form such a force, with the result that local defense associations known as the Volunteers were organized. These were to give the Patriots the great and special strength which was the decisive factor in winning Free Trade in 1779, and bade fair to give greater encouragement to radicalism in the future.

When Harcourt departed from Ireland in January, 1777, on the arrival of the new viceroy, Buckinghamshire, and before economic depression had become evident, it might have seemed to the superficial observer that the course of politics would continue to run smoothly. But the American Revolution hung like a cloud over Ireland because of the economic difficulties which the war would entail, so that Buckinghamshire, did he but know it, had a very hard road to travel.

The new incumbent was very different from his tired and ageing predecessor. He was John (Hobart), second Earl of Buckinghamshire, of Blickling Hall, Norfolk, once the residence of Anne Boleyn. Of Whig origin, he had served in the previous decade as ambassador to Russia and was admirably suited to a diplomatic career. Courteous and handsome, he had intellectual interests and was fond of social life. He very frequently attended the theater and, during his first six months in Dublin, much attention was paid by the press to his dinner engagements at the homes of leading members of the administration. A man of honor and integrity, he desired popularity and public esteem. Unfortunately in this very difficult period, his good qualities had their disadvantages in his role as viceroy. He was much too inclined to depend on his popularity and public knowledge of his good intentions. He did not make sufficient allowance for the fact that politics are a hard discipline under which men often pursue objectives regardless of personal friendship.[3]

Too trusting, he often did not notice the pitfalls that lie in the path of the administrator. This can be seen in his choice of Richard Heron as chief secretary, a man of only moderate ability and of middle-class background in an age when aristocratic connection was very important.[4] In Buckinghamshire there was a certain timidity and lack of toughness, serious defects in one holding an important political position; it was only under severe provocation that he would show indignation. He had the misfortune to be viceroy at a time when a ministry held sway in England—that of Lord North—which was often seriously indecisive and hesitant, and when a determined prodding from Ireland was necessary. Buckinghamshire had too mild a nature for such a situation.

However, his sincerity and pleasant personality won him favor in Ireland. Even the radical newspapers, though at various times denouncing his policy and administration, were never really personal in their attacks and they often praised him. Similarly, the Patriots in the Irish Commons who for reasons of political policy had to make Buckinghamshire's life a misery, always admitted that his administration was free from the "venality" of the regimes of his predecessors. At the time of his departure in December, 1780, the newspapers showed affection for him in contrast to their silence on the depature of Harcourt in 1777.

It was to his disadvantage that he was connected by marriage with two of the leading aristocrats in Ireland, Thomas Conolly and the Duke of Leinster. Previous viceroys had rented St. Wolstan's in Co. Kildare as a summer residence and Buckinghamshire continued this practice.[5]

This mansion lay across the River Liffey from the great country seat of Conolly (Castletown) and a few miles from Leinster's mansion (Carton), both exquisite examples of Georgian architecture. Thus, his contact with these aristocrats was particularly close. He was married to Conolly's sister, while Conolly's wife, a daughter of the second Duke of Richmond and sister of the third and contemporary duke, was an aunt of Leinster. These relationships might have been a great source of strength to the Viceroy but, unfortunately, though both were men of integrity, Conolly lacked judgment and Leinster had little political ability. The latter was much under the influence of his uncle, the radical English Whig, Richmond, and failed to give support when Buckinghamshire most needed it.

On his appointment as viceroy, Buckinghamshire received a long letter from Conolly, which seems to have had a deep influence on the early part of his four-year stay in Ireland. The Irish aristocrat pleaded for greater freedom from the British commercial restraints as essential to Irish prosperity which would ultimately redound to the wealth of Great Britain. The latter country had always treated Ireland with contempt (despite his English mother and wife, Conolly was very much an Irishman) and burdened her with taxes:

Lord Townshend came over here, to overturn the old aristocracy of the First Families of Parliamentary weight [i.e. the undertakers] which necessarily cost the Kingdom . . . a great sum. Lord Harcourt . . . has laid more upon us, than even Lord Townshend . . . and has continued to raise the *price* of members.

Conolly promised his assistance:

as far as I am permitted by my *first* connection, with a country in which I was born, and in the prosperity of which I am so deeply interested. I belong to no party here, I never did, or ever will. Altho' I have and expect to be tormented to make requests [for favors] to you, I shall uniformly decline it, meaning to be of service, but not of trouble to you.[6]

Despite his offer of assistance, he and Leinster did not commit themselves too readily to the new administration. From Castletown's famous "Long Gallery," where she spent much of her day, Conolly's wife, Lady Louisa, wrote to her sister, the dowager Duchess of Leinster. She told of the offers which the new Lord-Lieutenant had made for the support of the two:

His very civil, kind behaviour, both to the Duke of Leinster and Mr. Conolly, incline them to think they shall support him . . . but [they] . . . have taken care at the same time to keep themselves quite at liberty. However, I am in very great hopes that Lord Buckinghamshire has no *devilish* thing to do.

By *devilish* she meant, of course, any measure which would be considered totally opposed to the political principles of her husband. She then added that the Viceroy's power "hangs on a slender thread, for if things should go wrong in America, I suppose Lord George Germain will lose his power, and of course Lord Buckinghamshire will lose his chief support." [7]

The first year of the viceroyalty saw comparatively little political activity. The embargo on the export of provisions, laid in early 1776, was the running sore but Buckinghamshire could not be held responsible and he did his best to have it partly or wholly raised. The Irish Parliament did not meet until October so that there was little opportunity for political discontent to express itself for the first nine months of the year. Early reaction in Ireland to both the Lord-Lieutenant and his Chief Secretary was favorable enough, and there was little foreboding of the trials that lay ahead.

The first real test for the new viceroy occurred on October 14, 1777, with the opening of the Irish Parliament. In order to conciliate Patriot opinion, and on the advice of nearly all the leading members of the Administration, Buckinghamshire omitted any reference to America in the Speech from the Throne.[8] The omission won him the applause of Grattan in the Commons and Mountmorres in the Lords. The latter said that he would have opposed the Speech if it had made any hostile reference to the colonists, but he was pleased to see that the House was "no longer committed to the American Crusade." The wealthy Luke Gardiner, a representative for Dublin County and an independent supporter of the Administration, praised Buckinghamshire for having limited his appointments to Irishmen and for forming a connection with men of great landed property in Ireland.[9]

John Beresford, M.P. for Co. Waterford, a commissioner of the Revenue, a brother of the Earl of Tyrone, and one of the most influential members of the Administration, saw the omission of reference to America with distaste. He considered that this was a show of weakness and would avail the Viceroy nothing in the long run.[10] John Scott, who had just been appointed attorney-general on Buckinghamshire's nomination,[11] informed Heron, the Chief Secretary, that he considered the omission unwise but did not express his opinion officially.[12] Two years later, when Buckinghamshire's Government was facing ruin, Scott reiterated in the strongest terms his belief that this effort to placate pro-American sentiment was the first link in a chain of disaster. The second link was "a foolish rhapsody of Mr. Conolly's in the House of Commons, insulting every former Administration, and announcing that this Administration was to be a system of retrenchment." [13] North and Weymouth, the cabinet minister re-

sponsible for Ireland, accepted Buckinghamshire's defense
of the decision not to mention the colonies, but the King
saw it as a mistake and remarked sadly, "So America is
forgotten." [14]

Buckinghamshire disapproved of the manner in which
his two predecessors, Townshend and Harcourt, had conducted their Administrations—their extravagance and
lavish use of honors and emoluments. He intended

to give a degree of preference and to shew a becoming distinction to the men of the first character and influence, but
not to depend so far upon them or their connections as to disgust detached individuals; and above all things to spare the
public purse as far as discretion . . . will admit.[15]

Evidence that he tried to implement this policy comes in
a long series of admissions from Patriots in the House of
Commons during his four years in Ireland. Naturally
enough, retrenchment was not popular, as the Viceroy was
to learn, since "the plan of economy which preceding expense has rendered unavoidably necessary, must make me
some enemys." [16] This aspect of his viceroyalty was condemned by John Beresford, a hostile witness but one who
wrote with the sincerity of anger. In a letter in 1779, he
said that when Buckinghamshire arrived in Ireland, all
was well but

his private connections led him to other men, and they led
him to other measures. They persuaded him that the majority
obtained by Lords Townshend and Harcourt . . . had cost the
nation an immense sum, that it was to be governed by other
and cheaper means; that those persons connected with the
former Administration were not to be trusted, but that every
dependence was to be had upon men of virtue and integrity;
and that the Houses of Parliament were to be governed by the

appearance of public economy in the chief Governor, and every man left to himself[17]

The Lord-Lieutenant as good as admitted the substantial truth of this interpretation of the first year of his vice-royalty when he wrote in 1778 to his friend, Lord George Germain:

The immediate friends of the late Administration are disgusted at my not placing an implicit confidence in them, and cherish with others, whose expectations of emolument have been disappointed, a deep tho' secret dissatisfaction against that economy adopted first from principle, but which now, from necessity, must be adhered to.[18]

In February, 1776, acting on the instructions of the British Cabinet, the viceroy at this time, Lord Harcourt, placed an embargo on the export of provisions, unless intended for Britain and the empire (excluding the Thirteen American Colonies), or for the supply of the army or navy. It amounted, in effect, to a prohibition on the export of meat and butter to the European continent.[19] Its purpose was to ensure a ready supply of victuals for the armed forces and to prevent any being sent to the rebels in America. During the succeeding two years the charge was constantly made that the embargo was merely what the eighteenth-century called a "job," that is, a scheme to enrich one or a few at the expense of many. That the prohibition had a genuine public purpose is clear and will be discussed in the course of this chapter.

The Irish House of Commons reacted with several lively debates in which the Patriots gave full play to their rhetorical talents. Hussey Burgh, who could always be relied on for picturesque exaggeration, described the embargo as illegal and as an exercise of the royal prerogative of the kind which "had struck the Crown off one king, and Head off another." He accused the Government of wanting to fill the pockets of private English contractors. The anger over the issue can be gauged from the fact that the moderate Sir Lucius O'Brien joined in the attack by describing the proclamation as "a bad method of inducing the Irish to join Great Britain against America, to begin by infringing our Constitution." The Government's case was that the Crown had the right to lay an embargo in time of war, and the rebellion in America made it necessary. George Ogle mocked the plea of necessity:

The Highwayman robs you through *necessity,* and if you resist him, shoots you through the head from *necessity;* a man runs away with a pretty girl, through *necessity:* and if she refused to comply, he is under a *necessity* of ravishing her." [20]

The prohibition was made more stringent in the early winter of 1776 by the stipulation that all provision ships leaving for the British dominions must travel in convoy.[21]

Over the ensuing eighteen months protests against the embargo were constantly being made, usually by the mayor and merchants of Cork.[22] Shortly after the debates just described, the Irish Parliament was dissolved and a general election was held. The new parliament commenced its first session more than a year later, in October, 1777, and one of its spirited debates arose from an attack on the embargo. It took the form of a motion by the Patriot, Denis Daly, calling for an enquiry into the state of the provision export trade. He said that the country, particularly the south and west, had suffered greatly over the past two years, since the whole kingdom had been converted into a "magazine to support the unnatural war with the colonies." Ireland could expect nothing from a feeble British Government which was "making their designs to enslave America a pretense to oppress us." The recently appointed Prime Serjeant, Hussey Burgh, heretofore a leading Patriot, now tried to reconcile his former attitude by seconding Daly's motion on the dubious ground that it was merely an enquiry into trade and not an attack on the embargo. He considered that the embargo was legal and any debate on its legality would be unwise.[23] In consequence of Daly's motion, a committee of enquiry was set up. The situation was embarrassing for Dublin Castle, since even Robinson, Lord North's secretary, thought that the embargo had given rise to corruption.[24]

Meanwhile, the Lord-Lieutenant appealed to London for at least a temporary lifting of the embargo to enable current stocks of cattle and provisions to find a sale; not only the merchants and traders, but the landowners, he said, feared that the prohibition on the inferior kind of provisions, which went to the French and not to the army or navy, would mean a serious loss to the cattle trade and a consequent difficulty in collecting rents.[25] The reply from London stated that there could be no relaxation of the embargo since "the armaments still subsisting in the ports of France and Spain are carried on to such an extent that it is thought essentially necessary for the public security that the present embargo remain." [26] Therefore, it was decided by Dublin Castle to bring the deliberations of the provision trade committee to an end. A very vigorous debate was the result.[27]

The Administration argued that it was necessary to prevent supplies reaching the French, Spanish, and Americans. The distress caused by the embargo had been exaggerated; many of the low prices were due to speculation and overproduction in beef, and the increase in the export of pork had largely compensated for the decline in that of beef. John Hely Hutchinson, Provost of Dublin University and Secretary of State, said he had argued the case of his constituents (he represented Cork city), but the Crown had now decided upon the matter and the House must accept that decision and submit. If he had any doubts as to the legality of an embargo in time of peace, he had none in time of war, and rebellion was war.

The opposition was conducted with great warmth by John Forbes, Ogle, Grattan, Daly, and Newenham. They argued that the embargo was illegal and unnecessary, a great injury to Irish trade in causing, perhaps, the permanent loss of European and West Indies markets, and all for the selfish profits of Government contractors. The motion to terminate the committee's enquiry was passed by 137 votes to 80, but the fact that the minority was so large meant that political affairs were running in an unpleasant direction so far as Buckinghamshire was concerned.

Undaunted, the opposition renewed the attack a week later by demanding an inquiry into the activities of Robert Gordon, the commissary for the purchase of provisions for the supply of the armed forces. He was accused of "allowing corn to be landed without any entry, and selling it for private account." [28] That there was substance in the accusation is suggested by the fact that though the Administration succeeded in having the motion defeated, only Scott and Beresford stood firm on the Government's side; Foster, the Chairman of the Committee of Supply, and a strong supporter of the Administration, voted in favor of the motion,[29] and Hely Hutchinson left the House without voting. His conduct on the embargo had already given rise to uneasiness and had called forth a reprimand from the Lord-Lieutenant a few weeks before.[30]

The big disappointment for the Administration was that Hussey Burgh had not voted. In reporting to London, Buckinghamshire defended him on the ground that the Prime Serjeant was very reluctant to oppose any enquiry into an important matter, but there was every reason to believe that his future conduct would give full satisfaction.[31] Buckinghamshire had appointed Hussey Burgh to the office of Prime Serjeant and was, therefore, answerable for his conduct. He did not seem to realize that this, his second defection (the first was when he voted for Daly's committee of enquiry on December 9), might mean desertion later on. George III showed greater discernment:

The letters from Mr. Heron to Mr. Robinson only confirm an opinion I have long had that men who have been active in opposition rarely make useful servants to the Crown, of which the conduct of the Prime Serjeant is but too clear an instance.[32]

During the late summer of 1778, the embargo was relaxed, particularly as regards butter, and was lifted entirely at the end of December despite opposition by several of the ministers.[33] Why the British Cabinet should have decided to lift the embargo is impossible to say due to lack of evidence.

It is easy to understand that indignation was likely to arise from any embargo even if its necessity was fully appreciated. The normal course of trade was interrupted and merchants tended to find themselves at a serious loss until adjustments to the new conditions had been made. The necessity for provision ships bound for the British Dominions to sail in convoy obviously caused further difficulty. A frequent complaint was that the prohibition on the export to France might mean the permanent loss of the French market.

The Irish Commons' debates suggest that much of the indignation was directed against Robert Gordon for what were considered unfair or unsavoury practices. The early discussions on the embargo took place before its effect could be seen, but the second series—those of the early winter of 1777—reached their climax in an attack on Gordon's activities. The assault was renewed on March 11, 1778, when he again came under fire for dealing in supplies not intended for the armed forces. Even though provision merchants may have been prospering, one can appreciate their anger if the Government's agent was trading unjustly. The general indignation was expressed by Pery in a letter he intended for the benefit of the British Cabinet:

There is nothing which the people here would not submit to without repining, if they thought it necessary for the public service; but they are persuaded that all these measures are calculated for the emolument of a few private individuals; and I must confess that the public proclamations carry too much the appearance of it.[34]

One may conclude that even though the embargo may not have caused serious depression, it did provoke real indignation.

The charge, so often made during these three years, that the embargo was laid for the purpose of enriching certain contractors does not stand up to investigation. It is true that governments in the eighteenth century were conducted in a manner that the bourgeois administrations of the nineteenth and the democratic ones of the twentieth have considered very corrupt, but there was a limit to that corruption. Even private interests in that century would scarcely have been able to prevail against the political indignation and difficulties which the embargo engendered. There is nothing in the correspondence of statesmen to suggest that they thought of the embargo as being anything but necessary. Pery's letter of September 2, 1778, quoted above, might at first glance give the impression that he agreed that the embargo had its origin in private interest, but such cannot have been the case; his letter was intended for the British Cabinet and could only have been regarded as an unpardonable insult if it were thought to contain any suggestion that he doubted the bona-fide origin of the embargo. A man in a position to know its purpose was William Knox, the Under-Secretary for the American Colonies, an Irishman sincerely devoted to Irish interests and particularly to her commercial welfare. In a letter to Pery in October, 1778, concerning efforts to obtain some relaxation of the embargo, he refers to

the securing [of] a sufficient supply for our own forces, and the preventing [of] the French [from] availing themselves of our beef to victual their ships and colonies. The embargo effectually secures both; and if we cannot show some other way of doing it, I fear the embargo will not be removed.[35]

That the war, and not the trade restraints, was the chief cause of the depression was overlooked by the Patriots and by most others who clamored for Free Trade. By this term was meant the removal of the various restraints which the Navigation Laws and other British parliamentary enactments had placed on Irish commerce. Ironically, it was in governing circles in both Britain and Ireland that the removal of these restrictions was first mooted, and it was only when the British government failed to implement its intentions adequately that the subject was taken up vigorously by the Irish opposition leaders.

These restrictions were placed on Irish trade during the latter part of the seventeenth and the major part of the eighteenth century; most of them were part of the Navigation system, while some referred specifically to Ireland. It was forbidden to import goods from the British plantations into Ireland except through Britain; a corresponding prohibition was placed on the direct export of nearly all commodities from Ireland except provisions. Glass could not be exported at all. It was illegal to export raw wool and woollen goods to any country other than Britain; as regards the latter products, this restraint amounted to an embargo since Britain placed a high tariff on the import of woollen manufactures. The burdens most complained of were this virtual prohibition on the export of woollen goods and the refusal to allow direct import into Ireland from the plantations; the latter restraint continued to hamper direct export to the plantations, even after that right had been conceded in 1778, since an export without a corresponding import of commodities rendered shipping arrangements impractical. Linen was the only important manufacture allowed an unhindered export, and was actually encouraged by being permitted to benefit from a British bounty on linen exports.[36] Prior to the war, the effect of these restraints had been lessened by means of illicit trading with America and the European continent.[37] By cutting off this clandestine commerce, the war had brought about a depression for which the restrictions were blamed, and their removal became the great object of the nation in 1779.

Before proceeding further, it is necessary to consider the efforts made in 1778 to gain a considerable degree of commercial freedom. What Ireland demanded was an equality with British merchants, that is, to be placed on the same footing as Britain and to possess the same commercial rights. This involved being subject to whatever restraints Britain herself was bound by. The term to describe this equality was coined by Henry Flood in the Irish House of Commons in October, 1779, during the hectic debate on the address to the Throne, and the term was "Free Trade." [38] It passed from contemporary usage into history and, though not strictly accurate (equality in trading rights would be more exact), it is too venerable a term to be discarded.

The first real intrusion on the commercial restraints came in 1778. The effort was initiated by Buckinghamshire in an exploratory letter to North in July, 1777, in which he asked for some easing of the Navigation system so as to benefit Irish trade with the British ports on the African coast.[39] Valuable assistance came from William Knox, Under-Secretary for the American Colonies, who, since the summer of 1777, had been tugging at the sleeves of the Irish Administration in an effort to induce it to raise the subject with the British Cabinet. He had been asked by Sir Lucius O'Brien, a member for County Clare in the Irish Parliament and its expert on economics, for his opinion on what Ireland might ask of England.[40] Knox suggested that Ireland should request inclusion in the British Fisheries Act of 1775 and be allowed the direct import of sugar and rum and other West Indian products which she now had to import through Britain. He added that a visit to London by Heron would be useful as "personal solicitation does much more with great men than applications at a distance." [41] After further discussion and some prodding from Knox, the Lord-Lieutenant sent a new and more explicit request to Lord North for such concessions.[42]

In this letter Buckinghamshire suggested that an amendment might be added to the British Fisheries Acts of 1775 and 1776 so as to give bounties to Irish as well as British ships. In order to attain this end adequately, he asked that the British Parliament pass a measure bringing all Irish ships under the designation "British." In response to a further suggestion by Knox,[43] the Lord-Lieutenant followed up this letter by another on March 20, asking that Ireland be granted the concessions in trade now about to be proposed to the Thirteen Colonies, so that they "may not in any respect be put upon a better foot than Ireland." He was convinced as a result of conversations with some of the ablest men in Ireland that an enlargement of Irish trade was absolutely necessary to meet the increased costs of government and the annual drain of money from the country, particularly to Britain. The consequent enrichment of Ireland, he continued, would not only benefit Great Britain, but the Irish government and the British Empire in general.[44]

Opinion in high political circles in Ireland was now becoming animated; Heron reported Pery as saying that nothing short of a free trade (the term "Free Trade" had not yet become a technical one) would give real benefit to Ireland.[45] John Beresford wrote to Thomas Allan, a commissioner of the English Customs, at the outbreak of the French war:

The zeal and spirit of this country is up, and, if proper measures are adopted, great support may be had; but Great Britain must open her heart also, and spontaneously offer us some essential objects of trade; we are now their real support.[46]

The representations made to England by the Lord-Lieutenant and others produced their effect when Earl Nugent, an Irish peer resident in England, took up the matter in the British House of Commons. In obtaining the formation of a committee on Irish trade, he said that Britain's conduct towards Ireland had been impolitic and unjust, and that the present situation demanded a change. Burke and others supported him and his motion was passed *nem. con.*[47] Nugent opened the proceedings in committee with a speech in which he said that Ireland's loyalty in Britain's present difficulties deserved reward; she could be of much greater value to Britain, but for the impoverishing effect of the trade laws. Some opposition would arise, he feared, from the West India planters who were much under the thumb of merchants in England, and the merchants did not wish to lose the 2½ per cent commission they obtained on the sugars imported into Ireland through Britain.[48] Coming from one who was virtually a member of the Government, his speech was tactless in its hostility towards a large number of merchants. One can see why Knox expressed uneasiness about Nugent's handling of the sugar question and why he later was to refer to the intemperate zeal of the "Irish gentlemen" in England.[49]

Nugent proposed four resolutions: first, that Ireland be allowed the free export of all her products to the British plantations, wool, and woollen manufactures excepted; second, that Ireland be allowed the direct import of all products from the plantations, indigo and tobacco excepted; third, that the acts prohibiting the export of Irish glass be repealed and fourth, that the British duties on the import of Irish cotton yarn be removed.

The resolutions passed *nem. con.* and with little opposition in debate, receiving support from both Tories and Whigs. Lord North thought that these concessions would benefit Ireland and ultimately enrich the empire; "the Irish complained, and complained with justice," and the trade laws provided an opportunity of removing their grievances.[50] During further discussion in the Commons, Thomas Conolly, probably another of the intemperate "Irish gentlemen" to whom Knox was to refer, made the tactless point that the good of the empire should overrule any little injury that might be done to a part of Britain.

Before the end of April, there began to pour into the British House of Commons dozens of petitions against the Irish concession, mainly from Bristol, Liverpool, and Glasgow, and from other cities and towns in the counties of Somerset, Worcester, Stafford, and Lancaster.[51] Only a few came from London which "preserved the dignity of a great and majestic emporium, and continued uninfluenced by common opinion, and unmoved by popular clamour." [52]

From the resolutions there eventually emerged two acts; one allowed the export from Ireland to the British plantations of all products except wool and woollen goods, cotton manufactures, glass, and a few other articles; the other permitted the duty-free import into Britain of cotton yarn manufactured in Ireland.[53] The act allowing the export to the plantations stipulated that it would not come into force until the Irish Parliament had passed excise duties of the same kind as lay on the export of these commodities from Britain, that is, equalizing duties.

Buckinghamshire's pleas concerning the fisheries were answered with provisions that enabled Ireland to gain the full benefit of the Fisheries Acts of 1775 and 1776, and which stipulated that ships built in Ireland and owned by his Majesty's subjects in his European dominions would, be regarded as British-built.[54]

The most important resolution was the second—the right to import direct into Ireland from the plantations—and every effort was made to have this resolution enacted. The subject was debated at length in the British Commons on May 6, 1778, the opposition to the measure being led by Sir Cecil Wray.[55] He said he had no objection to admitting Ireland to a "free trade" if she would bear a proportionate share of the national burdens; her two million people provided a revenue of one million pounds or ten shillings per head, whereas Britain's six million provided twelve million pounds, or two pounds per head. While he would admit that Ireland had grievances—and here he made some shrewd points by referring to the Irish pension list, the sinecures, the absentees, and the Penal Laws—it was not right that British interests should suffer in order that trade restrictions be repealed. He moved that further consideration of the bill be postponed for three months, that is, that the bill be rejected. Nugent (with more of his "intemperate zeal") remarked that the opponents of the measure in Glasgow had acted in a manner that was "mean, unmanly, ungenerous, despicable, and even diabolical." Another Irish absentee peer, Lord Midleton, in referring to a report that the people of Manchester and Liverpool had decided to no longer be loyal should the resolution pass, remarked that these cities and Glasgow were "experienced in rebellion so abundantly that the Transition [to disloyalty] would be an object of easy accomplishment." The remark was clever but tactless.

North gave his support to the bill and warned that it would be unwise to disappoint the Irish now that their hopes had been raised by what had been done in the Commons; Ireland deserved generosity from Britain. But the great speech on the bill was Burke's. He threw himself into the fray with all the argument and rhetoric that he could summon. He considered that Ireland's loyalty to Britain entitled her to demand not pity but justice, not generosity but wisdom. Other places, experienced in rebellion, might become disloyal if these concessions were granted (a more tactful reference than those of Nugent

and Midleton to the protesting cities), but Ireland's
loyalty would be constant. Yet, her reward would be continued subjection because it was the British policy of the
day to be "Proud to the humble and humble to the
Proud." The comparison of the revenue of the two kingdoms on a basis of population was erroneous, since Ireland
had but a fraction of the wealth of England: "You tax
candles in England. But there are two hundred thousand
houses in Ireland, in which probably a candle such as
you tax, was never lighted. The taxes must follow wealth
and not precede it." Even if granted commercial equality
with Britain, Burke continued, the great difference in
capital would necessarily mean that Ireland could never
become as rich as England. The cheapness of labor in
Ireland gave her no advantage, for experience every day
showed that where labor was dearest the manufacturer
was able to sell at the lowest price. Then came a condemnation of the old mencantilist conception when Burke
added that men must have a "strange opinion of the extent of the world, who believed that there was not room
enough in it for the trade of two such islands as these."

Finally, he referred to the fact that he was acting against
the wishes of his constituents in the part he was taking,
but, he felt, in conformity with their interests. Should his
conduct lead to the loss of his seat at Bristol, this loss
would serve the useful purpose of showing that a member
was adhering to principle against interest and popularity,
and that constituents were exercising their right to reject
their representative, not from corrupt motives, but in
their belief that he was acting against their judgment and
interest.

Despite the victory of the supporters of the bill on this
occasion, May 6, 1778, by 126 votes to 77, the measure
was killed on May 25 by an amendment for adjournment

proposed by Sir George Yonge. This was not a trick
motion which caught the supporters of the bill napping,
since it had already been decided to abandon the bill due
to the strength of the opposition.[56]

Pery and Sir Lucius O'Brien had gone to London and
assisted Knox in preparing and negotiating the concessionary measures.[57] Knox applied himself to smoothing the
ruffled feelings of English merchants and manufacturers,
and suggested compromises in the bills which could satisfy
opponents and yet retain sufficient substance in the concessions.[58] He blamed Irish members of the British Parliament for provoking further hostility in Britain:

The violence of some of our friends excited such a jealousy
of the determined purpose of the gentlemen connected with
Ireland, to carry matters with a high hand, and allow no compromise or modification, that a spirit was rising which would
soon have put an end to all our expectations.[59]

Confirmation of his view is found in a letter to Buckinghamshire from Edward Bacon, a commissioner of the
Board of Trade: "The over zeal of some gentlemen was
very injudicious . . . on the outset, in the first resolutions of the committee and raised such a storm as augured
very bad consequences." [60] Nugent, Midleton, and Conolly had been tactless and needlessly provocative. Their
speeches contrasted sharply with the restrained and diplomatic, yet forceful, delivery of Burke.

At first glance it is amazing that the British Government should have considered sweeping away the greater
part of the mercantilist restrictions on Irish trade. Only
the decision to grant major concessions to America—part
of the conciliatory offer carried to Philadelphia by Carlisle
in the spring of 1778—could have induced the Government to consider the proposals in regard to Ireland. No

doubt the desire to ensure Irish support now that France was entering the war, encouraged the adoption of the plan. But the deluge of petitions from the towns, combined obviously with pressure on members of parliament by constituents (such as Burke resisted), overcame the Government's intentions.

In practice, the concessions actually made were not of great value, largely because of the rejection of permission to import goods into Ireland direct from the plantations. When Nugent announced in June his intention of again moving for this right in the next session of parliament, he said that permission to export alone would be useless since Ireland could not afford to give long credit, and could speedily recover payment only by a corresponding import.[61] In assessing the value of the concessions granted, it is necessary to consider two letters which Edmund Burke wrote in April. In the first he said:

Do not be afraid. The things pretende [d to be done] for Ireland are frivolous; and if they were considerable, they [have not] capital to carry them on. They are intended to keep Ireland from diverting you with another rebellion.

A few days later he wrote:

These things are mere triffles [sic]; and known to be such, by those from Ireland, who seek, and by the Ministers here, who consent to them. But they are merely to satisfy the minds of the people there; to shew a good disposition in this country; and so prevent the spreading of universal discontent and disaffection.[62]

What he says gives one a shock until it is realized that he was writing to Richard Champion, a merchant of Bristol, and the letters were intended for circulation. He therefore had a purpose in minimizing the extent of the concessions. He wrote these letters a month before it was decided to abandon the direct import measure which certainly would not have been a minor concession. Three weeks after writing to Champion, he made his great speech in the Commons; both his speech and the debate were serious affairs and certainly not conducted in the interest of frivolity. Furthermore, he would have scarcely provoked the anger of his constituents merely on account of "trifles." Nevertheless, the two letters do cause one to reappraise the concessions and to remember that the omission of wool and woollen goods meant that Ireland's most important trade grievance was being left unattended.

During the course of these bills through the British Parliament, the Irish administration feared the bad effects on Ireland if the measures should be rejected.[63] For a while in May, it looked as if riots might break out in Dublin, but the danger passed.[64] Indignation was not confined to the lower classes, and great disappointment was expressed when the import bill was abandoned. At first, the bill's abandonment caused alarm, but it was soon realized that serious disturbances would not ensue, and that the right to export to the plantations had given much satisfaction.[65] Beresford agreed to a large extent with Heron's view that this concession had pleased moderate men, but added the warning, "If private dissatisfaction should work up disappointment, and inflame the distressed, it will go great lengths."[66]

The Irish newspapers were usually not too optimistic about the passing of all the concessions and maintained a detached attitude. Hope tinged with scepticism concerning their passing, and suspicion of the sincerity of the British Government, set the tone of newspaper editorials and correspondence. When the import measure was abandoned, ineffective attempts were made to start a non-importation movement, but they were not taken up seriously.[67] Yet the outburst that was to come in 1779 cannot have been created in that year alone; resentment must have smouldered. In May, 1778, Beresford had warned that there were gounds for anxiety in the disappointment over the failure of the import bill, and Pery, in a letter which he wrote in October to William Knox, and which dealt with the commercial issues, said that the situation in Ireland was bad and that serious trouble lay ahead.[68]

The depression resulting from the war had made itself acutely felt in Dublin by the beginning of 1778. Among the manufacturing workers unemployment was rife, the situation having become so serious that a relief fund was organized under the patronage of the Lord-Lieutenant who personally subscribed £100. Over £4,000 was raised, the principal donors, who gave £105 or £100, being: Lords Hertford (a former viceroy), Rockingham, Hillsborough, Meath, Donegall, Nugent, Milton, Egremont, the Duke of Devonshire, and Thomas Conolly.[69] Lord Meath asked every peer to buy a suit of Irish clothes for himself and each of his servants, while William Burton, a prominent landlord, held a special breakfast for members of the nobility and gentry who then toured the shops and purchased Irish goods. Buckinghamshire gave a great ball at which the guests wore clothes of Irish manufacture, an event which stirred journalistic imagination. That the age of chivalry still lived (Burke had not yet reflected!) was proved by the *Dublin Evening Journal* when it stated that the five hundred ladies at the ball "might vie with equal number, for beauty and politeness, in any part of the globe." Some months later, however, the same newspaper beat a retreat from gallantry by suggesting that the workmen would benefit if the nobility and gentry were to pay their bills. References were frequent to similar efforts to promote the purchase of native goods, including the formation of a club whose members would wear no clothes but those of Irish manufacture.[70]

The depression led to restriction of credit and the danger of widespread bankruptcies. In April the Government was obliged, in order to maintain public confidence, to give official backing to Finlay's Bank in the form of a statement inserted in the newspapers.[71] A month later, Sir Edward Newenham reported that, within a space of ten days, two banks and nineteen merchants had failed.[72]

Politically speaking, the most vital significance of the depression lay in its effect on the financial position of the Administration. For nearly a decade expenditure had exceeded revenue, and deficits had been met by borrowing on an unprecedented scale. The two years ending March 25 of 1775 and 1777 had been particularly unfavorable. The deficits—£190,000 (about 25 per cent of revenue) in the former year, and £130,000 (about 15 per cent of revenue) in the latter—had been met by loans.[73] The succeeding year, 1777–1778, saw a reduction of the deficit to £83,000, but the last months of this financial period, that is, the spring of 1778, witnessed what Heron called a "great sudden and unexpected fall" in the revenue.[74] Even this difficulty might have been surmounted if the Government had been able to borrow, but such was not the case; subscriptions to recently issued public loans had fallen off to almost nothing. The Administration found it impossible to obtain sufficient money from Dublin banks, and felt it necessary for Lord North to intervene if money were to be raised in London. In one of his letters to North appealing for assistance, Buckinghamshire referred to

a general distress for money throughout all ranks in the city [Dublin], no balance in the [Irish] Treasury, and scarcely any

in the hands of the several collectors, and the receipt of His
Majesty's revenue having fallen lower than has been known
for many years.[75]

What made the situation so desperate was the increased
military commitments, particularly the encampment of
the army for summer training, that resulted from the
entry of France into the war. In an attempt to relieve the
situation, the Lord-Lieutenant suspended payment of "all
salaries and pensions, civil and military, Parliamentary
grants, clothing arrears, etc., [and] of all other ordinary
payments." [76] but this saving was not sufficient and, if
money were not forthcoming from London, the military
measures "so absolutely necessary for the defense of this
kingdom [Ireland], must be obstructed in such a manner,
that it cannot be said how fatal the consequences may
be." [77] Finally, a loan of £50,000 was obtained from the
Bank of England, and on the arrival of this money in
Dublin, the Viceroy gave the order for the encampment
of the troops a month later than had originally been
planned.[78]

The immediate crisis had been surmounted, but the
financial difficulties of the Government remained. The
revenue continued to be inadequate, and the same difficulty in finding the money for the encampment of the
troops was again experienced in the summer of 1779. The
operation was held up for over a month until the British
Government had sent across £50,000. As in 1778, the
Viceroy was forced to suspend payment on many of the
Administration's commitments.[79]

For the government the real disaster arising from this
crisis was the inability, owing to lack of money, to implement the Militia Act, passed by the Irish Parliament in
the early summer of 1778. Confronted with the danger

of a French invasion, and in the absence of any militia under governmental auspices, a large number of voluntary military associations were formed in the second half of 1778 which had come to be known as the Volunteers before the end of that year. It was the Volunteers who gave to the Patriots that vital power which forced the British Government to grant Free Trade and completely altered the proportion of forces in Irish politics.

NOTES FOR CHAPTER III

1 T. S. Ashton, *Economic Fluctuations in England 1700–1800* (London, 1959), pp. 100, 130, 136.

2 See Appendix A.

3 On his death, the *Gentleman's Magazine* (Vol. LXIII, Part II, 1793), pp. 867–68, paid him the following tribute: "Private society has seldom experienced a greater loss than it has suffered by the death of this amiable nobleman. Placed in a most arduous situation, at the critical period of 1779–80 as Lord Lieutenant of Ireland . . . few, if any, of his predecessors conducted themselves with more propriety, or encountered greater difficulties. Conciliatory manners, elegant national [sic] hospitality, without intemperance or profusion; generosity, founded on its true basis, justice and economy, were the fair characteristics of Lord Buckinghamshire's administration; and he possessed, in an eminent degree, the qualities of a man of rank and fashion—politeness with ease, and dignity without pride."

4 Heron was Lord-Treasurer's Remembrancer in the Court of Exchequer and came from a legal family, his father and two brothers holding the recordership of Newark. His genealogical data in Burke's *Peerage and Baronetage* (London, undated but circa 1841–42, p. 514) gives no indication of any distinction or aristocratic influence. He was described in 1780 by an important political observer as a mill-stone around the viceroy's neck. (William Knox, Under-Secretary for the Colonies, to Germain, May 26, 1780, HMC, Stopford-Sackville Papers, I, 270).

5 The house is now a boarding school conducted by the Sisters of the Holy Faith.

6 November 27, 1776, Heron Papers.

7 Brian Fitzgerald, ed., *Correspondence of Emily, Duchess of Leinster* (Irish Manuscripts Commission, Dublin, 1957), III, 253–56.

8 Buckinghamshire to Germain, October 13–15, 1777, Heron Papers.

9 HJ, October 17, 1777.

10 Beresford to Thomas Allan, a commissioner of the Irish Revenue, Oct. 14, 1777, *Correspondence of the Rt. Hon. John Beresford,* ed. William Beresford (London, 1854), I, 16–20.

11 Heron to Robinson, October 13, 1777, Heron Papers.

12 Buckinghamshire to Germain, October 13–15, 1777, Heron Papers.

13 Scott to John Robinson, November 21, 1779, *Beresford Corr.,* I, 81–84.

14 Germain to Buckinghamshire, October 23, 1777, Heron Papers.

15 Buckinghamshire to Germain, February 2, 1777, Heron Papers.

16 Buckinghamshire to Germain, June 27, 1777, Heron Papers.

17 Beresford to Robinson, October 13, 1779, *Beresford Corr.,* I, 53–60.

18 August 23, 1778, HMC, Stopford-Sackville Papers, I, 251.

19 *Dublin Gazette,* February 6, 1776.

20 HJ, February 7, 9, 23, 1776.

21 *Dublin Gazette,* November 5, 1776.

22 Harcourt to Weymouth, November 15, 1776; Buckinghamshire to Weymouth, June 28, 1777, July 9, October 30, 1777, SP, 63/455, f. 182, SP 63/457, ff. 147, 219, SP 63/458,fffl 153–55.

23 HJ, November 3, 1777; Buckinghamshire to Weymouth, November 1, 1777, SP 63/458, f. 164; Buckinghamshire to Germain, November 1, 1777, HMC, Stopford-Sackville Papers, I, 247.

24 Robinson to Heron, October 2, 1777, Heron Papers.

25 Buckinghamshire to Weymouth, October 30, 1777, SP 63/458, ff. 153–55.

26 Weymouth to Buckinghamshire, November 27, 1777, SP 63/458, f. 205.

27 HJ, December 12, 1777.

28 HJ, December 17, 1777.

29 HJ, December 17, 1777; Buckinghamshire to Weymouth, December 17, 1777, SP 63/458, ff. 274–75.

30 Buckinghamshire to Germain, November 28, 1777, HMC, Stopford-Sackville Papers, I, 247–48.

31 Buckinghamshire to Weymouth, December 17, 1777, SP 63/458, ff. 274–75.

32 George III to Robinson, February 7, 1778, Add. Mss., 37833, f. 216.

33 Weymouth to Buckinghamshire, August 20, September 4, December 24, 1778, SP 63/461, ff. 47, 93, 324; Heron to Buckinghamshire, March 22, 1779, Heron Papers.

34 Pery to Heron, September 2, 1778, *Memoirs of the Life and Times of Henry Grattan*, ed. Henry Grattan the Younger (London: 1839–1846), I, 335.

35 October 9, 1778, HMC, Emly Papers, I, 200.

36 Curiously enough, when Free Trade had been granted, this bounty was continued.

37 The restraints are described in some detail by George O'Brien, *The Economic History of Ireland in the eighteenth century* (Dublin and London, 1918), p. 173 *et seq*.

38 *Grattan Memoirs*, I, 384.

39 July 28, 1777, Heron Papers.

40 Anonymous [William Knox], *Extra Official State Papers* (Dublin, 1789), pp. 188–89.

41 Knox to O'Brien, August 23, 1777, Knox, *Extra Official*, p. 188.

42 Heron to Knox, September 27, 1777; Knox to Heron, February 9, 1777, Knox, *Extra Official*, p. 193; Buckinghamshire to North, February 20, 1778, Knox, *Extra Official*, p. 197.

43 Knox to Heron, March 14, 1778, Knox, *Extra Official*, p. 205 *et seq*.

44 *Grattan Memoirs*, I, p. 298 *et seq*.

45 Heron to Knox, March 21, 1778, Knox, *Extra Official*, p. 207.

46 *Beresford Corr.*, I, 21–24.

47 British House of Commons, April 2, 1778, *Parliamentary History*, XIX, 1100–1106.

48 British House of Commons, April 7, 1778, *Parl. Hist.*, XIX, 1107 *et seq*.

49 Knox to Heron, March 28, 1778, Knox, *Extra Official*, pp. 212–216; Knox to Heron, May 4, 1778, Knox, *Extra Official*, pp. 224–28.

50 British House of Commons, April 7, 1778, *Parl. Hist.*, XIX, 1107–1113.

51 *British Commons Journal*, XXXVI, 938 *et seq*.

52 *Annual Register* (London, 1778), p. 176.

53 18 Geo. III, c. 56 and c. 55.

54 18 Geo. III, c. 55.

55 This account of the debate is taken from the *Parliamentary History*, XIX, 1115–24.

56 *Parl. His.*, XIX 1123–26; Heron to Knox, May 22, 1778, HMC, Knox Papers, p. 234.

57 Beresford to Allan, April 4, 1778, *Beresford Corr.*, I, 27–28; Knox to Heron, April 21, 1778, Heron to Knox, April 25, 1778, Knox, *Extra Official*, pp. 218–21.

58 This is shown in numerous letters between Heron and Knox

in Knox, *Extra Official*, pp. 212–39 and also in Heron to Porten, May 10, 1778, SP 63/460, f. 64.

59 Knox to Heron, May 14, 1778, Knox, *Extra Official*, pp. 234–36.

60 June 4, 1778, HMC, Lothian Papers, pp. 331–32.

61 *Parl. Hist.* XIX, 1126.

62 Burke to Champion, April 11, 14, 1778, *The Correspondence of Edmund Burke*, Vol. III, ed. George H. Guttridge (Cambridge University Press, 1961), 427, 429–30.

63 Heron to Knox, May 6, 1778, Knox, *Extra Official*, pp. 228–29.

64 Buckinghamshire to Germain, May 12, 22, 1778, Heron Papers; Heron to Robinson, May 13, 1778, Heron Letter Book.

65 Heron to Knox, May 22, 24, 1778, HMC, Knox Papers, pp. 234–35.

66 Beresford to Allan, May 25, 1778, *Beresford Corr.*, I, 31–34.

67 DEJ, May 21, 23, 26 and June 23, 1778; FJ, May 23, 1778. Sir Samuel Bradstreet urged the establishment of such a movement in the Irish Commons on June 5, 1778.

68 Beresford to Allan, May 25, 1778, *Beresford Corr.*, I, 31–34; Pery to Knox, October 23, 1778, HMC, Knox Papers, pp. 235–36.

69 HJ, May 13, 1778; FDJ, August 27, 1778; FJ, June 11, 1778.

70 HJ, May 18, 1778; DEJ, February 5, May 21, 1778; DEJ, February 19, May 19, 30, 1778; FDJ, February 19, 1778; DEP, August 6, 1778.

71 DEJ, April 9, 1778; HJ, April 15, 1778; Lifford to Pery, April 9, 1778; HMC, Emly Papers, I, 196–97.

72 Newenham to Dartmouth, May 15, 1778, HMC, Dartmouth Papers, pp. 240–41.

73 See Appendix A.

74 Heron to [Porten], May 25, 1778, SP 63/460, ff. 145–46.

75 April 30, 1778, *Grattan Memoirs*, I, 321–22.

76 Buckinghamshire to North, May 16, 1778, *Grattan Memoirs*, I, 324–25.

77 Buckinghamshire to North, April 30, 1778, *Grattan Memoirs*, I, 321–23.

78 Buckinghamshire to Weymouth, June 3, 6, 1778, July 4, 1778, SP 63/460, ff. 180, 205–206, 322.

79 Buckinghamshire to Weymouth, June 5, 27, 28, 1779, July 3, 12, 1779, SP 63/465, ff. 75, 181, 179, 249, 367; North to Pery, August 3, 1779, MC, Emily Papers, I, 201–202, Heron to Robinson, August 20, 1779, *Beresford Corr.*, I, 46–51.

IV

War with France and the Formation of the Volunteers

In the middle of March, 1778, the British Government was officially informed by the French ambassador in London of the Franco-American treaties of friendship and commerce. This meant war with France. The British Parliament was informed of this position on March 17, and both Houses immediately passed addresses of loyalty to the king. The Whigs proposed amendments calling for the dismissal of Lord North's ministry on grounds of incompetence, but without success.[1]

The Irish Parliament greeted the news with an outburst of loyalty and showed little of the discontent voiced by the English Whigs. Even before the legislature received official notification, the Commons passed a vote of loyalty to the king which was proposed by a leading Patriot, Denis Daly. When the addresses that corresponded to the English addresses of March 17 were introduced, they were voted for with the same enthusiasm. Grattan and the Duke of Leinster tried to provide a Whig opposition similar to what had been done in the British Parliament, but they were unsuccessful.[2] The Patriots for the most part stood four-square behind the Administration now that France was the enemy. The Protestant Parliament had no intention of toying with disloyalty now that there existed the possibility of a (Catholic) French invasion.

Similar protests of loyalty poured in from counties and principal towns.[3] Sir Edward Newenham, a leading Patriot and opponent of the Government, did everything possible to encourage addresses of loyalty, even to the extent of opposing Grattan's attempt to interfere with the Commons' address.[4] Nearly all these resolutions were simple declarations of zeal for the Government in the present emergency, references to France and the Bourbons being frequent. In two places—Carrickfergus and King's County—a discordant note was struck by a reference to the restrictions on Irish trade. At the Dublin county meeting an amusingly impudent but ineffective attempt was made, probably by the picturesque radical, Napper Tandy, to pass censure on Lord North's ministry.[5]

Owing to the delicacy of their position with respect to the possibility of a French invasion (in the Commons Hussey Burgh and John Scott, the Attorney-General, had expressed confidence in Catholic loyalty),[6] the Catholics were on their mettle. Consequently, they were quick to present an address to the Lord-Lieutenant signed by three hundred of their number, including the six peers—Fingall, Gormanston, Trimblestown, Dillon, Cahir, and Kenmare—and Anthony Dermott, the Secretary of the Catholic Committee. It was a simple statement of loyalty, making no explicit reference to either America or France.[7] The only hostile reference to America in any of the addresses, Catholic or Protestant, came from the Catholics of Newry.[8] In the British Commons on March 17, in the debate on the loyalty address, Thomas Conolly (he had a seat in both the British and Irish Houses) said that in the southern parts of Ireland at least 150,000 Catholics were ready to aid any effective French invading force.[9] This statement must not be taken too seriously, since Irish political leaders were at that time in London pressing for commercial concessions, and were likely to stress the need to conciliate Ireland, and, furthermore, Conolly was inclined to make foolish speeches.

What the attitude of the mass of Catholics was, is impossible to say with any degree of confidence. Even contemporaries could only hazard speculative opinions. In all probability they lacked political consciousness and were illiterate to an extent that makes it virtually impossible for the historian to assess their opinions, but, were the French to have landed a strong force, traditional feelings might have erupted and then anything might have happened.

Presbyterian sentiment, which had been strongly opposed to the British Government on the American war, somersaulted into loyalty once the French entered the arena. Buckinghamshire hailed their new outlook in a letter to Weymouth: "By accounts received from very good authority the idea of a French war has not only altered the language but the disposition of the Presbyterians." [10] William Steel Dickson, the celebrated Presbyterian preacher who had condemned the American war as a mad and wicked crusade on the part of the British Government,[11] took a very different line when confronted with the possibility of a French invasion: "Should necessity call us forth to oppose the jealous enemies of our liberties and religion, we are ready to prove ourselves the steady friends of the constitution and the rights of our country." [12]

War with France made the proper defense of Ireland a matter of urgency. Weymouth immediately instructed Buckinghamshire to obtain a vote of credit from the Irish Parliament to meet the increased military expenditure.[13] A grant of £300,000 was passed against some ineffective opposition from Grattan, who felt that half that sum should be sufficient. Hussey Burgh thought that the voting of the larger sum would have the effect of impressing the country's internal as well as external enemies—an indication that anxiety about internal loyalty still existed.[14]

According to the Lord-Lieutenant there were 12,921 men on the Irish Establishment, 3,039 of whom had been sent to America, leaving a balance of 9,882 in Ireland. As this latter force was not complete, the actual strength in Ireland was 8,871. It was proposed to recruit some 2,500 men in Ireland, to which would be added two regiments from Britain totalling about 2,300. Thus, it was expected that in due course, and with the present complement brought up to full strength, the army in Ireland would number nearly 15,000. The cost of maintenance for two years of the two British regiments and the 2,500 men to be recruited in Ireland, together with the cost of encamping the entire army for five months of summer training, was estimated at £298,000. This figure would be an addition to the current military expenses.[15]

Therefore, the French entry into the war had the effect of laying a substantial burden on the fiscal resources of the Irish government, resources already depleted by the economic depression. Between 1769 and 1782 the Irish revenue was greater than £800,000 for only one year.[16] These extra military expenses dealt the Administration a heavy blow which had grave political consequences. It was only with the aid of special financial assistance from London that Dublin Castle was able to provide for the most essential military needs in 1778 and 1779. As elsewhere described,[17] the Government's inability to organize a militia through lack of funds led to the formation of the Volunteers.

Even before war had broken out with France, George Ogle, the energetic Patriot, had prepared a militia bill, and on March 19 had obtained leave from the Irish Commons to introduce it. He had put through a similar measure in the previous session of Parliament, but it had been rejected by the English Privy Council as unnecessary, too expensive, and likely to interfere with army needs.[18] In supporting his motion on March 19, Ogle said that in the event of war with France and a consequent invasion, it would be necessary to have a militia to deal with the large number of disloyal people in Ireland. He clearly had in mind a force that would be exclusively Protestant.[19] There was no opposition in the Parliament to the raising of some form of military force, but much discussion took place on the question of whether it should take the form of a militia or of independent companies. The Lord-Lieutenant preferred the latter, which if organized on a limited scale, would cost no more than a militia—some £35,000 for a force of 4,500 men for two years. He thought that unless there was an invasion, they would merely be needed for maintaining law and order in areas from which the military had been withdrawn.[20] Ogle was indifferent as to which type of force should be organized, and only desisted from adding a clause for the raising of independent companies when he was informed that the king had the right to do this in times of danger.[21]

Some of the peers in the Irish Privy Council objected to a militia on the grounds that in the south it was unnecessary due to the presence of the army, and it might be difficult to form a militia there because of the small Protestant population; in the north it would be composed of men likely to sympathize with a resistance to the payment of "rents, tithes and assessments." The peers considered that the intention of Ogle's measure might be more effectively aided by the formation of independent companies by the larger landowners.[22] The Lord-Lieutenant transmitted the heads to London with the recommendation that they be passed, since their rejection would produce much disappointment, and it might be necessary to raise a militia if the formation of independent companies should prove impracticable.[23] The English Privy Council added a clause, suggested by Pery and recommended by Buckinghamshire, that Protestant Dissenters be allowed to take commissions in the proposed militia.[24] The measure thus amended was sent back to Dublin and passed by the Irish Parliament, receiving the royal assent from the Viceroy on July 1, 1778.

The proposed independent companies bore no resemblance to the force voluntarily organized towards the end of 1778 and known as the Volunteers. The former would have been organized under state supervision, and would have served with the army on army rates of pay, but without any obligation to serve overseas. The cost of such a force would have been close to four times that of a militia of comparable numbers. That was why Buckinghamshire thought that independent companies would have to be maintained on a much more limited scale than had been suggested by the Irish House of Commons.[25]

In spite of all the fuss, the Militia Act was never implemented, essentially because of the Government's financial difficulties. The raising of a force, even of the most limited size, would not justify the cost which the Lord-

Lieutenant estimated at about £38,000 a year. In a report to Weymouth on December 12, 1778, he gave this as the main reason why he had not organized a militia; additional factors which supported his decision were the lateness of the season and the hope that this force might not be necessary. He believed that the Government would be unable to organize and maintain such a force unless additional funds could be obtained.[26] It is clear from this report and from his correspondence in the early part of 1779, that Buckinghamshire failed to appreciate the political power inherent in the Volunteers.

The entry of France into the war rendered urgent the formation of a militia, or some sort of independent companies. Their contribution of local support to the regular army in repelling an invasion would be important. This support would be of special significance as a means of providing resistance against an enemy landing in a particular locality, pending the arrival of regular army units. Such locally organized bodies would be well suited to dealing with the populace should the latter show a disposition to join the French in a common cause. Even without any pro-French sympathies in the people, there would be a grave necessity to maintain law and order, and to ensure the defense of property, not only in the area under attack, but throughout the country, since whole provinces, in the event of invasion, might be denuded of army garrisons. Even the concentration of the regular troops in particular places for summer training involved this danger.[27] It was to be expected that when the Government was unable to array some form of local force, the vacuum should be filled by voluntary bodies.

There was, of course, nothing new in the formation of these forces for defense against invasion or internal disorders. But the latter part of 1778 witnessed their growth and extension throughout the country on an unprecedented scale. Even before the Militia Act had been passed, such corps were being organized. In May volunteering activities were reported from Dublin, Cork, and Belfast.[28] In fact, corps were being formed in Belfast some months earlier.[29] In July, Lord Shannon's "regiments" in Cork were mentioned as expressing hostility to the Catholic Relief Bill.[30] Nevertheless, these reports did not mean much, and it is only with the approach of autumn that these military bodies became numerous and widespread. In October a contingent calling itself the Dublin Volunteers was organized under the command of the Duke of Leinster,[31] and one can take this event as marking the establishment of the Volunteers as an important national force.

The proceedings of this group of associations can be followed in the editorials, news items, insertions, and correspondence in the press. On February 1, 1779, the Patriot member of parliament, George Ogle, presented colors to the Wexford "regiment of Independents" and paid tribute to their zeal in having prevented the internal broils with which many other parts of the country were currently distressed.[32] On March 23, the Dublin Volunteers (Leinster's corps) paraded and "went through their different evolutions, with a regularity and exactness, which would have done honour to any veteran corps." In pronouncing this eulogy, the *Dublin Evening Post* expressed pride in such activities when "civil broils and foreign enemies threaten the empire, and a corrupt ministry are trying every means to sap the basis of our once glorious constitution." [33] The Whiggish tone of most of the Volunteers is suggested by this newspaper when it adds that the different associations throughout the country are determined to protect the constitution and the blessings of the

Glorious Revolution against an "insidious set of evil counsellors," another name for Lord North's ministry.

Throughout the spring and summer of 1779 the newspapers continued to praise the Volunteers. Leinster reviewed the Dublin Volunteers at least once a month. In
August the Eyrecourt Volunteers in County Galway paraded under their commander, Lord Eyre, and the Enniscorthy Volunteers caused a correspondent in the Dublin
Evening Post to go into raptures in praise of their excellence and the patriotism of their commander, Sir Vesey
Colclough, the other member of parliament for County
Wexford:

When we consider the *Enniscorthy Corps* as the first raised in
Ireland—when we consider them pointing out a laudable example, which has been followed by the respectable inhabitants
of most counties in the kingdom; when we consider the sum-
mit of military discipline to which they have attained . . . we
must allow that real patriot, Sir Vesey Colclough, worthy
every honor and eulogium.[34]

A sobering note was struck by a correspondent in the
same newspaper a week earlier with a warning against
"that false security which public shows are apt to excite in
a people," that the times are fraught with danger, and
while "we are indulging ourselves with the glare of useless
processions, the enemy may be on the coast, ready to awake
us from our fatal inattentions."

The most impressive tribute to the growing importance
and strength of the Volunteers comes from the numerous
county meetings which placed notices in the press announcing their intention of forming Volunteer corps. The
first of these gatherings to advertise this intention were
the "Gentlemen and Inhabitants" of County Meath on
July 12, 1779. Other meetings followed until by the end

of September they had been held in ten counties and advertisements had been placed in the press.[35] Meetings were probably held in most of the other counties, since the lack of an announcement in the press would not mean that a meeting had not been held. Cork, Galway, Down, and Antrim had many corps but there is no report of any such assemblies in these counties.

It is difficult to say, even approximately, just how many men were enrolled in the various corps. Members of parliament who wished to point to the might of the force talked of 40,000 Volunteers, but they probably exaggerated. The newspapers were more modest. The *Dublin Evening Post,* the most useful of the newspapers because of the coverage given to news and editorial comment, gave the number in 1779 as 10,000 in April, 18,000 in July, 47,000 (obviously an error of some kind) in August, and 19,000 in September.[36] These figures were probably substantially correct (excepting of course the figure of 47,000) since the Lord-Lieutenant reported the Volunteers in May as not exceeding 8,000, while the sober-minded Beresford thought in October that they numbered not less than 25,000.[37] The various Volunteer groups were much too disconnected and their growth too spontaneous to enable anyone to make an accurate calculation. The *Dublin Evening Post* asked repeatedly that commanders should send in a report of the size of their units so that an estimate might be made, but no estimate was ever published.

The Volunteers were a group of Protestant associations in which Catholics were at first either not admitted, or merely tolerated in small numbers. The members constantly celebrated, to an extent which makes one wonder just how formidable they would have been in the event of a French invasion. Their "loyal toasts" were nearly all of a Whiggish Protestant type, and included bumpers to the House of Hanover, the Glorious Revolution, the siege of Derry, and the battles of the Boyne and Aughrim. The Eyrecourt Volunteers celebrated the accession of the Hanoverian regime "by which our religious and civil rights are insured to us and our posterity." [38] The anniversary of the battle of Culloden was celebrated by Sir Vesey Colclough's corps in Wexford who "had not been on parade since King William's birthday." [39] It was reported that various corps intended to commemorate William's birthday, November 4, and to make it a special occasion in honor of "their great deliverer" since the people were determined to show a "truly Whig spirit" against the "Toryism of the Court." [40] At a Boyne celebration in the following year,

one of the sons of Mars having sacrificed rather too liberally at the shrine of Bacchus . . . fell a prostrate worshipper of the Glorious Memory, and was carried off the field a victim of enthusiastic loyalty. [41]

The new "military" force was not without its oddities:

An event in the County Kilkenny, now caused great commotion and filled all the newspapers in England and Ireland— Sir John Blunden and the new raised Volunteers fell out— they burned him in effigy, and he in contempt warmed himself at the fire. [42]

Both the bibulous and more serious celebrations of the Volunteers were of such a Whiggish and Protestant nature that one would hardly expect to see many Catholics among them, quite apart from the fact that it was illegal for Catholics to bear arms. That these organizations were composed almost completely of Protestants is borne out by several events that occurred in 1779.

The first of these incidents took place in May, 1779, when the alarm of a French invasion induced the Catholics of the Waterford area to consider forming themselves into military associations, but they were discouraged from doing so by Lord Tyrone, the head of the Beresford family and the principal aristocrat in that part of Ireland. He considered that the formation of Catholic corps

would raise such a noise at this, and the other side of the water [i.e. in England] as must distress Government; but I convinced the leaders to change their ideas, and understand they will, in an address to Government, offer their assistance to join with the Protestant inhabitants, in case of any enemy's landing, to defend the country in whatever manner Government shall please to point out.[43]

Early in June, 1779, as a result of an erroneous report that the French had landed in Bantry Bay, the military in Cork city were ordered to march towards Bantry while the Volunteers were arrayed for the policing of the city. "A great number of Roman Catholic gentlemen immediately offered themselves as volunteers, to join with their Protestant fellow-citizens, and were well received." Later the Passage Union Volunteers (near Cork city) formally thanked their "Roman Catholic neighbours who so loyally and spiritedly offered to join them on . . . the alarm of . . . the French having landed in Bantry Bay." The Clonmel Association of Volunteers thanked the Clonmel Catholics for having offered their services "which offer the Association accepted of, and as the alarm appears to have been groundless, the necessity of troubling those gentlemen consequently discontinues." [44] In describing the events the (Protestant) Bishop of Cork praised the Cork Volunteers among whom "there were a few Roman Catholics who desired to be admitted and were accepted." [45] The obvious conclusion is that Catholics in Cork and

Clonmel and, presumably, in most parts of the south of Ireland, were not normally in the Volunteers and were admitted, if at all, only in times of extreme danger.

In the midland town of Longford, a county meeting was held on July 27, 1779, and the inhabitants decided to form corps. When it was learned that the Earl of Granard, a local aristocrat, had admitted Catholics into his own corps, a second meeting was held at which it was decided that only Protestants should be admitted to the new corps.[46] On September 14 a Roman Catholic is mentioned in the *Freeman's Journal* as having suggested that Dublin Catholics should emulate their co-religionists in Dingle, a small town in Co. Kerry (one suppresses a smile at the thought of Dingle being cited as an example to the second city of the British Empire!), by uniting with Protestants in the defense of Ireland against French and Spaniards. The implication is that in Dublin, Catholics were not enrolled in the force, at least not in any significant number.

In August, 1780, in the Irish Commons, Sir Boyle Roche described the Volunteers as "composed in general of the Protestant tenantry of Ireland." [47] There is virtually nothing in either newspapers or correspondence in 1779 and 1780 to merit challenging the substantial truth of Boyle's description. After 1780, a change set in and Catholics were admitted more readily, but the force remained essentially Protestant.

Interesting sidelights on the Volunteers come from two Catholics, Rickard and Maurice O'Connell. The former was a rather wild young officer in the French army. He was embittered by having been prevented by the Penal Laws from pursuing a profession in his native land. Also, he felt the contempt of the professional soldier for the amateur:

Would to God . . . that we were at this moment 200,000 strong in Ireland. . . . I would kick the Members [of Parliament] and their Volunteers and their unions and their Societies to the Devil! I would make the Rascally spawn of Damned Cromwell curse the hour of his Birth![48]

Rickard's cousin, Maurice O'Connell of Derrynane, Co. Kerry, received a request from Robert Fitzgerald, M.P., the Knight of Kerry, to assist in the formation of a corps of Volunteers:

I have been thinking of a scheme for preventing the Barony of Iveragh from being the asylum of the rogues and vagabonds of the other parts of the country. The Associations of Volunteers have done wonders all over the Kingdom, in civilising the country and quelling lawless proceedings. Why should not a Corps be raised in that Barony? . . . The gentlemen of property of your religion, uniting with the Protestants, might soon raise a body of men, I should imagine, that might be relied on for executing the above purpose.[49]

O'Connell's reply was very definite:

I am fully convinced that the Roman Catholic gentlemen of Iveragh would readily unite with their Protestant neighbours . . . to form a Corps did they think such a measure would meet the approbation of the Legislature. They would, in common with every Catholic of standing in Ireland, be exceedingly happy by every means in their power to give additional weight and strength and security to the kingdom; but what can they do while the laws of their country forbid them the use of arms? Under such circumstances, I look upon it to be their duty to confine themselves to that line of conduct marked out for them by the Legislature, and with humility and resignation wait for a further relaxation of the laws, which a more enlightened and liberal way of thinking, added to a clearer and more deliberate attention to the real interests and prosperity of the country will, I hope, soon bring about.[50]

There is double irony in O'Connell's letter. He was taking sweet revenge on the Parliament by showing a wonderful respect for its anti-Catholic legislation, thereby saving himself the trouble and expense of helping to organize a Volunteer corps. This meticulous reverence for law had not prevented him from adding to his patrimony over a long period by engaging in contraband.

A few years later, in 1782, Nemesis overtook O'Connell when he was caught red-handed by an unusually diligent revenue officer. On his journey home from Derrynane the officer was attacked and almost killed by a party of O'Connell's tenants, furious at losing their share of the contraband. As a result, Maurice and his brother Morgan (father of Daniel O'Connell, the leader of the movement for Catholic Emancipation a generation later) were charged with instigating attempted murder. They were almost certainly innocent, being much too wise in their generation to perpetrate anything so blatantly foolish. There followed a warrant from the Chief Justice of the King's Bench, Lord Annaly, committing the brothers to prison without right of bail.

Fortunately, the O'Connells had a friend in Dominic Trant, a leading barrister, who prevailed upon his brother-in-law, John Fitzgibbon, M.P. (the future lord chancellor), to persuade Annaly to cancel the warrant. Thus, they were granted bail, and at the next assizes the Grand Jury threw out the charge, and all ended peacefully.

Trant's letter to Fitzgibbon on the subject gives an insight into the "backdoor" toleration which Catholics in the eighteenth century often enjoyed, particularly if possessed of influential friends. It is also an amusing testimony to the fact that dealing in contraband, or what the nineteenth century so primly called smuggling, cast no slur on a man's reputation. Trant describes the accused as

gentlemen of reputation and consequence . . . of character and considerable property . . . of probity and honour . . . of a very ancient Roman Catholic family, which has preserved a remnant of its former property thro' all the Revolutions of this Kingdom.[51]

A primary function of the Volunteers, and one readily undertaken, was the maintenance of order and the support of the civil authorities. They filled the role of a police force in conducting offenders to the courts and to prison, suppressing lawless groups and sometimes assisting with the collection of tithes.

During 1779 and 1780 the newspapers made constant reference to these activities of which two characteristic examples can be mentioned. One was the tribute paid by the *Dublin Evening Post* of April 27, 1779, to Sir Vesey Colclough's corps, the first formed in Ireland "on the constitutional plan of independence." Their conduct was such that had it been imitated earlier, "we should not have heard of the houghers or White-Boys, of whom they entirely rid the county of Wexford, almost as soon as they appeared in it." In the summer of 1779, a certain Mr. Trench was reported as expressing gratitude to

the Earl of Clanricarde and the gentlemen of his corps; to Lord Eyre and the gentlemen of his corps; to Mr. Carleton and gentlemen of the Athlone Volunteers; and also to the neighbouring gentlemen, for their readiness and alacrity in coming to Ballinasloe on hearing of the riot at the wool-fair of said town; and their diligence in taking, securing and conducting to Galway gaol, many of the promoters of the said riots.[52]

In his important letter to Weymouth of December 12, 1778, concerning his omission to organize a militia or independent companies, Buckinghamshire explained that the fear of invasion had induced the maritime towns to organize local forces for their own protection and that this practice had spread to the inland parts of the country. These forces [the Volunteers] consisted of Protestants usually under the direction of "persons of distinction" and appeared to have nothing in view but "the defense of their properties against an attack, either foreign or internal." They had applied to him for arms and ammunition but, since they were illegal bodies, he had refused to comply. On the other hand, he had not attempted to suppress them, because their conduct had been conducive to public order, and because it might be dangerous to interfere with them in the absence of any state militia.[53]

The Lord-Lieutenant did not appreciate the vital importance of what was taking place. His letter of December 12 conveys the impression that these voluntary organizations enjoyed his approval because they supported civil order. His attitude was still complacent two months later:

The numbers of the associated companies greatly exceed my expectations, they have grown up insensibly, but none of the servants of the Crown seem to think them dangerous.[54]

Uneasiness was first felt in England, and the Lord-Lieutenant was obliged to gather more exact information. On February 21, 1779, he wrote to Pery at his home in Co. Limerick:

As there is some solicitude in England respecting the Independent Companies [i.e. the voluntary or military associations as they were usually called at this time], you would oblige me much in procuring me nearly a correct account of the number of men under that description in the parts of Ireland where you stand most intimately connected, and how they are commanded.[55]

Since the Viceroy's principal counsellors in Dublin Castle had advised him not to be alarmed at the spread of these organizations, one cannot accuse him of gross neglect, or of blindness in failing to perceive the great menace they were to become. Nevertheless, a shrewder observer would have been less complacent. The advisers most influential with him were Irish servants of the Crown—Pery, Scott, and Hussey Burgh—and it may well have been that as Irishmen, either connected closely with the landed classes or in a position to purchase estates, they saw with understandable approval the formation of a force which appeared to be bringing civil order into rural life. Those Crown servants who were English were not very influential with the Viceroy, excepting the unimpressive Heron. The most important of them was Lifford, the lord chancellor, but he was an easygoing man who made no attempt to play any major role in politics. Buckinghamshire's relatives, Leinster and Conolly, very probably shared the Irish Crown servants' approval of the Volunteers, especially since the two of them were very prominent organizers of Volunteer corps.

The continued financial embarrassment of the Administration made it impossible, even as late as May, 1779, to form a militia or take over the Volunteers and bring them under some sort of official control. The latter course would involve the provision of arms and uniforms, an expense which the Lord-Lieutenant considered would be too much for "our exhausted treasury." [56] Since they were a force with no legal right to exist, the Viceroy had to be careful to give them no formal recognition though he claimed, in defending his conduct, that he had given them as much discouragement as prudence would permit "when the arm and good-will of every individual might have been wanting for the defense of the State." [57] Offers of assistance by Volunteers were definitely but tactfully refused. In May, 1779, Lord Clanricarde, a prominent aristocrat in the west of Ireland, offered the services of the Clanricarde Volunteers to the Government in the event of invasion.[58] The Lord-Lieutenant's chilling reply was typical of official policy:

. . . as the associations of numbers of armed men, formed under their own regulations in different parts of this kingdom, cannot, as His Excellency is advised, be justified by law, it would not be proper for His Excellency to give any encouragement or sanction to them. At the same time, his Excellency cannot but be pleased with the zeal intended . . . and, in case of an actual invasion, would think himself bound to call upon all his Majesty's subjects qualified to give aid and assistance . . . in such a manner as his Majesty's servants shall judge to be best adapted for that purpose.[59]

In the summer of 1779, strong pressure was put on the Lord-Lieutenant to distribute arms to the volunteers due to the hostile intentions of Spain which had led to a declaration of war in June. His first reaction was to give a polite refusal, but later he changed his mind and decided to meet the need by obtaining authority from the Irish Privy Council in July to distribute old militia arms to

the governors of the several counties of this kingdom, for the better preservation of the peace and safety thereof, upon application for that purpose, and upon their giving an acknowledgment in writing, containing an engagement to return the same when demanded.[60]

As a result of this decision, 16,000 arms were issued, 500 to the governor of each county.[61]

Every care was taken that this action should not convey any legal recognition of the Volunteers. The minute of the Irish Privy Council's decision makes no mention of military associations or any suggestion as to what the governors are to do with the arms.[62] Heron's reply to Charlemont's request for arms as governor of Co. Armagh is similarly discreet, and limits itself to saying that "his Excellency has no objection to your lordship's distributing that number [500 arms] to such persons as you may think proper for the purposes aforesaid." [63] By placing responsibility on the governors for the distribution of the arms, the Administration was able to satisfy the demand for arms and yet continue to refuse formal recognition to the Volunteers.[64] The government's action also meant that the arms were being distributed in a manner that ensured, as far as possible, that prominent aristocrats would supervise the distribution and be responsible for the use of the arms after they had been issued. Once handed out to the Volunteers there was of course, not too much that anyone could do, whether it be the government or a great lord, to ensure that the arms would not be used for purposes which Dublin Castle would not approve. This excessively discreet way of doing things was not very dignified and only advertised the Government's fear of the Volunteers and its financial inability to meet the requirements of the present situation.

Much the same difficulty was experienced in the summer of 1779 over the encampment of the military, as had been experienced in 1778. Towards the end of May the Lord-Lieutenant was advised by London to encamp the army. He could not do this, since the Treasury had a balance of "Blank," so he applied to the Bank of England for a loan of 50,000 guineas.[65] Some weeks later, he was directed to encamp the whole army except for the numbers necessary to garrison forts and towns.[66] After receiving this instruction, the poor man complained to his friend Germain that the "military gentlemen are tearing me to pieces for the money which they know I have not. . . ." [67] The Viceroy's plea was answered not by a loan from the Bank of England, but by £50,000 from the British Government. Buckinghamshire had made the most impassioned pleas for the loan,[68] and the bank must have refused him since he had to obtain the money direct from the British Treasury. Lord North's letter to Pery illustrates the exceptional straits to which poverty had led the Irish Administration, and also shows that the British Cabinet was at last aware that the Irish situation was getting desperate:

The proposition of applying British money to the support of the Irish army is so new and unprecedented that I could not immediately come into it. Nothing certainly deserves so sacred a regard as the appropriation of Parliamentary grants; and, therefore, it was natural that I should pause before I consented to apply any public money to a service to which none had ever been applied before. But, upon a full consideration of the matter, I think myself well justified in the step I have taken, and hope that what we send will at least be sufficient to put your army in motion.[69]

The question naturally arises as to what social classes the Volunteers belonged. From the constant references in the press to their activities, it is clear beyond contradiction that their commanders were of the landlord class and were usually owners of large estates. But what of the rank and file? In general, newspaper accounts implied that the Volunteers were composed of men of some substance in rural areas, and merchants and professional men in the towns. Their consistent support of civil order against lawless elements in both town and countryside makes it abundantly clear that they were not made up of the lower classes.

In July, 1779, Buckinghamshire described them as mostly composed of "either tradesmen or farmers" [70] (in the eighteenth century "tradesman" usually meant shopkeeper). As it has already been pointed out, Sir Boyle Roche described them in August, 1780, as "composed in general of the Protestant tenantry of Ireland." On April 8, 1780, the pro-Government *Faulkner's Dublin Journal* said that the Volunteers might easily become a danger to the state if led by an ambitious man, but, happily, they maintain law and order which is what happens when a force is composed of propertied men. The *Dublin Evening Post* in the same week described them as "the proprietors of the land." On July 20, it stated that it was mainly the "middling ranks of society" which started the Volunteers.

In his memoirs Lord Charlemont, the commander-in-chief of the Volunteers, described them as having been "in effect the people." [71] It must be remembered that the expression, "the people," had a very elastic meaning in the eighteenth century, but usually indicated men who were owners or tenants of property.

Lord Shannon was the leader of many Volunteers corps in Cork city and county. In August, 1779, in regard to a plan to bring them under state supervision and enable them to take the field with the army in case of invasion, he wrote:

But tho' the original institution of the independent corps was for the sole purposes of protecting their families from being violated and plundered in case of the apprehended risings of the lower class of people, for keeping the country quiet, and preserving peace in cities, and towns, they are [now] further willing to assist the army. . . .[72]

Sir Edward Newenham, commander of the Dublin Liberty Volunteers, described his men as freeholders of the county and freemen of the city of Dublin.[73]

In June, 1779, the Dublin Volunteers wrote a letter to the London *Morning Post* protesting against the report that they were tailors, starving weavers, shopkeepers, and apprentices. They maintained that their officers were gentlemen and the rank and file were "virtuous men." [74] When Luke Gardiner enrolled his servants in his own corps, some of the Volunteers objected though the *Dublin Evening Post* thought he did right.[75] In 1781, the Dublin hairdressers, finding that the majority of their number were precluded from joining the Volunteers, decided to form a corps of their own. The news drew the snobbish comment from the *Hibernian Journal* of May 14, 1781:

No doubt they will make a formidable Light Cohort, especially when we consider that no People are so used to Smelling Powder, that they are peculiarly calculated for scratching the Common Enemy, and that slaughter is so familiar to them, that the destruction of Thousands has long made them esteem Killing no Murder.

Major-General Edward Maxwell, commander of the army in the north of Ireland, and a man who knew that area intimately,[76] described the Volunteers in northern towns as "chiefly composed of tradesmen and mechanics, who ". . . [could] be usefully employed in quelling riots, when a foreign enemy is in the country." [77] The north was the only part of Ireland in which the Protestants were really numerous, but the presence in their midst of a large

Catholic minority—often a local majority—meant they could not afford to play any role that would be radical in a social sense. Maxwell believed that they had "a rooted hatred of the French as the supporters of the Popish religion" but were under no apprehension of the "Papists, who are here very poor, and kept in subjection." [78] In 1783 a meeting of delegates of forty-five corps in Ulster described their force as consisting of "the several gradations of Nobles, Commoners, Merchants, Yeomen and Mechanics." [79] While the Volunteers in the northern towns included artisans, these workmen were likely to support the propertied middle classes, and with their Catholic neighbors "very poor, and kept in subjection," one can see why.

In conclusion, one might quote Lord Shelburne's description towards the end of 1779 of the Volunteers as composed of "the nobility, gentry, merchants, citizens, and respectable yeomanry: men able and willing to devote their time, and part of their property to the security of their country." [80] It remains to consider whether the Volunteers were conscious of their corporate strength and their middle-class composition, and to what extent this awareness influenced their political thinking.

In September, 1780, the Galway City Volunteers, in reply to a charge that Volunteers should not discuss political questions, protested that

a whole people self-armed, self-paid, are not to lose the citizen in the subordinate character of the soldier, nor suffer those very arms, which have given weight to their opinions, to be used as a conclusive argument against their forming any opinions at all.[81]

A few weeks later, a correspondent said that in the north of Ireland

the companies will not be *officer-rid,* since some of them have
protested against their [officers'] proceedings and resolutions
at large, others against the election of a *Chaplain,* without
their consent, and a third have got their officer to declare his
signature a *forgery.* I am heartily glad to see such gentry exposed when they would pretend to give the sense of the
people . . . [when only] giving their own.[82]

In the *Hibernian Journal* of March 30, 1781, a writer addressed the Volunteers, apparently of Ulster:

Invest no man among you with too much power, or any permanent rank, least you should be deceived . . . as you have
nearly all the Freemen and Freeholders in the Province enrolled among you, and the nature of your associations leading
to a more perfect communion and intercourse one with another, you can, with infinite ease, at the next general election,
reject ever[y] man, who has betrayed the interests of his
country.

On April 10, 1781, the Freeholders of Co. Tyrone were
addressed by a correspondent in the *Dublin Evening Post*
who besought them to attend a county meeting for the
nomination of candidates for parliament, and urged on
them

the necessity of boldly throwing off your subjection to landlords. . . . Attend the meeting, and pass judgment freely
on those proposed; let it not be a meeting of what are called
gentlemen only . . . he among you who is only worth 40
shillings a year, has equal right as he who hath five thousand . . . [at present you have a golden opportunity since]
the nation is a Camp of Soldiers armed in your cause.

In the summer of 1781 the activity of the Volunteers
underwent a change. Reviews lasting one day, as in former

years, were replaced by manoeuvres and parades very
often extending to two or three days. These were held in
various centers all over the country—in Dublin, Belfast,
Cork, Limerick, Londonderry, Bellewstown, Ennis, Galway, Carlow, Tallow, Wexford, Newry, and Monaghan.
The number of men taking part were reported in the
press as being much greater than those in the parades of
former years. The manoeuvres at Belfast were hailed as a
"scene of military grandeur beyond all powers of description." The second most numerous gathering took place in
Phoenix Park outside Dublin. On July 26, the *Dublin
Evening Post* published a map of Belfast and its environs
(an unprecedented event in contemporary journalism) to
illustrate the manoeuvres in that area. Charlemont took
the salute at the more important gatherings, while lesser
manoeuvres were presided over by Leinster, Tyrone,
Shannon, and Muskerry.

The enthusiasm at these manoeuvres seems to have been
further promoted by what is often described as "traditional Irish hospitality." In July, 1781, Conolly reviewed
1200 Volunteers at Toome, Co. Londonderry, in the vicin-
ity of which he owned a large estate. At the conclusion, he
entertained each Volunteer to "a Pye, a Bottle of Porter,
and a Bottle of Punch." When preparations were being
made for the great manoeuvres outside Dublin in June,
1781, the *Hibernian Journal* made a patriotic plea for the
consumption of Irish liquors so that if the Volunteers "are
doomed to undergo actual inebriation, then they shall
enjoy the Reflection of its being effected by the Produce
of their own Country."

The newspapers could be very candid in description of
crimes of indecency, but they encouraged a high standard
of propriety, even in connection with Volunteers activities. The crowds expected to attend the review in the

Phoenix Park were so great that *Faulkner's Dublin Journal* of June 5 warned that

No female who regards her reputation, should go unprotected, for not only the arts of seduction will be put in practice, but from the various inclinations predominating in such an aggregate mass of persons, little decorum or delicacy need be expected.

This concern for seemly behaviour was not limited to crowded meetings, but extended even to the domestic scene:

A correspondent declares it his opinion, that no exertions to restrain the insolence of servants can have any great effect, while masters make so *free* with their female servants, and mistresses with their *male*.[83]

And now we must return to a more serious consideration of contemporary events.

It requires but little imagination to understand the enormous impression which the parades in the early years and the manoeuvres in 1781 must have created in the minds of Volunteers. Formerly, most of them would probably have known little of the political world while going about their business in their own locality. The local landlord, who organized the corps, would have been their leader economically and socially. Their political horizon would very probably have been bounded by his mansion, which was known in Ireland as the Big House. From 1778 local and county parades brought the Volunteers together with other corps, and enabled them to extend their knowledge of politics and to realize that there were other great men in the county besides their own leaders. In 1781 they found themselves encamped for two or three days with thousands of other Volunteers drawn from half a province.

Also these "military" activities were taking place at times when political topics were being discussed everywhere, and political feelings were running deep. It would be surprising, to say the least, if these corps were not to experience a sense of corporate power, and if their members were not to return to their native parishes in a very different frame of mind. That such was the case can be proven.

In 1782, a letter to a newspaper stated that "the people, as freeholders, never yet had decisive influence; as Volunteers, they have." [84] On the question of parliamentary reform, a correspondent in the *Dublin Evening Post* of June 15, 1782, said:

Every Volunteer at this instant feels and exults in his own consequence: Did he feel this ardour for liberty, this independence upon rank and wealth before he became a Volunteer? Does he expect that when the corps he belongs to disbands . . . that he will hold the same share of the national power which he does at present? No! the instant he lays down his arms, . . . his consequence and all his rights as a man and citizen fall into the hands of a few, who influence the boroughs which return the majority of Parliament. . . . [Should parliamentary reform be attained] no little interest between landlord and tenant will then subjugate the latter to a blind dependence on the owner of his farm. A yeomanry will by degrees arise, which will diffuse liberty and industry through every class of the inhabitants of Ireland.

Nor did the change in status of these men pass unnoticed by the upper classes. A social butterfly called Dorothea Herbert has described an entertainment by the Earl and Countess of Tyrone at Curraghmore, their great mansion in Co. Waterford:

The Volunteers were invited to a Grand Dinner at Curraghmore given on purpose for them, many were the laughable

stories told of them—One eat salt with his grapes and sugar
with his walnuts, another offer'd Lady Tyrone a well aired
chair, which he (a very fat man) had sat on.[85]

This social event occurred as early as 1780 but it indicates
the power of the corps. Men who supplied the upper
classes with "laughable stories" would not have been
entertained in Curraghmore unless its noble owner had
come to respect their political importance. A more general picture of the new attitude of the landlord classes was
painted, no doubt in extravagant colors, by the *Dublin
Evening Post* on August 1, 1782:

The pains now taking by many of our Nobility and Gentry,
who have for some years past gone at the wrong side of the
post, to glean a small portion of popularity; has thrown some
of them in situations truly ridiculous; for those proud satraps,
who whilom [formerly] treated all their dependents, tenants
and neighbours, with the most supercilious haughtiness and
contempt, are to be seen in all parts of the country meanly
crouching, in the most abject manner, to the crowd, going
from door to door of every farm-house, even cabin, and kindly
enquiring after the health and welfare of families, who have
had hitherto no other knowledge of their lords and masters,
than frequent instances of their tyranny and oppression.

The effect on the rank and file of the Volunteers, that is
on large numbers of middle-class people in town and
country, is attested by an article in an English newspaper
which was transcribed in the *Freeman's Journal* of May
17, 1783:

Military discipline, which in other institutions, teaches a
slavish subordination, has given to us a new lesson of equality.

The aristocracy is taught, even by its own vanity, to court the democracy. The intercourse between the officer and the private Volunteer softens the sentiments of the one, and elevates those of the other. What a difference was there between the English yeoman and the Irish tenant! . . . How much has volunteering done in two years? The poorest Volunteer feels himself a member of a free, and of a strong state; his ideas expand, his character is ennobled. He begins to love and to enforce the laws. He is no longer a timid slave, who conceals his substance, but a free subject, proud that he can afford an uniform.

An historical writer, Sir Jonah Barrington, who was in the Volunteers as a young man, has described the effect of the movement on the various strata of society:

The Volunteer system now becoming universal in Ireland, effected an important and visible change in the minds and manners of the middle and lower orders of the people; by the occurrence of new events, and the promulgation of novel principles, their natural character became affected in all its bearings, and acquired, or rather disclosed, new points, which at that period tended to promote their prosperity, but eventually formed the grand pretence for the extinguishment of their independence. . . .

The familiar association of all ranks, which the nature of their new military connections necessarily occasioned, every day lessened that wide distinction, which had theretofore separated the higher and lower orders of society—the landlord and the tenant—the nobleman and the artisan—the general and the soldier—now, for the first time, sat down at the same board—shared the same fare—and enjoyed the same conviviality. The lower orders learned their own weight in the community—the higher were taught their dependence upon the people—and those illiterate minds which had never before conceived or thought on the nature of political constitutions, or the fundamental principles of civil government, now learned from the intercourse and conversation of their superiors, the rudiments of that complicated but noble science. . . .

They had now, by the constant discussions of political subjects in every rank of society, acquired a capacity of acute reasoning on constitutional controversies, their native eloquence breaking forth at every meeting nourished their native ardour, and almost every peasant became a public orator. . . .

[In 1782 and later years] the armed Volunteers had now assumed a deliberative capacity. Political subjects became topics of regular organized discussion in every district in Ireland and amongst every class and description of its population. They paraded as soldiers and they debated as citizens.

It must be remembered that Barrington [86] felt that the Act of Union, which abolished the Irish Parliament, was a disaster. Thus he depicted the country in the decades before the Union in glowing colors and exaggerated the virtues and influence of the Volunteers. The bulk of that force, as already shown, was composed of the middle classes, so that Barrington is too loose in his terminology in attributing its membership to "the middle and lower orders." Even when full allowance has been made for his anti-Union feeling and enthusiastic inaccuracy, it is still apparent from what he says, that the Volunteers had created a new consciousness among classes which had hitherto been virtually outside politics. All the contemporary evidence presented in the foregoing pages proves that his conclusions, though highly colored, are for the most part true. Additional information on the new political consciousness of the middle classes is to be found in the agitation for parliamentary reform in 1783.

NOTES FOR CHAPTER IV

1 *Parl. Hist.*, XIX, 914 *et seq.*; FJ, March 26, 1778.

2 HJ, March 30, 1778; Buckinghamshire to Weymouth, March 29, 1778, SP 63/459, ff. 217–20.

3 The addresses from six towns and more than half the counties are in the viceroy's correspondence in the (London) Public Record Office (SP 63/460, ff. 461 and 462). Dublin County and Dublin City passed addresses but they are not in this correspondence (DEJ, March 31, April 2, 1778). Similarly, other meetings may have voted addresses of which there is no trace in the official files.

4 Newenham to Lord Dartmouth, April 21, 1778, HMC, Dartmouth Papers, p. 240; HJ, March 30, 1778.

5 DEJ, April 2, 1778.

6 HJ, March 25, 30, 1778.

7 SP 63/462, f. 20.

8 SP 63/462, ff. 24–25.

9 *Parl. Hist.*, XIX, 944.

10 March 29, 1778, SP 63/459, ff. 217–220.

11 McDowell, *Irish Public Opinion*, pp. 41–42.

12 J. C. Beckett, *Protestant Dissent in Ireland, 1687–1780* (London, 1948) p. 101.

13 SP 63/459, f. 149.

14 HJ, April 1, 1778.

15 SP 63/459, ff. 276–80, 284, 288–89.

16 See Appendix A.

17 See pp. 63–64.

18 Buckinghamshire in his letter to Weymouth of April 21, 1778, *Grattan Memoirs*, I, 300–304.

19 The *Hibernian Journal* of January 28 applauded Ogle for his intention to introduce a "Protestant militia bill;" because of his hostile attitude to Catholic emancipation, it is inconceivable that he would have countenanced their being recruited into a militia.

20 Buckinghamshire to Weymouth, April 21, 1778, *Grattan Memoirs*, I, 300–304.

21 *Ibid.*; Irish Commons, March 26, 27, April 2, 1778 (HJ, March 27, 30, April 3, 1778). The royal prerogative was not clear since Buckinghamshire in his letter of April 22 asked North to have the constitutional position clarified.

22 Buckinghamshire to Weymouth, April 21, 1778, *Grattan Memoirs*, I, 300–304.

23 *Ibid.*; Buckinghamshire to North, April 22, 1778, *Grattan Memoirs,* I, 305–307.

24 Buckinghamshire to Weymouth, May 1, 1778, SP 63/460, ff. 27–29, 31; Buckinghamshire to North, May 1, 1778, *Grattan Memoirs,* I, 323; SP 63/460, ff. 229–230.

25 This description of the proposed independent companies is taken from the Irish Commons' debates on the Militia measure and from Buckinghamshire's letter to Weymouth of April 21, 1778.

26 Buckinghamshire to Weymouth, December 12, 1778, SP 63/461, ff. 328–30.

27 This point is explicitly made by Buckinghamshire in his letter to Weymouth of December 12, 1778.

28 DEJ, May 7, 12, 28, 1778; FDJ, May 14, 1778.

29 R. E. Burns, "The Belfast Letters, the Irish Volunteers 1778–79 and the Catholics," *Review of Politics,* XXI (October, 1959), 682.

30 DEJ, July 23, 1778.

31 DEP, October 10, 1778; FJ, October 13, 15, 1778.

32 DEP, February 18, 1779.

33 DEP, March 25, 1779.

34 DEP, August 12, 1779.

35 DEP, July 31, August 24, 28, September 11, 21, 23, 28, 1779; FJ, July 31, 1779; FDJ, August 10, 1779.

36 DEP, April 20, July 29, August 14, September 7, 1779.

37 Buckinghamshire to Weymouth, May 23 (erroneously published as May 24), 1779, *Grattan Memoirs,* I, 347–49; Beresford to Robinson, October 24, 1779, *Beresford Corr.,* I, 67–73.

38 DEP, August 5, 1779.

39 DEP, April 27, 1779.

40 DEP, October 7, 1779.

41 DEP, July 4, 1780.

42 *Retrospections of Dorothea Herbert, 1770–1789* (London, 1929), p. 57.

43 Tyrone to John Beresford, May 28, 1779, *Grattan Memoirs,* I, 352–53.

44 HC, June 7, 10, 1779.

45 Bishop of Cork to General Irvine, June 5, 1779, SP 63/465, f. 85.

46 DEP, July 31, August 26, 1779; FJ, August 24 and 28, 1779.

47 HC, August 17, 1780.

48 Rickard O'Connell to Maurice Leyne, August 20, 1779, M. J. O'Connell, *The Last Colonel of the Irish Brigade* (London, 1892), I, 223–24.

49 February 1, 10, 1780, O'Connell, *Last Colonel,* I, 264.

50 *Ibid.,* 265–66.

51 Trant to Fitzgibbon, December 31, 1782, O'Connell, *Last Colonel*, I, 309–311.

52 DEP, August 19, 1779.

53 SP 63/461, ff. 328–30.

54 Buckinghamshire to Germain, February 15, 1778, HMC, Lothian Papers, p. 345.

55 HMC, Emly Papers, p. 200.

56 Buckinghamshire to Weymouth, May 24, 1779, *Grattan Memoirs*, I, 347–49.

57 *Ibid.*

58 *Grattan Memoirs*, I, 355.

59 Thomas Waite, Under-Secretary to the Lord-Lieutenant, to Clanricarde, June 5, 1779, *Grattan Memoirs*, I, 355–56. Clanricarde had offered to raise 1,000 men who "will swim in their own blood in defence of his Majestiy and their native country."

60 Buckinghamshire to Weymouth, July 23, 1779, *Grattan Memoirs*, I, 367–68.

61 HMC, Charlemont Papers, I, 52–53.

62 A copy of the minute was enclosed with Buckinghamshire's letter to Weymouth of July 23, 1779.

63 Heron to Charlemont, September 25, 1779, HMC, Charlemont Papers, I, 355.

64 The governorship of a county was an honorary office in the nomination of the viceroy. The nominee was nearly always a landed aristocrat.

65 Buckinghamshire to Weymouth, June 5, 1779, SP 63/465, f. 75.

66 Weymouth to Buckinghamshire, June 24, 1779, SP 63/465, f. 141.

67 Buckinghamshire to Germain, June 28, July 4, 1779, HMC, Lothian Papers, pp. 352–53.

68 Buckinghamshire to Weymouth, June 28, July 3, 1779, SP 63/465, ff. 179, 249.

69 August 3, 1779, HMC, Emly Papers, I, 201–202.

70 Buckinghamshire to Heron, July 9, 1779, Heron Papers.

71 HMC, Charlemont Papers, I, 73.

72 Shannon to Buckinghamshire, August 15, 1779, Heron Papers.

73 DEP, September 7, 1779.

74 DEP, June 29, 1779.

75 DEP, August 31, 1779.

76 General Irvine to Buckinghamshire, June 29, 1779, SP 63/465, f. 216.

77 Maxwell to Irvine, June 27, 1779, SP 63/465, ff. 218–219.

78 *Ibid.*

79 DEP, July 8, 1783

80 *Parl. Hist.*, XX 1159. The occasion was a debate in the British House of Lords on Irish trade. It suited Shelburne's purpose to be complimentary to the Volunteers but there is no reason to doubt the substantial sincerity of his statement. The owner of a large Irish estate, his family was of Norman-Irish origin and he had visited Ireland some months before making this statement.

81 DEP, October 10, 1780.

82 DEP, October 19, 1780.

83 HC, August 30, 1781.

84 DEP, July 30, 1782.

85 *Retrospections of Dorothea Herbert,* p. 59.

86 Sir Jonah Barrington, *The Rise and Fall of the Irish Nation* (Dublin, 1863), pp. 84–85, 161, 311.

V

The Catholic Relief Act of 1778

During the last decade of the seventeenth, and the early decades of the eighteenth century, a series of enactments known as the Penal Laws were passed by the Irish Parliament. The primary purpose of these laws was to place and retain in the hands of (Anglican) Protestants all political, administrative, and, as far as possible, economic power. The result was that Catholics were debarred from holding any political, legal, or administrative office, from sitting in parliament or town corporations, and from the franchise. They could not enter the legal profession, the army or the navy, though, in practice, they were recruited into the rank and file of the two armed forces. They were legally prohibited from teaching in schools and from sending their children overseas to Catholic schools. Special stress was laid on the ownership of landed property: a Catholic could neither buy nor lease land for a long period; at his death the law required that his estate be gavelled, that is, divided equally among his sons. The eldest son by conforming to the established (Anglican) church—the Church of Ireland—was entitled to have his father made a life-tenant, and, on the latter's death, could claim the entire estate regardless of the rights of his younger brothers.[1]

It is estimated that Catholics still owned some 15 per cent of the profitable land at the beginning of the eighteenth century,[2] but the Penal Laws were successful enough in their operation to gradually render this proportion much smaller. In 1772 the viceroy, Lord Townshend, was able to say that "at this day there is no Popish family remaining of any great weight for landed property."[3] Though undoubtedly the substantial truth, his statement was inaccurate since there still existed at least one large estate, that of Lord Kenmare.[4] Townshend's opinion was borne out by Lord Charlemont in his memoirs where he states that "the greatest part of the old Catholic gentry had, either from conviction or convenience, conformed to the established and ruling religion," and "the restrictive laws which were meant to operate to the diminution and impairment of Catholic property, had amply produced the desired effect."[5]

As a partial compensation for this decline in landed property there occurred during the course of the eighteenth century an accumulation of wealth in the hands of Catholic merchants. Mrs. Maureen Wall, the authority on Catholics in eighteenth-century Ireland, says that in the period around 1780, Catholics formed "a not inconsiderable part of the business population of Dublin;" large numbers of them were "persons who had some stake in the country, and . . . were particularly interested in leasing or in buying property."[6] The importance of this wealth can be seen in the several attempts made in the Irish Parliament between 1760 and 1773 to enable Prot-

estant landowners to mortgage their estates to Catholics.[7]
In expressing opposition to such a proposal in 1772,
Townshend said that it would "give the Popish creditors
such a control over those who are in debt as may in particular times operate very strongly." [8] Charlemont states
in his memoirs that much of the increasing wealth of Ireland at this time enriched Catholic merchants and

Principally in the southern and western counties, could not
fail to raise a considerable Catholic party . . . even in elections on account of its riches and consequent influence of
importance sufficient to be courted by one or other of the
candidates. Hence arose a sort of Popish patronage in both
houses of parliament. . . ." [9]

An example of a wealthy Catholic, a landlord, who had
influence in elections can be found in Maurice O'Connell
of Derrynane, Co. Kerry. In 1783 he received the following request:

My brother-in-law, Mr. Fitzgibbon, has declared himself a
candidate for the County of Limerick at the next general
election. May I request that you will be kind enough to
exert yourself for him, as I flatter myself you would for me
on a similar occasion.[10]

It is ironic that this Fitzgibbon was the future lord chancellor and ultimately so virulently anti-Catholic and so
ruthless that he became perhaps the most hated man in
eighteenth-century Ireland. It is equally ironic that
Maurice O'Connell should have been the uncle of Daniel
O'Connell, the leader of the movement for Catholic
Emancipation.

When the repeal of some of the Penal Laws regarding
property was being discussed in the Irish newspapers in

the spring and early summer of 1778, much was said about the wealth of Catholics. A supporter of the repeal wrote: "As they are not permitted to realize their fortunes [by buying land], they will always have a power in ready money that may be dangerous." In the *Freeman's Journal* of May 30, 1778, an opponent described the Catholics as having almost all the money of the nation in their hands, and stated that they were supposed to have already spent (by the end of May) £30,000 to procure the passing of the Relief Bill. He expressed the belief that they were prepared to spend an additional £100,000. Another correspondent referred to the bribery of members of parliament with "those immense sums, so openly raised, and so liberally distributed." The fear was frequently expressed that if not granted relief, wealthy Catholics would emigrate and bring their money with them either to Britain, where they could now buy estates, or to America. Concerning the latter country, there was the contrary view that Catholics would not be welcomed in the strongly Protestant Thirteen Colonies. Buckinghamshire believed that the fear of prosperous Catholics emigrating was a real one among Protestants.[11] It was also held that some Protestants supported relief in order to find a larger market for the sale of their estates.

In considering the Catholic Relief Act of 1778, it is important to bear in mind this behind-the-scenes influence of Catholic money. Another factor in their increasing financial and political importance was the Catholic Committee. It was founded in Dublin in 1760 and was composed mainly of merchants and landlords. Representative of these elements throughout the country, it applied itself to removing grievances and to obtaining a repeal of the Penal Laws. It is indicative of the increasing importance of the middle classes that the merchants played a more important role in the committee than the landlords.[12]

The first official sign that a new day was dawning was an act passed in 1774 by the Irish Parliament enabling Catholics to testify their loyalty by taking an oath which included a declaration of allegiance to the king and a denial that the pope possessed any temporal authority in Ireland. The oath conferred no explicit benefit, but it did give the Catholics a certain legal status, valuable for the future. The same year saw the passing in England of the Quebec Act which gave a partial establishment, including the right to levy tithes, to the Catholic Church in Canada. A basis for concessions had thus been laid in the legislatures of both Great Britain and Ireland. As already described, the leading Catholics presented a petition of loyalty in 1775 that was prompted by the outbreak of the American Revolution. The opportunity provided by Britain's growing difficulties in America was too good to be missed, and Irish Catholics began to press tactfully for some redress of their grievances.

In October, 1777, an address, signed by more than three hundred of the principal Catholics, was presented to Buckinghamshire for transmission to the king. The latter gave it a favorable reception and the Viceroy was asked for his opinion as to what relief might be given.[13] Though expressing sympathy for the Catholics, he neglected to answer this request, perhaps because he considered the subject a very delicate one.[14] About the end of February, 1778, Heron was approached by a Catholic of "considerable fortune and distinction," Richard Talbot of Malahide Castle, Co. Dublin, who handed him a draft of a bill for Catholic relief. Buckinghamshire said, with some exaggeration, that the document comprised "a repeal of almost all the Popery Laws" and consulted Protestants who had been foremost in assisting Catholics. He accepted their view that to grant any concessions now would be unwise and probably "cause a flame."[15] The King accepted the

Viceroy's advice and agreed that nothing need be done.[16]

It is significant that Weymouth's letter conveying the King's decision was written on March 28, two weeks after London had learned of the Franco-American treaties. Thus, the American difficulties and the virtual entry of France into the war were not sufficient to produce a Catholic relief measure.

On March 12 what was probably a feeler was put out in the Irish House of Commons when James Fitzgerald moved for leave to introduce heads of a bill which would enable Catholics to take long leases to "build in towns and villages." The opposition proved too strong—Foster and the Patriots, Ogle and Bradstreet, being some of the opponents—and the motion was withdrawn.[17] Clearly there was little chance of concession in the near future, and matters would have remained static but for the action of the English Whigs.

In a discussion in the British Commons on Irish trade on April 7, the Whig, Thomas Townshend, expressed the hope that relief would be granted to Irish Catholics in order to promote their loyalty. He "hated the Romish religion for its persecuting spirit, but he would not on that account wish to be a persecutor." Lord North expressed sympathy and thought that the Irish Parliament would redress Catholic grievances. Charles James Fox considered that if the British Parliament were to repeal its own laws, it would set an example to the Irish legislature; he believed that the principles of the Protestant religion necessitated tolerance for both Catholics and Protestant Dissenters. Burke held that the Penal Laws in Ireland did not operate against Catholicism—since that religion was already established, each parish having its priest and each diocese its bishop—but only against Catholic property. The rich Catholics suffered while the poor were unaffected. The Americans, he continued, had established a religion that was neither Catholic nor Protestant: it was the Christian religion.[18]

This public support for concession was followed up in the British Parliament by two bills introduced in the middle of May which went through with little opposition and received the royal assent in early June.[19] The first was a relief measure for English Catholics, and the second repealed two statutes of Queen Anne's reign prohibiting Catholics from buying forfeited Irish estates. The latter bill was a necessary preliminary to the passing of any legislation in Ireland which would allow Catholics to buy land. Both were Whig bills, the former piloted through Parliament by Sir George Savile and the Marquis of Rockingham, the latter by Lord Richard Cavendish and Lord Effingham, but both received strong Tory support. Savile considered the laws against Catholics, clerical and lay, as cruel and inconsistent with Christian ideas. John Dunning thought the "speculative religious principles" of the Catholics no threat to the safety and tranquillity of the state. The Irish Parliament, he said, had a few years past framed an oath [the Act of 1774] enabling Catholics to testify their loyalty, and they were willing to take this oath. The Lord Chancellor, Bathurst, and the Lord Advocate for Scotland, Henry Dundas, gave Tory support and Lord Beauchamp, another Tory, hoped that this bill would induce the Irish Parliament to make similar concessions.[20]

Pery, the Speaker of the Irish Commons, who had been in London, arrived back in Dublin on April 30, 1778. He informed Buckinghamshire that the King had expressed the hope that some reasonable concessions should be granted to Catholics in the current session of the Irish Parliament. The Lord-Lieutenant immediately agreed to consult the Crown servants without delay in order to draw up a plan to be submitted to the King.[21] At the same time, activities were under way independent of the Government for proposing a relief bill to the Irish Commons.[22] Less than a week later, William Knox, the Under-Secretary for the American Colonies, informed Heron that the Irish Government lay under censure in British political circles for their neglect of the Catholics.[23] The proceedings in the British Parliament, even apart from the wish expressed by the Crown, had an immediate effect on Ireland, and resulted in the introduction of a relief measure in the Irish Commons before the end of May.

That these English parliamentary activities were the prime cause of the change in Irish political circles is borne out not only by the course of events, but by the explicit statements of Buckinghamshire, Gardiner, Pery and Hely Hutchinson, all of whom were in a position to understand the issues involved.[24] The British Government may well have been encouraged to adopt a concessionary attitude due to the importance of placating Irish Catholic sentiment in a troubled world, but three months before the entry of France into the war, the King had already expressed himself in favor of concessions. The Quebec Act and the Irish (Oath) Act of 1774 had demonstrated an attitude of tolerance towards Catholics long before there was any real fear of an international war. Thus, the British support of relief was a quickening of an existing tendency rather than the development of a new policy. There was also the political and economic influence of Catholic wealth to which reference has been made, but this purely Irish factor was a "constant," and it was the British intervention which played the decisive role.[25]

In regard to the relief measure being introduced to the Irish Commons, Buckinghamshire on May 24, 1778, asked London for instructions since "there is a prospect of a

warm opposition, particularly to the Gavelling clause."
He added that both he and the [Protestant] Primate considered that the Catholics should be allowed to enjoy, as
far as circumstances would permit, the same rights in both
kingdoms.[26] Weymouth considered this opinion a sound
one and left it to the Lord-Lieutenant to decide what
relief could prudently be given.[27]

Before dealing with the measure in the Irish Parliament, it is of interest to investigate more fully Irish public
opinion on the subject as evinced in pamphlets and the
newspapers.

The talk of concession produced a controversy in the
spring of 1778 which raged through the summer. Issues
such as Free Trade and the right of the British Parliament
to legislate for Ireland could produce only poor debates in
newspaper columns. It was difficult to argue convincingly
in Ireland that the country should not be allowed freedom
in trade, or that its parliament was a subordinate one.
Catholic relief, on the other hand, was a godsend to the
controversialist interested in politics or religion (and who
was ever interested in *neither!*), and printers' ink flowed.
Scores of letters were published in the newspapers and
every aspect of the subject was threshed out *ad-nauseam*.

One of the first targets was the Catholic Bishop of
Ossory, John Troy, whose pastoral, calling on Catholics
to be loyal and condemning the American rebels, appeared in February, 1779. As a Popish bishop he was informed that he had no right to be anywhere but in jail.
Another writer considered that, when a Popish bishop
would publish such a pastoral, it was small wonder that
lay Papists should become so haughty as to present addresses which had been ignored, take oaths which had not
been trusted, and seek concessions which had been refused.
Most opponents of relief were less insulting if not less de-

termined. Some argued that it was still unsafe to place power in the hands of those who had been identified with lawless activities in recent years and who thus showed that their religious principles had not changed since 1641 when they massacred and oppressed Protestants. The dispensing power of the pope, the lack of necessity to keep faith with heretics, and the allegiance to the Stuarts were points at issue. Supporters of concession argued that these doctrines had long ceased to be part of the beliefs and loyalties of Catholics; that the Penal Laws, though perhaps necessary when enacted, were not required now that the lives and property of Protestants, and the established church, were no longer in danger. Others emphasized the loyalty of Catholics over the years, particularly during the rebellions of 1715 and 1745, and asked that such behavior be rewarded. They were now perfectly loyal and the state needed their full support against possible invasion. Reference to this danger provoked the statement in the *Hibernian Journal* on March 11 that Catholic relief, a subject

in which the interests and passions of men must be deeply involved, is at this time peculiarly improper, and whoever [introduces it] . . . at so critical a season . . . can be no friend either to the security or peace of the country.

Discussion of the subject was ill-advised when "the Empire is convulsed to her very foundation, and we are at the eve of a French and Spanish war, if not an invasion from these Popish countries." The danger of invasion was used as an argument by both sides.

One Protestant supporter of concession saw no difficulty with the laity, but warned against allowing the clergy to be educated abroad or to accept Papal dictation. He ended his letter with the arrogant suggestion that priests should "abrogate their unnatural celibacy, promote decaying population, and let the Catholic ladies of Ireland, enjoy in its full extent, *their benefit of clergy*." Frequent references were made to the oppression of Protestants in Catholic countries such as France. There was much play with the idea that Popery was friendly to "arbitrary power" thereby having found favor with the government of George III. This argument was voiced again and again during the summer and autumn once it had been seen that concession was being supported by Dublin Castle. Hostility to Catholic relief in Ireland, to the Quebec Act, and to the British Government's American policy were thus combined.

Pamphlets on the subject produced little that was not in the newspaper correspondence.[28] One writer in support of relief leaned over backwards to show how innocent his co-religionists had become. He attacked the *Court* of Rome in contra-distinction to the *Church* of Rome. To the former he attributed responsibility for the past misdeeds of Catholics, but maintained that in this enlightened age the Papacy had been stripped of its power and the Pope was now accepted as only the head of the Church.[29] The same view was expressed in the *Hibernian Journal* on February 27: "Heretofore the temporal power of Rome was so great, that it became a terror to such Protestant states as had many popish subjects . . . [but now] this elevated Ecclesiastic . . . hath, by a happy change of times, fallen back to his primitive *Spiritual* power only."

The matter became practical politics on May 22 when Luke Gardiner gave notice in the Commons that he intended to propose a measure of Catholic relief in regard to landed property.[30] Ogle immediately objected on the ground that a motion designed to benefit the Catholics had already been withdrawn because it was considered too late in the session for its passage. Monck Mason admitted

the truth of Ogle's statement, but felt that "the circumstances of this Country with regard to Popery are entirely
changed. There is a bill in Great Britain . . . that makes it
absolutely necessary to proceed at this moment." Yelverton
deemed concession necessary for fear Catholics would
emigrate to England now that relief was being granted
there, and bring their money with them.

Three days later Gardiner obtained leave from the
House to introduce heads "for the Relief of his Majesty's
Roman Catholic Subjects of Ireland." He repeated Yelverton's argument that if no favors were granted, the Catholics would emigrate with their wealth to the freer atmosphere of England. Barry Barry (his first and last names
were the same) seconded the motion because he believed
the Catholics would invest their money in land and thus
support the Protestant Establishment: "I have always considered pecuniary property to be the most dangerous in
case of rebellion." Ogle objected that at this late hour introducing a relief measure was like

burying the Constitution by Torch light, and the Protestant
interest along with it. . . I am perfectly of the opinion of
Voltaire. Morality is the same in every country, because it is
the work of God but religion differs in every country, because
religion is the work of man. . . . Has the Romish Church
changed her spirit; has the Romish Church changed her
principles?

Gardiner's heads gave Catholics the right to buy land and
repealed the hated gavelling and conforming clauses which
enabled the eldest son to get control of the whole of his
father's property by becoming a Protestant.

At the end of the debate, Sir Edward Newenham, the
champion of the Presbyterians, obtained leave to introduce heads of a bill for the relief of Protestant Dissenters.

On June 5 the heads were received and committed (that is, discussed by the members in session as a committee). Ogle again objected, this time with the statement that "the flood gates of Popery will be laid open." Newenham warned: "We are going in the space of one week to repeal those laws which took years to perfect."

On June 15 Newenham, having withdrawn his heads on behalf of the Presbyterians, introduced an amendment to Gardiner's measure for the repeal of the sacramental test. He was supported by Robert Stewart, Richard Longfield, and Ogle who savagely attacked Gardiner's measure as subversive of the Protestant Establishment in church and state. Scott (the Attorney-General) and Conolly opposed Newenham's amendment for fear it would endanger the passing of the whole bill. Monck Mason spoke heatedly in support of the measure without the addition of the amendment:

The first consequence . . . will be an influx of wealth from every quarter of the Globe. The next consequence will be an immediate increase of the value of your estates, which are now sold for nineteen years purchase. . . . Religion did not sit so lightly on the plain, and honest people of Ireland, as upon the more interested people of England. To the honour of the Roman Catholicks in Ireland, those laws have been entirely ineffectual. . . . in seventy-six years they have produced but five thousand converts out of six millions of Papists that must have inhabited this country during that time.

After an exhausting discussion the debate was adjourned.

Newenham's amendment was an embarrassment not only because it added to the Irish difficulties, but also because it raised the question of Protestant Dissenters in England. To attach this amendment to a Catholic bill was appropriate, since the sacramental test in Ireland had

originally been added in London to an anti-Catholic bill
passed by the Irish Parliament in 1704. The addition had
been directed against the Irish Presbyterians and had been
accepted by the Irish Parliament because of the Parliament's anti-Catholic zeal at the beginning of the century.
Because of Poyning's Law, the excision of the test clause
from the bill as sent back by London, would have meant
the rejection of the whole measure.[31] Newenham was undoubtedly sincere in his concern for the Presbyterians, but
he had no interest in Catholics. His burdening Gardiner's
measure with the sacramental amendment meant that if
the Protestant Dissenters were not to be granted satisfaction, he had no compunction about seeing Catholic relief
shot down.

On the next day, June 16, Newenham stated that his
constituents (he sat for Co. Dublin) wished him to oppose
Catholic relief. Grattan now entered the debate for the
first time. Ironically, the man who was later to become the
foremost champion of Catholic claims in the Irish and
British parliaments opposed the measure vigorously. He
objected to giving Catholics the right to purchase land in
fee simple [i.e. outright purchase] because it would give
them power, but approved of permitting them to take
long leases. He also wished to see the gavelling law retained. Concerning emigration he said: "If you were to
pass as many laws as you please, you would not be able to
make the climate, and government of Ireland as tempting
as the climate, and government of America." He thought
Presbyterians more likely to emigrate if the Catholics were
given too much toleration.

In reply to his critics Gardiner stated:

I believe they [the Catholics] have large sums of money in
their hands . . . [but] I can't think they will ever possess one

twentieth part of the land. Will they take their money out of the Trade? I say not, only men that have large capitals. Every man that has his Trade makes from ten to twelve p. cent. He must have recourse to Trade to form a capital before he can make a purchase.

Newenham's amendment concerning the sacramental test was passed by the very close vote of 111 to 108. There was strong hostility to the repeal of both the gavelling clause and the clause which gave exclusive inheritance rights to the conforming eldest son.

In the course of debate Newenham made the interesting comment that "there are not above 25 Dissenters out of two thousand electors in the county of Dublin." Scott admitted that "I was bred a Dissenter, sprung from Dissenting loins" but he was nevertheless opposed to burdening Gardiner's bill with the Test clause. The heads were passed but experienced much the same reception in the Irish Privy Council before they were transmitted to London on June 25. Buckinghamshire considered that several peers in the Council allowed Newenham's amendment to pass only because they believed it would be rejected in London. It was undoubtedly used by the opponents of Catholic relief as a means of having Gardiner's measure defeated.[32]

The right to purchase land was the most controversial part of the measure. The ownership of certain lands involved the right to appoint candidates to administrative and legal positions, and the owners of most boroughs could nominate members of parliament. Thus, there was danger in giving Catholics the right to buy land. Yelverton, Hussey Burgh, and others suggested ways in which this impediment could be circumvented, but the problem was finally solved when Ogle proposed that Catholics not be permitted to buy outright, but only on leases of up to 999 years. The protagonists of the measure were forced to accept this limitation for fear of having the entire measure rejected.[33]

From the first, the Lord-Lieutenant believed that Gardiner's relief measure would have a difficult passage and that discretion demanded that the Government's support should be of only a limited kind.[34] A few days later he asked Weymouth for explicit instruction as to how far he should support the measure since he was becoming alarmed at the strength of the opposition.[35] The British Cabinet deemed it wiser to limit his role to giving moral support to concession for fear of offending opinion in the Irish Parliament by appearing to interfere.[36] As difficulties mounted, the Irish Administration found itself becoming more deeply committed to the support of the measure.[37] In fact, it would very probably have been defeated in the Commons had the Administration not intervened.[38] When the problems connected with the sacramental test amendment became apparent, Buckinghamshire suggested to Germain that London should allow it to pass in order not to antagonize the Presbyterians.[39] A few days earlier he had informed Germain:

Nothing since my arrival in Ireland, . . . has given me so much uneasiness as the Popery Bill, from the first of its being in agitation every effort has been exerted to excite the factious and to alarm the timid.[40]

The ease with which the two bills concerning Catholic Relief had passed through the British Parliament meant that there would be no difficulty in London with Gardiner's "heads" if they were concerned merely with Catholics. However, all efforts nearly came to grief in England

because of the test clause, as revealed by the correspondence of Edmund Burke. He strained every sinew in order
to obtain the Government's approval for the measure,
with or without the test amendment. In a letter to him
the Attorney-General, Alexander Wedderburn, later Lord
Loughborough, made the interesting statement:

I suspect the passage of the papist-bill will not be so smooth
as I wish; and that I shall be obliged to break the silence I
meant to observe, and write something upon the test. . . .
was not occasional conformity once prevented in Ireland? . . .
Is not the sacramental test at present merely used [in Ireland]
as in England, to qualify for acceptance, without any obligation to receive it during the possession of an office? And is
not there, in fact, an act from session to session to allow
farther time to qualify? [41]

Some two weeks later Burke reported to Pery on his
conversations with North and the new Lord Chancellor,
Thurlow. The Prime Minister favored the retention of
the sacramental test because he believed in the Anglican
establishment in church and state, and because the repeal
of the test would be opposed by the Anglican clergy in
England; furthermore, its repeal in Ireland would lead to
a corresponding demand in England. Burke replied that
the Whigs did not intend to move for its repeal in England, though, if it were proposed, he himself would give it
his support. He added that what was done in Ireland need
not affect England since,

Presbytery was established in Scotland. It became no reason
either for its religious or civil establishment here. In New
England the Independent Congregational Churches had an
established legal maintenance; whilst that country continued
part of the British empire, no argument in favor of inde-

pendency was adduced from the practice of New England. Government itself lately thought fit to establish the Roman Catholic religion in Canada; but they would not suffer an argument of analogy to be used for its establishment anywhere else.[42]

Finding that North did not appear to be impressed with this reasoning, Burke concentrated on the bill's Catholic issues and found his arguments more acceptable. He pointed to the danger of allowing Catholic relief to be defeated merely because the Dissenters' test clause was linked to it, thereby making the Dissenters the "arbitrators of the fate of others."

In Burke's opinion the Lord Chancellor was well disposed to the Catholics and listened enthusiastically when he pointed out how disgraceful it would be for the Government to allow a measure, recommended by itself, to be defeated merely because the opposition had used skillful tactics. Thurlow admitted that if Catholics and Dissenters were to bargain with each other for concesssions from the Government, it would be a "perpetual nursery of faction." In ending his letter to Pery, Burke declared that it all now rested with the Cabinet and if the measure should fail "you are a witness that nothing on our part has been wanting to free so large a part of our fellow-subjects and fellow-citizens from slavery, and to free government from the weakness and danger of ruling by force." [43]

The Cabinet cut out the test amendment and sent the heads (which can now be designated a bill) back to Dublin. Following the example of the British Commons on Savile's relief bill, the Cabinet changed the title "Roman Catholic subjects" to "subjects professing the Popish religion," an indication that religious antagonism still flourished.[44] In the Irish Commons the bill met bitter hostility. Ogle, Robert Stewart, and Sir Richard Johnston did their best to procure its defeat. Fitzgibbon reiterated his objection to the repeal of the right of the eldest son to inherit the whole estate by conforming; in future the son could be punished by his father for becoming a Protestant. In supporting the bill, Yelverton pointed to his own very Protestant background:

I am of an English family by the maternal and paternal lines and from my tenderest connections. I was born, and educated in the Protestant Dissenters. I have no Popish connections of any kind.

Conolly spoke warmly in support of the bill: "I have always seen every thing for their [the Catholics'] relief spurned by this House, always stifled here." Newenham defended himself against the charge that he had introduced the test clause merely to have the measure defeated: "I objected to taking the Sacramental Test to hold an office, holding that last incompatible with the Christian religion." Grattan drew a comparison between Ireland and Canada where the Popish religion had been established as a counterbalance to the Protestant colonists. The same tactics were now being employed by Britain's Tory Government in Ireland to divide Protestant from Catholic, and Anglican from Dissenter. Hely Hutchinson rebutted this argument with the assertion that the "Canada bill moved from Administration," but Gardiner's measure was "founded in Great Britain" and proceeded from the Opposition, "from Whigs not from Tories."

In the Irish Lords the Lord Chancellor and the Duke of Leinster spoke in favor of the bill while Ely, Carysfort, and several bishops spoke against it. Bellamont denounced it bitterly as the action of an English ministry which had expelled America from the empire and now wanted to destroy Ireland: disrespect was shown to Presbyterians while Papists were being nestled in the bosom of government. The Church of Ireland prelates were divided, five voting for and seven against.[45]

The passing of the bill, the first great intrusion on the Penal code, was hailed by Pery as "of more real importance to our country, than any law which has passed during my time." [46] The act virtually allowed Catholics to buy land (on leases of 999 years or up to five lives) and bequeath their property as they wished; the conforming eldest son was relieved of his power to lay hands on the entire estate. Burke joined in the celebrations, though future years scarcely saw fulfilled the happy effects he prophesied:

The Irish House of Commons has done itself infinite honour. . . . the far greater weight of the abilities and eloquence of the House was on the side where eloquence and ability ought ever to be, on the side of liberty and justice. You are now beginning to have a country; and I trust you will complete the design. You have laid the firm, honest, homely rustick of property; and the rest of the building will rise in due harmony and proportion. I am persuaded that when that thing called a Country is once formed in Ireland, quite other things will be done than were done whilst the zeal of men was turned to the safety of a party, and whilst they thought its interest provided for in the distress and destruction of everything else. Your people will begin to lift up their heads, and walk and think like men.[47]

Buckinghamshire heaved a sigh of relief and informed Germain that no legislative measure of a more intricate and delicate nature had ever been enacted in Ireland.[48] Lord Hillsborough wrote his congratulations on having gotten through the longest and most difficult session of Parliament I ever remember in Ireland. Your success in it is very much to your own honour, and gives very great pleasure to your friends.[49]

The act, which had been confronted with determined opposition in both houses of the Irish Parliament, and had nearly been defeated in the Commons, owed its success to the Administration and particularly to Pery, and to various other members, Whig and Tory, such as Gardiner, Conolly, and Leinster. These three and Yelverton were the only Patriots to be prominently identified as its supporters: the Patriots as a whole were unsympathetic, and in the case of Grattan and Ogle decidedly hostile. It was small wonder that Irish Catholics should be so effusive in protesting their gratitude to a Tory administration as to provoke the indignation of Burke who, with justice, saw this as unfair to the English Whigs whose actions had precipitated the concession. A year later, he sent a reprimand to the Catholic leader in Dublin, John Curry, to the effect that Irish Catholics should remember that the persons primarily responsible for the Relief Act were English Whigs—"those who are the furthest in the world from you in religious tenets, and the furthest from acting with the party [the Tories] which, it is thought, the greater part of the Roman Catholics are disposed to espouse." Having warned that they should not return "hostility for benefits received," he admonished them to "interfere as little as possible with the parties that divide the state." [50] In other words, they must not attempt to play politics. It is clear from Curry's reply that Burke was concerned with Whigs in Ireland as well as in England. Curry denied the charge of ingratitude and explained the Catholics' failure to express their gratitude to "those noblemen and gentlemen, both here and there, for the important services they had done us" as due to quite a different cause.[51]

The fact that Burke was so concerned is proof that the Catholic Relief Act had redounded to the benefit of the Tories despite its Whig origin. Six months after the passing of the measure, Buckinghamshire was able to report that "the Roman Catholics are in the highest good humour," while in September, 1779, Lord Shelburne wrote from Ireland:

I find all classes in this kingdom much more animated about America than in England. In every Protestant or Dissenter's house the established toast is success to the Americans. Among the Roman Catholics they not only talk but act very freely on the other side. They have in different parts entered into associations, and subscribed largely to levy men against America, avowing their dislike of a Constitution here or in America, of which they are not allowed to participate.[52]

The enactment testified to the growing feeling of security among the Protestants and sounded the death-knell of lingering fears that dispossessed Catholic families still yearned for a Stuart restoration. In high political and parliamentary circles the subject was debated on grounds of expediency and political principle, and there was little or no reference to theology. Such was not always the case with the general public, since press correspondence often bristled with biblical quotation.

The joy of Catholics in Ireland was obvious. Abroad, one of the most influential members of the "wild geese" in the French army, Lieut-Col. Daniel (later, Lieut-Gen. Count) O'Connell, expressed his delight in a letter to his brother, Maurice O'Connell of Derrynane:

A Revolution so unexpected and so long wished for must needs procure, in course of some years, an accession to the power and prosperity of the Kingdom of Ireland, and unite in one common Sentiment of loyalty the hearts of that long-oppressed and long unfortunate Nation. One step more still remains to be made—I mean the Liberty of spilling their blood in defence of their King and Country. I doubt not 'twill soon be granted tho' no motive cu'd ever induce me to bear arms against France, where I early found an Asylum when refused one at home.[53]

Superficially, it would seem that the measure had no connection with the other events of Buckinghamshire's viceroyalty. In reality, however, there was a common denominator in the activity of the middle classes. The earlier efforts to procure relief concerned the right of Catholics to take mortgages on Protestant estates. Townshend and Charlemont testified to the comparative insignificance of Catholic landlords, but enough has been said in this chapter to show that Charlemont's consciousness of the growing political power of Catholic merchants was soundly based. Hostility to the Relief Act was directed primarily to the right of buying land: it was not the remnants of a former aristocracy who mattered in this connection, but merchants with money to invest. The great practical argument of supporters of the bill was the economic loss to the country, should the wealthy urban Catholics purchase property abroad if not allowed to invest their money in land at home. When Burke wished to effect a change in the political affiliations of Irish Catholics, he wrote not to the scion of a noble house, but to a Dublin medical practitioner, John Curry. Wealth and political importance among the Catholics were now centered in the burgeoning middle classes.

NOTES FOR CHAPTER V

1 These laws are described in Lecky, *History*, I, 145 *et seq.*

2 J. G. Simms, *The Williamite Confiscation in Ireland, 1609–1703* (London, 1956), p. 160.

3 Townshend to Rochford, April 10, 1772, Lecky, *History*, II, 192–93.

4 Owing to a succession of only sons, the Kenmare estates had not been affected by the gavelling law.

5 HMC, Charlemont Papers, I, 43–45.

6 Mrs. Maureen Wall, "The Catholic Merchants, Manufacturers and Traders of Dublin 1778–1782" *Reportium Novum*, II (1959–60) 300–302.

7 Lecky, *History*, II, 191–93.

8 *Ibid.*, 193–94.

9 HMC, Charlemont Papers, I, 45–46.

10 Dominic Trant to Maurice O'Connell, May 28, 1783, O'Connell, *Last Colonel*, I, 311–312.

11 Buckinghamshire to Germain, May 27, 1778, Heron Papers.

12 I am indebted to Mrs. Maureen Wall (formerly Miss Maureen MacGeehin) for permission to read her valuable study: "The Activities and Personnel of the General Committee of the Catholics of Ireland, 1767–84," (M.A. major dissertation, 1952, Department of History, University College, Dublin).

13 Weymouth to Buckinghamshire, December 6, 1777, Lecky, *History*, II, 197; SP 63/458, f. 227.

14 Buckinghamshire to Weymouth, December 15, 1777, SP 63/458, f. 277.

15 Buckinghamshire to Weymouth, March 4, 1778, SP 63/459, ff. 109–110.

16 Weymouth to Buckinghamshire, March 28, 1778, SP 63/459, f. 177.

17 FJ, March 14, 1778.

18 FJ, April 16, 1778; *Parl. Hist.*, XIX, 1107–1113.

19 Geo. III, c. 60 and c. 61: Weymouth to Buckinghamshire, May 31, 1778, SP 63/460, f. 160.

20 FJ, May 23, 1778.

21 Buckinghamshire to Weymouth, early in May, 1778, Heron Papers.

22 Buckinghamshire to Germain, May 5, 1778, Heron Papers.

23 Knox, *Extra Official*, pp. 230–31.

24 SP 63/460, f. 143; *Correspondence of the Rt. Hon. Edmund Burke,* ed. C. W., Earl Fitzwilliam, and R. Bourke (London, 1844),

II, 223–24, 233–37; [John Hely Hutchinson] *The Commercial Restraints of Ireland considered* . . . (Dublin, 1779), p. 203.

25 Dr. Robert E. Burns in his valuable article "The Catholic Relief Act in Ireland, 1778" (*Church History*, June, 1963) sees the reasons for the passing of the act somewhat differently. Had he been aware of the letter of Buckinghamshire to Weymouth of early May, 1778, his interpretation might have been closer to mine.

26 SP 63/460, f. 143.

27 Weymouth to Buckinghamshire, May 31, 1778, SP 63/460, f. 160.

28 Anonymous, *A Sketch of the History of Two Acts of the Irish Parliament,* (London, 1778). Anonymous, *Humble Remonstrance for the Repeal of the Laws against the Roman Catholics with Judicious Remarks for the General Union of Christians.* (Dublin, 1778). This pamphlet deals with theological rather than political matters. Anonymous, *A Roman Catholic's Address to Parliament* . . . (London, reprinted Dublin, 1778). This work refers to English rather than Irish Catholics.

29 *Historical remarks on the Pope's temporal and deposing power* (Dublin, 1778).

30 The description of the parliamentary proceedings on the Catholic Relief Bill is taken from Sir Henry Cavendish's "Irish Parliamentary Debates."

31 Beckett, *Protestant Dissent,* p. 43 *et seq.*

32 Buckinghamshire to Weymouth, June 20, 1778, *Grattan Memoirs,* I, 329–32: Gardiner to Burke, August 11, 1778, *Burke Corr.,* II, 233–37.

33 Gardiner to Burke, August 11, 1778, *Burke Corr.,* II, 233–37.

34 Buckinghamshire to Germain, May 22, 1778, Heron Papers.

35 May 24, SP 63/460, f. 143; Buckinghamshire to Germain, May 27, 1778, Heron Papers.

36 Germain to Buckinghamshire, May 30, 1778, Heron Papers; North to Buckinghamshire, June 1, 1778, Heron Papers; Weymouth to Buckinghamshire, May 31, 1778, SP 63/460, f. 160.

37 Buckinghamshire to North, June 21, 1778, Heron Papers.

38 Heron to Porten, June 17, 1778, SP 63/460, ff. 269–60.

39 June 24, 1778, Heron Papers.

40 June 21, 1778, Heron Papers.

41 July 2, 1778, *Burke Corr.,* II, 226–27.

42 Burke to Pery, July 18, 1778, *Writings and Speeches of Edmund Burke* (Boston, undated) VI, 199–206.

43 *Ibid*

44 *British Commons Journal,* XXXVI, 989; Weymouth to Buckinghamshire, July 24, 1778, SP 63/460, f. 354.

45 DEP, August 13, 1778.

46 Pery to Burke, August 11, 1778, *Burke Corr.,* II, 232.

47 Burke to Pery, August 22, 1778, HMC, Emly Papers, I, 199.

48 August 23, 1778, HMC, Stopford-Sackville Papers, I, 251–52.

49 Hillsborough to Buckinghamshire, August 22, 1778, HMC, Lothian Papers, p. 337.

50 Burke to John Curry, August 14, 1779, *Burke Corr.,* II, 291–95.

51 Curry to Burke, September 4, 1779, *Burke Corr.,* II, 305–308.

52 Buckinghamshire to Germain, January 14, HMC, Lothian Papers, 343–44: Shelburne to Richard Price, September 5, 1779, Edmond Fitzmaurice, *Life of William, Earl of Shelburne* (London, 1876), III, 57–58.

53 October 5, 1778, O'Connell, *Last Colonel,* I, 207–208.

Derrynane, Co. Kerry (East front), home until 1949 of the O'Connell family. The only surviving Gaelic "Big House," it was the home of Eileen O'Connell, author in 1773 of the "Dirge of Art O'Leary," considered probably the finest lament in modern Gaelic literature; of Daniel, Count O'Connell of the French army; and Daniel O'Connell, the leader of the struggle for Catholic Emancipation. This part of the house was added to the original structure at various times between 1745 and 1825. It is now the property of the Commissioners of Public Works.

ERRATA

In the illustrations, the captions for Grange Cuffe, Co. Kilkenny, and Thornberry (formerly Prospect House), Clonderlaw, Co. Clare, are transposed.

The caption for Kilbrack, Doneraile, Co. Cork, should read: Kilbrack, Doneraile, Co. Cork. Slightly larger than the usual middle-class farmhouse, it was the home of the Creagh family. Of gentry connection, the Creaghs became Protestants about 1750. Kilbrack was later the home of Captain Boycott (from whom the word "boycott" derives) for a short time. The present owner is Mr. Patrick Walsh. (Liam O'Brien, Mallow)

Derrynane, Co. Kerry (North front). Built in 1745, though somewhat altered since then, it is the oldest part of the present house.
It is believed to have been the first slate-roofed house in this remote
and lonely part of Ireland.

Derrynane Harbor, Co. Kerry, from which contraband was shipped to and from France in the eighteenth century. As part of the "cargo," recruits (popularly known as "Wild Geese") for the Irish brigades in the French army and seminarians were smuggled to the continent (see Appendix C).

Ballyowen (or Newpark), Cashel, Co. Tipperary. A gentry home, it was erected about 1750 by the Pennefather family. They owned the borough of Cashel and thus nominated two members to the Irish House of Commons. The present owner is Mr. Frank Mc-Can, whose family purchased the house in 1864.

Castletown, Celbridge, Co. Kildare, home of Thomas Conolly, M.P. The largest house in Ireland, it was built for William Conolly, M.P., Speaker of the Irish House of Commons, and completed in 1728. The identity of the architect is uncertain, but Sir Edward Lovett Pearce was at least connected with its construction. The present owner is Lord Carew, M.C., descendant and representative of the Conolly family.

The staircase in Castletown. The Baroque Georgian plasterwork dates from about 1760. (Thomas P. Gunn, Dublin)

The Long Gallery, Castletown. Painted in the Pompeian manner about 1780, it is a room of exceptional charm. (Thomas P. Gunn, Dublin)

The gothic tower built in 1778 in honor of George Washington by Sir Edward Newenham, the radical but slightly eccentric M.P. for Co. Dublin. Erected beside his home, Belcamp, Raheny, Co. Dublin, the tower originally bore an inscription which included the words: "Oh, ill-fated Britain! The folly of Lexington and Concord will rend asunder, and forever disjoin America from thy empire." Newenham's home is now part of a boarding school run by the Oblate Fathers.

Late eighteenth-century street in Dublin, showing typical houses of landlords, successful barristers, and wealthy merchants.

Headfort, Killarney, Co. Kerry, the home from 1810 until 1911 (when it was demolished) of the McCarties. A Catholic family, accepted as being of aristocratic Gaelic ancestry, they were reduced by the confiscations and penal laws to the position of middle-man, holding a long lease of an estate of small farms. The thatched portion dated from the eighteenth century, if not earlier, while the slated part was added in the early nineteenth century.

Lisfuncheon, Ballyporeen, Mitchelstown, Co. Cork, home of the Hickey family, Catholic tenants of this farm since about the middle of the eighteenth century. The present owner is Mr. Owen Hickey.

Thornberry (formerly Prospect House), Clonderlaw, Co. Clare, the home of a Protestant tenant farmer, Chartres Brew, until 1780. It then became the Church of Ireland (Anglican) rectory and was probably enlarged to its present size. It was demolished about 1950.

Grange Cuffe, Co. Kilkenny, erected about 1760 and occupied by an agent to the Cuffe (Lord Desart's) estate until 1800. It was then rented, as a farm of 350 acres of good land, to the Catholic Patrick Corr, whose family were then hoteliers and shopkeepers in the local small town of Callan. The present owner, John Francis Corr, is a descendant of Patrick.

Ballysheehan, Mallow, Co. Cork, a four-roomed house unchanged since the eighteenth century when it was occupied by the Protestant Vincent family. A member of this family was a steward (lesser agent) of Lord Doneraile, a local landlord. The present owner is Mr. Peter Sheehan. (Liam O'Brien, Mallow)

Kilquane, Castletownroche, Co. Cork, occupied by a Protestant family named Atkins, a branch of a local landlord family, from about 1775 to the 1840's. In 1829 the resident, Mr. Atkins, sheltered Charles Daly, a suspect hunted by police and bloodhounds in connection with the "Doneraile Conspiracy" (involving a famous trial in which Daniel O'Connell dramatically and successfully defended a large number of men in danger of conviction because of unjust court procedure). By a true but deliberately misleading statement, Atkins induced the police to seek Daly elsewhere, thus enabling him to escape. The thatched roof was recently covered with galvanized iron. The present owner is Mr. Patrick O'Riordan. (Liam O'Brien, Mallow)

Ardelly, Skahanagh, Doneraile, Co. Cork, farmed throughout the eighteenth century by the Protestant family of White, related to the local Protestant landlord family of Grove-White. In the nineteenth century the house was slated and improved by a barrister, Francis Evans, who used it as a summer residence. The present owner is Miss Mary Hunter, whose family purchased the property in 1890. (Liam O'Brien, Mallow)

Kilbrack, Doneraile, Co. Cork. Slightly larger than the usual
middle-class farmhouse, it was the home of the Creagh family. Of
gentry connection, the Creaghs became Protestants about 1750.
Kilbrack was later the home of Captain Boycott (from whom the
word "boycott" derives) for a short time. The thatched roof was
recently covered with galvanized iron. The present owner is Mr.
Patrick Walsh. (Liam O'Brien, Mallow)

Rockfield, Oran, Co. Roscommon, home of the White family since its erection about 1780. The first occupant was Thomas White, a Catholic farmer, who leased this farm of 163 acres, one-third of which is arable. This stone house consisted originally of three rooms and an attic and was later enlarged. The present owner is Thomas' descendant, James H. White. (Abbey Studios, Roscommon)

VI

The Free Trade Movement

I

After the conclusion of the parliamentary session of 1777–1778, the political situation did not return completely to the calm that normally ensued after the prorogation of parliament. Nevertheless, most of the excitement had died down by winter, and the beginning of 1779 bore little sign that it was to become a dynamic year in Irish history. That it did so, was due, in the first instance, to activities in the British Parliament. Just as statesmen in England had virtually initiated the movement for a lifting of the restrictions on Irish commerce in 1778, and the Irish Catholic Relief Act had been triggered by what was happening in the British House of Commons, it was the resumption of British parliamentary debates on Irish affairs which gave the great impetus to the Free Trade movement in 1779.

On January 19, 1779, the Irish peer, Lord Nugent,

moved in the British Commons that there be laid before the members an account of the trade between Britain and Ireland since 1768. His motion was a preliminary one, he said, to bringing in a bill for granting further relief to Irish commerce. He painted the economic condition of Ireland in the most vivid colors:

Want and poverty were visible everywhere throughout the kingdom: manufactures were at a standstill; and famine had so overspread the country, that nothing but the calamities of our people at Calcutta during the dreadful scarcity of provisions there, could equal the present situation of the Irish.

He then proceeded to attack the "narrow policy of confining the trade of an empire to one part," a system unknown in Europe and now discontinued even by the Spanish. Ireland's poverty lessened her value to Britain as a customer of British manufactures; now that America was irretrievably lost (even though she might return to her allegiance, she would be an impoverished, debilitated America), it behooved Britain to care for the remainder of the empire. If something were not done, Ireland would be lost to Britain by famine or emigration. His motion was adopted.[1]

It was publicly known in Ireland that Nugent and other "Friends of Ireland" were about to press for the repeal of some of the commercial restrictions, and in recognition of his services, Nugent was granted the Freedom of the City of Dublin.[2] The first sign that something serious was afoot in Ireland came a few weeks later when the Dublin Evening Post on February 4, 1779, suggested that nearly £2,000,000 would be kept at home and circulated among "our famished traders and manufactures" if the Irish Parliament would establish "a general asso-

ciation against the importation of English manufactures."
The *Freeman's Journal,* two weeks later, called on the
merchants of Ireland to have no dealings with such of
their English and Scottish counterparts as should sign any
petition against "an extension of the Irish trade." A week
later, on February 27, a letter appeared in the same newspaper demanding action:

There are twenty thousand manufacturers starving. . . . Let
them starve and be damned, whilst we have an English ware-
house in every corner of the town, and whilst scores of
Scotch pedlars are permitted to vend their manufactures
daily in the streets of Dublin.

A further injection of energy came from London when
on February 15 Lord Newhaven moved in the Commons
for a committee to consider the laws restricting Irish trade.
His purpose, he said, was to give Ireland the right to import direct from the West Indies, without which the export trade granted her last year was of little value. Economic distress had made emigration the only solution for
the Irish. When he had had a seat in the Irish Parliament,
he had procured a return which showed that in two years
16,000 people had emigrated. The Americans had benefitted to such an extent that General Washington was able
to "oppose our armies with our own Irish subjects, whom
our own narrow policy had driven from their country."
Lord North considered any enquiry into Irish trade imprudent. It was surprising that further concessions should
be asked before the effect of the indulgences already
granted could be observed. He thought that further privileges could not be granted without doing material injury
to Britain. Burke "raged at the idea" that it was not
prudent to enquire into the state of Irish trade; the

narrow policy towards Ireland was such as had lost America and would yet lose Ireland, not by rebellion or invasion, but by a political and commercial, death. Lord Beauchamp underlined the need to pacify Ireland by suggesting that the existence of 20,000 Volunteers was a subject worthy of the attention of the House.[3]

On March 10 Newhaven again brought up the subject in the British Commons. He moved that the House go into committee on March 19 to consider the restrictions on the Irish import of sugars from the British colonies and plantations. In support of his case he provided statistics: over the past two years the exports from Britain to Ireland had decreased by £155,000, of which linen represented £75,000; during a period of ten years the annual exports from Britain to Ireland were £2,057,000 while the imports into Britain from Ireland amounted to £1,353,-000. Thus, the average annual balance in favor of Britain was £704,000, which meant that in ten years Britain gained a balance of £7,040,000 on her Irish trade. Nugent, Beauchamp, Thomas Townshend, and Welbore Ellis gave a mixture of Whig and Tory support to Newhaven's motion which was passed by 47 to 42. In the debate the existence of 20,000 Volunteers was put forward, as it had been on February 15, as a reason for granting concessions.[4]

On March 12 a motion in the British Commons on imports from the West Indies gave rise to another debate on Irish trade. In response to a warning from Thomas Townshend not to drive Ireland into rebellion, North said he was very friendly to Ireland; he had appointed natives of that country to Irish offices usually held by Englishmen, had never even thought of increasing the Irish pension list, and had not been inattentive to her commercial interests in the last session.

Burke had no mercy and no regard for good intentions

when he rose to denounce the Prime Minister's handling
of government and loss of America. What care had he of
Ireland when he allowed 11,000 men there to arm without
authority! His government, continued Burke, was in a
chaotic condition, one example of which was the divergent
lines of conduct in Irish affairs between the Premier and
Beauchamp, the former opposing concessions, the latter
supporting these same concessions.[5] On March 23, 1779,
the radical *Dublin Evening Post* was even less appreciative
of the unhappy North, and praised Burke for having attacked the Prime Minister and "set his administration,
both in a just and contemptible light. Lord North . . .
asserted, that he had given places to the natives (very
condescending) and that his sentiments concerning us
were well known (too well, truly) ."

Despite Burke's aspersions, North's concern for Ireland
was genuine enough and one result of that concern was
the Government's decision in March, 1779, to take on the
payment of the 3,000 soldiers on the Irish establishment
serving in America. The cost was estimated at about
£70,000 a year, and the concession was explicitly made to
meet Buckinghamshire's repeated requests to repair the
depleted state of the Irish treasury.[6] In Ireland the British
action excited little public comment except for the *Dublin
Evening Post's* statement that England deserved no thanks
for this apparent generosity. She had been forced to undertake this expense simply because Ireland was unable to
find the money.[7]

For the first half of the year 1779, the Chief Secretary
was in London pleading the necessity for the grant of commercial concessions to Ireland. His correspondence with
his master, Buckinghamshire, shows that there was little
hope of obtaining any *major* relaxation of the Navigation
system. North was prepared to free Ireland from some of

the restraints, such as the prohibition on the importation of sugar direct from the West Indies, but only if Buckinghamshire could guarantee that Ireland would make no further demands. The latter however, was unable to give any such guarantee.[8]

One can see the difficulty of North's position in having to deal with both the jealousy and fears of British traders and manufacturers, and the ill-defined demands of Irish political and economic circles. His feeling that Buckinghamshire was not being sufficiently firm showed that he had not fully accepted the latter's warnings about the deterioration of the Irish Government's position. Earlier in March, the Lord-Lieutenant had warned Heron, who was in London in almost daily contact with North, that

the time no longer exists when measures may be carryd by little intrigues and feeding the rapacity and flattering the vanity of Individuals, when something has been done to give satisfaction to the nation in general, such helps may have a secondary operation.[9]

In Ireland the decks were cleared for action by the debates in the British Commons, and the gun that opened fire was a meeting of the Grand Jury and Freeholders of Co. Galway on March 27, 1779. They decided not to import or buy any goods produced in Manchester because of that city's "narrow and selfish" opposition to commercial concessions. They also decided that, should "the addresses from this kingdom [Ireland] to the Throne prove fruitless," the resolution would extend to the goods of Britain as a whole.[10] In the same week vigorous calls for action appeared in the press. A correspondent in the *Freeman's Journal* wrote on March 27:

It does but expose us to the imputation of folly, meanness, and cowardice to beg . . . the enjoyment of our *natural in-*

alienable rights [an American note is sounded here] . . . which it will be virtue in us in part to recover, by entering into a *Non-Importation Agreement.*

Two days later, the *Hibernian Chronicle* published a letter which it described as written by a member of the Irish House of Commons:

Do you think the inhabitants of Cork would enter into an association to make use of our own manufacture only? If this could be done all over Ireland, the dirty little manufacturing towns here [Great Britain], instead of sending insolent circular letters to every Member of the British Parliament, would employ themselves in writing to entreat the passing our Bills into laws, which nothing but fear will ever procure us.

The example of Galway was infectious, and during the ensuing six months at least fifteen counties and the cities of Dublin, Kilkenny, Waterford, and Wexford held similar meetings. These were usually composed of the grand jury, and "Gentlemen and Inhabitants" and were convened under the chairmanship of the high sheriff. These were important gatherings because they clearly represented the propertied classes. Some twenty meetings were reported in the press, usually in the form of paid insertions, but it is probable that many additional meetings were held but not publicly reported. The decisions arrived at always included a determination to buy only Irish goods and a resolution to boycott any trader who should sell British goods was usually added. Some meetings went further and admonished Irish manufacturers to use the favor to good effect, and not attempt to increase prices, or produce shoddy articles.

The non-importation agreements were entered into throughout the country, but not in the north of Ireland;

in Ulster only the fringe counties of Monaghan and Cavan joined the boycott. Those engaged in the linen manufacture, which was centered in the North, feared the emergence of a counter non-importation movement in Britain against the purchase of Irish linen. Belfast made an unsuccessful attempt to take up the movement,[11] the Grand Jury of Co. Down refused to join, and a correspondent in the *Dublin Evening Post* admitted that the northern counties had not entered into non-importation associations, but, nevertheless, their principal inhabitants were determined to buy only Irish goods.[12]

The most radical and important agreement was entered into at Dublin on April 26 at a meeting which described itself as the "Aggregate Body of the Citizens of Dublin." This gathering elected a committee, which henceforth styled itself as the Committee of the Aggregate Body and consisted of seven members, including the two radicals, Alderman Horan and James Napper Tandy. Its first resolution described the miserable state of the country, its poverty and emigration, and castigated Britain for preventing Ireland from enjoying her natural wealth; worse still, Britain "even tantalizes us with imaginary schemes of improvement and insults us with a permission to cultivate our own soil"—a reference to the Tobacco Act.[13] The meeting went on to denounce the avarice of those in Britain who opposed commercial concessions to Ireland, and ended on a decision to refuse to import any British products that could be produced or manufactured in Ireland.[14]

The tone of its resolutions, the violence of the denunciations, and the determination shown in the non-importation decision gave this meeting a vigor not equalled elsewhere. The Lord-Lieutenant regarded its resolutions as "of such dangerous tendency," that he consulted with the

Lord Chancellor, the Prime Serjeant, and the Attorney-General as to taking legal action. The Lord Mayor was also consulted, but he deemed the matter of small consequence, and, as result, it was decided that repressive action by the Government would only make a disagreeable situation worse.[15] This decision was approved by London which, however, warned Buckinghamshire to do everything possible to alleviate the effect which this meeting might have, and to try to calm the public mind.[16] There were no immediate repercussions as far as Buckinghamshire could judge, and he breathed a sigh of relief.[17]

But he was wrong. The Committee of the Aggregate Body showed a surprising toughness and perseverance during the following six months. On May 29 it commenced a systematic publication of the names of all importers of British goods. Henceforth, such names appeared regularly until it was announced in December that the British Government had decided to grant freedom of trade. Buckinghamshire was alarmed and informed Weymouth that this publicizing of names

is probably calculated for the abominable purpose of drawing the indignation of the mob upon individuals, and is supposed to be the act of the very meanest of the faction. As this circumstance gives disgust to all reasonable people, means may probably be found to put a stop to it.[18]

Even in expressing anxiety at this turn of events, the Lord-Lieutenant was still able to comfort himself with the thought that "the associations to wear only Irish manufacture may, I rather believe, be considered as merely temporary, and will soon dwindle into nothing." [19]

The power of this dynamic little group was seen when one of their original members, Jeremiah D'Olier, a silversmith, objected to the publication of names and resigned, only to become the object of their attentions. A week after the first publication he felt obliged to insert in the *Hibernian Journal* a transcript of various cancellations of orders placed in Britain, and he appended a copy of his affidavit testifying to the truth of his statement.[20] Two months later in advertising his wares, he was careful to assure his customers that he did not import British goods. In October a woollen draper, Ralph Smyth, inserted a similar affidavit in the *Hibernian Journal*. In December James King, a mercer, published a sworn statement to the same effect, to which was added a statement from some twenty-five merchants, including the prominent manufacturers, Benjamin Houghton and Richard McCormick, paying tribute to him as "incapable of practising any low cunning or deception." [21]

As the year wore on, advertisements for the sale of goods showed an increasing tendency to stress the fact that the articles were of Irish manufacture. Towards the end of the year no merchants were so indiscreet as to boast of an array of imported goods, though they often had done so in the spring. One example was the June advertisement of Michael Murphy, a button seller, who stocked "the greatest variety of fancy buttons ever imported into this Kingdom." Three months later his advertisement is so worded that one gets the impression that to import a button is the last thing he would think of doing. The victims of the campaign included a merchant named John Lee, who felt obliged to assure the public in an advertisement that he had desisted totally from importation even though "my enemies are industriously circulating reports, that I persist in the importation of musical instruments."[22]

The popular anger aroused by the first insertion of importers' names in the press can be seen in the riots that occurred in Dublin on June 1 when a mob attacked the premises of three merchants, at least two of whom, John Ball and Stephen Stock, had been on the proscribed list.[23] Ball was forced to mend his ways because the Journeymen Silk Weavers thanked him a few months later for his readiness to "give us indubitable and satisfactory proofs that you have not brought over any broad or narrow silk goods in your late importation," and drove home a threat of boycott by describing themselves as his friends so long as he continued faithful to the non-importation agreement.[24]

Pressures were brought to bear by organizations other than the Committee of the Aggregate Body. In the *Freeman's Journal* of June 17, a group of woollen drapers published a statement, with their signatures attached, to the effect that they would sell only articles of Irish manufacture "except such goods as have received invoices of and are now on the way, the date and amount of which invoices have been exhibited to the Committee of Woollendrapers, and an account taken of the same."

All this evidence proves that the determination not to import British goods was a very considerable force in Dublin business life. Whether the county and town meetings outside Dublin were equally effective, it is difficult to say. Until well into the summer, the Dublin newspapers were complaining of the continued importation of British wares, and suggestions were being made for more effective prohibitions. These complaints tended to grow less frequent as autumn approached, and in the late summer various assertions were made that the movement was effecting a great increase in the employment of manufacturing workers, and was making itself felt in England and Scotland.[25] However, statements of this kind often tended towards wishful thinking.

That the movement to check or abolish British imports was not wholly effective can be gleaned from several letters in the press. One of them was written by the Committee of the Aggregate Body complaining that a consignment of goods had been imported in what appeared to be fictitious names, and suggesting that the firm of Bell and Medlicott were the actual importers. In their defense the accused published an affidavit stating that the goods did not belong to them, and added

should any outrage be committed in consequence of the liberty they have taken with our names, or may hereafter take, that we shall undoubtedly look upon them, the said Committee, to be fully answerable for the same.[26]

An anonymous correspondent defended Bell and Medlicott and expressed doubt as to the ability of the Committee to prevent imports from taking place, since the prohibition in Dublin would merely lead to the introduction of goods through other ports.[27] Another writer said:

There have been certainly goods imported since the signing that Association; but there are several warehouses and shopkeepers who have not signed it, that are at liberty to do as they please to the no small injury of those who restrained themselves, merely to give bread to many of their Fellow-creatures who were starving for want of it.[28]

From all the foregoing it may be seen that the non-importation agreements were neither universally adopted, nor completely effective. Nevertheless, their very existence, and the indignation they provoked are, in themselves, a tribute to their strength. The fact that the British Parliament received in 1779 no petitions against concessions, such as poured into it in 1778, is a proof that efforts in

Ireland had made their mark in Britain. How far this change was due to the existence of the Volunteers, or the influence of the non-importation measures, it is difficult to say, but it seems more probable that the latter would have had the greater effect on manufacturing circles in Britain; any loss or interruption in trade would have been immediately and acutely felt, whereas the danger of the Volunteers would probably have seemed comparatively remote to the business community.

This interpretation of the effect of the boycott on British goods is borne out by the comments of leading statesmen. Heron wrote of "those combinations for wearing their own manufacturers, the continuance of which for any time must prove very injurious to those of England." [29] In September Buckinghamshire described the non-importation agreements as "more rigidly adhered to than could have been imagined." [30] Another important witness whose opinion in this matter has a special weight is Lord Charlemont. He became the Commander-in-Chief of the Volunteers a year or two later, and naturally regarded that force as the great means by which Ireland gained her objectives. Furthermore, as a landed aristocrat, he was unlikely to lavish praise on a movement that was mercantile rather than aristocratic, and which was not essentially related to the Volunteers. Yet in his memoirs he pays a great compliment to it by saying:

The association was general and effectual, numbers even of our gentry entered into it. . . . Importers were compelled to quit their injurious traffic by the dread of infamy, and, still more, of popular fury.

He further describes the movement as having given "employment and consequent bread to our own starving man-

ufacturers," and as having impressed upon the English the
consideration that even without granting concessions, they
were in danger of losing the Irish market.[31]

Historians have underestimated the importance of this
movement: Lecky, in his *History of Ireland in the Eighteenth Century*, merely mentions the fact that resolutions
were intered into.[32] A recent authority on Anglo-Irish relations of this period, Professor Herbert Butterfield, is
more conscious of the boycott's importance, but describes
it as having operated "perhaps somewhat as a hindrance
of hindrances, by the mere fact that they [the non-importation agreements] struck directly at the obstinacy of
the vested interests in Great Britain." He goes on to say
that they were "ragged in their consequences, and limited
in their staying-power." [33] As he, as well as Lecky, did not
make a study of Irish newspapers (he was interested primarily in the English side of Anglo-Irish affairs), Professor
Butterfield did not know of the perseverance of the radical
Committee of the Aggregate Body, nor of all the other
evidence in the newspapers which make "ragged in their
consequences, and limited in their staying-power" an
understatement.

There is another aspect of the movement which has
been largely overlooked—its effect on public opinion and
popular emotion. There is no concrete evidence which
could describe this effect, and no contemporary has passed
comment on it. Nevertheless, it requires only a little
imagination to consider what an enormous influence in
provoking popular interest and excitement must have
been exerted by the various meetings, and by the regular
publishing of names by the Committee of the Aggregate
Body. Some of these gatherings published resolutions attested by hundreds of people, many of whom had probably never before seen their names in print and had never

been so close to participating in political agitation. The Dublin newspapers were circulated through most of the country,[34] so that the excitement must have been widespread. One can easily imagine that the lists of importers and the charges against individual merchants must have kept the political emotions of Dublin manufacturing workers simmering. It is but reasonable to conclude that the political crisis which was building up through the summer of 1779 owed much to the non-importation movement, and much more than has been realized.

II

The Irish problem was to create a furor in the British Parliament when the Marquis of Rockingham moved, on May 11, 1779, for an enquiry into Ireland's economic position. He proposed

That this House, taking into consideration the distressed and impoverished state of the kingdom of Ireland, and being of opinion, that it is consonant to justice and true policy, to remove the causes of discontent by a redress of grievances; . . . doth think it highly expedient that this important business should be no longer neglected . . . that his Majesty would . . . direct his ministers to prepare and lay before Parliament such particulars relative to the trade and manufactures of Ireland, as may enable the national wisdom to pursue effectual methods for promoting the common strength, and commerce of his Majesty's subjects in both kingdoms.[35]

He prefaced his motion with a long speech in which he dealt first with Ireland's financial position over the previous twenty years—the increasing cost of administration, the necessity to resort to loans, and the decline in revenue of recent years. In 1777 the expenditure exceeded revenue

by £260,000,[36] and in 1778 the Irish Government could
not even raise money on loan. For the eleven years ending
in 1777, Britain exported to Ireland upwards of £6,500,-
000 more than Ireland exported to Britain. But in 1778
British exports to Ireland were under £1,500,000, a de-
crease of more than 25 per cent from the year 1777. It was
in Britain's interest to have Ireland more prosperous. He
was informed by a large manufacturer of woollens in
Yorkshire that woollen exports to Ireland had fallen considerably, and that the manufacturer had been assured
that if he were to go now to that country he could not be
sure of safety for "either his property or his person."

The poverty of Ireland could be seen, continued Rockingham, in the fact that the British Government had had
to take on the payment of troops on the Irish establishment serving in America (it was ironical that a measure
thought likely to appease Irish sentiment should furnish
an argument in favor of further concessions). The Government had neglected Ireland; concession had been made
to the Catholics, but the Dissenters had been treated with
contempt by the excision of the sacramental test clause
from the Catholic Relief Act of 1778. Concessions should
be granted to Irish trade on every principle of "gratitude,
interest and sound policy." The great unifying factor
there was the determination not to import British manufactures. Ministers in Britain had greatly erred in neglecting the defense of Ireland and allowing the Irish to organize illegal armed companies even though the latter had
acted properly in attempting to defend themselves when
neglected by government. Finally, Rockingham used the
threat provided by the existence of the Volunteers when
he said that he had every confidence that they would defend their country against invasion but wondered how far
the "same spirit might be exerted in resisting oppression
and injustice from any other quarter."

The motion was immediately opposed by Weymouth on the ground that the House had not sufficient data before them and, anyway, such a motion should more properly come from the Commons. The Duke of Chandos approved of all but the part which censored the Government. Rockingham owned a large Irish estate, and Chandos made full use of this fact by describing as a principal cause of Irish distress the rents which that country had to pay to absentee landlords. The rapier found its mark since the marquis was provoked into indirect reply by venomously stressing the danger of the "formidable military associations" which should be considered if the Government intended to adhere to their "former system of oppression and injustice."

Lord Townshend, a former viceroy of Ireland, considered that Ireland merited every indulgence which "justice dictated, and generosity and national gratitude rendered a positive duty on the part of a great nation." Even though it might hurt his personal interest as a landowner in a manufacturing county—Norfolk, he would never countenance measures founded on a "narrow or partial scale of politics." He considered the two countries as one and their peoples as bound by the same aim—the prosperity of the whole. He did not believe that Ireland would ever resort to violence leading to a separation from England. A much greater danger was that the Irish would emigrate to America in large numbers if not granted concessions. He was extremely sorry to find "his early information respecting Washington's army had proved so fatally true, and that we had been in part baffled in our attempts to subdue our rebellious colonies, by the great number of Irish emigrants, who, driven by poverty and oppression from their native country, were compelled to enlist in the rebel army."

Rockingham rose a third time and stated that the Volunteers in Ireland amounted to more than 10,000 men "all acting under illegal powers, under a kind of supposition that all government was at an end." The American war had commenced in addresses and petitions which, when a deaf ear had been turned to them, were followed by non-importation agreements. There had then ensued an oppressive policy which led to ruin. Let not the same mistake be made in regard to Ireland.

The Duke of Manchester stressed the danger of allowing the French to offer the Irish "independency and a free trade." The policy of France was to come as

friends to succour and relieve; no longer as the foes but the friends of human kind, come to vindicate the rights of injured and oppressed nations. This was her policy respecting America, and this he feared would be her policy respecting Ireland.

A timely generosity to Ireland was the way to forestall the French plan.

Lord Gower, Lord President of the Council, proposed an amendment to Rockingham's motion which excised censure on the Government for neglecting Ireland, and, in this amended form, the motion was passed *nem. con.*

Lord Shelburne supported the amended motion but retained the right to express his personal strictures on the Government. He considered the Irish people loyal, and when armed,

an enraged mob, of whom there was not a man but would defend his country against the common enemy, should any attempt be made on it. As for the [non-importation] associations, they could do no harm to Great Britain; and upon their knowing that government and the parliament here [in Britain] intended them some relief, they would soon be dissolved.

There was always a touch of the *enfant terrible* about Shelburne, and this was demonstrated by his use of the term "enraged mob." It gave great offense in Ireland, appearing in the account of the debate in the Irish newspapers. From the context it is clear that the unhappy description was not meant to be abusive, but merely to give vividness to the assertion that the Volunteers were really loyal, but had been driven by English oppression into a state of fury.

Shelburne did not go as far as most of the Whigs with respect to Ireland. He considered that commercial restraints were not the sole cause of her economic difficulties; British manufacturers were not illiberal but had been disturbed by

persons zealous in the cause of Ireland, who had alarmed them by representing that the Irish were to be allowed to import the raw materials for manufactures, paying less duty on them than the English, which would ruin the manufacturers of Liverpool, Manchester, Yorkshire, Norwich, and other parts of England.

One cannot help wondering about the wisdom and patriotic sincerity of Rockingham and his Whig colleagues in making such speeches. Their oratory could only have the effect on Irish minds which would lead to greater difficulties for the British Government. One can understand how the Whigs had come to be hated by George III who inevitably had difficulty in appreciating honesty of purpose in an opponent. It seemed now as if the Opposition in the British Parliament was determined to leave no stone unturned in order to bring down Lord North's Administration. To induce in the Government and in manufacturing circles a sense of urgency concerning Irish affairs was excellent, but to stir up smouldering fires in Ireland was quite a different matter. Soon the Irish tinder was bursting into flame.

As Buckinghamshire had foreseen, the references in the debate to the power of the Volunteers as an instrument to procure commercial concessions led to an immediate increase in recruiting.[37] Early in the summer of 1779, he had come to realize the political menace of the Volunteer movement.[38] Viscount Barrington, a Tory, declared: "The present opposition is more wickedly factious than those of former times." [39] By May 23 the Lord-Lieutenant had become thoroughly alarmed:

I had been assured very lately, that the spirit of the Independent Companies began to subside; that some individuals grew disgusted at the expense; others complained of giving up so much of their time without any pecuniary consideration and, consequently, that many of those bodies would soon moulder away; but, on the contrary, within these few days, intelligence has reached me, that additional companies are forming; and it has been asserted, that this arises from the insinuations which are daily circulated in the public prints, that the idea of their numbers may conduce to the attainment of political advantages to their country.[40]

On May 29 the unfortunate Lord-Lieutenant referred to the baneful effect on "Irish patriots" of the English Whig expressions,[41] which he described a short while later as "plausible, though wicked insinuations." [42] It was only after May that the Volunteers began to assume really large proportions; in late July they were estimated at 18,000, in September at 19,000, while in October Beresford gave the figure as not less than 25,000.[43] In July, county meetings began to organize the movement on a large scale,[44] and in August Beresford reported that "the country is arming from one end to the other." [45]

In consequence of Rockingham's amended motion, Buckinghamshire was instructed to transmit to London "your opinion together with such information and materials as may lead to the forming of a proper judgment on a point of such serious concern as the welfare of the kingdom of Ireland." [46] He immediately set about obtaining the views of leading members of the Dublin Castle Administration and a few others, and over the course of the succeeding six weeks forwarded them to London.

The British Parliament had not yet finished with Irish affairs. On May 26 Lord Beauchamp proposed a motion in the Commons on Irish trade grievances similar to that passed in the Lords on May 11. North acquiesced and the proposal was passed *nem. con.* Thomas Conolly, who had a seat in both parliaments, gave a recruiting boost to the Volunteers by describing them as loyal to England, but

with all their loyalty, he would not be answerable for them, nor for any body of men who, with arms in their hands, felt themselves aggrieved and saw they had nothing to hope from the superintending power of the empire.[47]

Lord Shelburne showed that he had no intention of letting the Cabinet slumber when on June 2 he moved in the Lords for information on what had been done since May 11 about Irish grievances.[48] He requested that the British Parliament be kept sitting and the Irish Parliament be assembled so that "the national wisdom might collectively interpose for the redress of the grievances of Ireland." In a long speech he censured the British Government for its delay in attending to Irish affairs, and made a spirited attack on North for his statement a few days before that Ireland's protests were ill-timed and could be dealt with in the next session of parliament. Did North want another war in order to provide his family with new

honors, or was it mere laziness? "Did the noble lord long
to be at leisure to feast on turtle?" The American war,
Shelburne continued, had started on less provocation than
that given to Ireland. The latter had "shut up her trade
from us, refused to have intercouse with us, and had already formed very alarming combinations." She had resorted to every measure adopted by America, except
actual rebellion, but now everything was to be feared
since the Irish might soon be in arms. Camden called on
the Government to convince the Irish that it was sincere;
action was needed, not empty promises. Other peers took
part in the discussion which reached an even more emotional level than the debate of May 11.

The persons consulted by the Lord-Lieutenant in re-
sponse to his instructions were John Hely Hutchinson
(Provost of Dublin University and Secretary of State),
Edmond Sexton Pery (Speaker of the Irish Commons),
Walter Hussey Burgh (Prime Serjeant), Sir Lucius
O'Brien, John Foster (Chairman of the Committee of
Supply in the Irish Commons), Lord Annaly (Chief Justice
of the King's Bench), Marcus Paterson (Chief Justice of
the Common Pleas), Lifford (Lord Chancellor), and the
Commissioners of the Revenue (Lord Naas, Monk Mason,
Lord Clifden, Sir Hercules Langrishe, and Robert Waller
—Beresford was not included because he was on a visit
to London and in verbal communication with North and
Robinson). Henry Flood refused to submit a statement on
the grounds that he had not been able to investigate the
official records, and the Primate (Protestant Archbishop of
Armagh) declined because he felt that as a prelate he was
not in a position to proffer such advice.[49]

The opinions can be divided into four groups: those of
Annaly and O'Brien, the joint report of the Revenue
Commissioners, those of Hely Hutchinson, Pery, Hussey

Burgh and Foster, and finally the opinion of Lifford in which he summed up the views of all the others (which had been given to him for perusal) and then stated his own view.

The first two, Annaly and O'Brien, saw the commercial restrictions as the greatest, but by no means the only impediment to Irish prosperity. They were more or less agreed that even full freedom to trade would not by itself produce the desired result, since the Irish people were badly in need of some regulation of their economic life. Annaly saw a major factor in "the idleness and licentiousness of the lower class of people." O'Brien said that a free trade "would neither remove the distresses nor . . . the discontents of this country, without a great variety of operative regulations . . . many of which . . . should be entered on immediately." The Combinations Act, which O'Brien piloted through the Irish Parliament in 1780 for the purpose of preventing journeymen's restrictions on the freedom of masters, indicates the sort of regulations to which he was referring, and, gives a clue to what Annaly meant by "idleness and licentiousness."

The second group of opinions were those of the Revenue Commissions. They cited as "the heaviest weight against the improvement of this country" the absentee rents paid to owners residing in England. Since the Seven Years War, much English money had been invested in Irish estates thus increasing the drain of money from Ireland. The lower rates of interest in England induced English investors to buy land in Ireland and also encouraged Irish individuals and the Irish Government to raise loans in England. The result had been a greatly increased flow of money out of Ireland in rents, annuities, and interest.

Another cause was the increase in population which had

not been balanced by a corresponding increase in employment. Emigration had been heavy since the Glorious Revolution and had increased since 1763 but not so much as
to effect a reduction in population. The comment of the
commissioners on emigration to America is interesting:

The temptations to emigration from this country to America
have always been very great, from the exceeding cheapness
of land there, the high species of art and manufacture; to
which has gradually been added the inducement from relationship and connection with former settlers. Partial discontents on this side have somewhat contributed to the same
effect; arising perhaps from failures and disappointments in
a limited trade, or from disagreement in religious opinions.
In America every handicraft is sure of employment, and
every religious profession finds an established Communion in
some of the colonies.

The commissioners saw the immediate source of the
depression in the American Revolution. The war with the
colonists had put a stop to emigration from Ireland to
America and had cut off the Irish export trade to that
country. The result was unemployment among the manufacturing classes. Their plight would have been very great
but for the relief afforded by charity and the enlistment
of many artisans in the army. The end of the war, however, would not bring a solution, since when peace would
come, emigration would be very heavy and the flow of
skilled workers to America would not only impoverish
Ireland, but would hinder the return of prosperity by
establishing rival manufactures in America. Great Britain
also would suffer from this expected emigration from
Ireland.

The remedy lay, according to the commissioners, in a
freeing of trade. The concessions granted in 1778 were important but useless because of the interruption of the

American trade. Even at the best of times, the right to export could have little value without a corresponding right to import. Without the latter "a return of money for our goods cannot be expected." One great benefit from direct import would be a diffusion of commerce over the whole country, whereas at this time, it was confined to the more eastern ports; from Londonderry in the north, round by Belfast. Newry, Dublin and Waterford, to Cork in the south—Limerick being the only western port of importance. A larger population in the west would ensure more submission to the laws particularly the contraband laws, thus facilitating the collection of revenues.

Though they did not explicitly say it, the commissioners obviously considered a free export of woollen goods to be vitally important for Irish prosperity since they observed that because

our wool is of a coarse staple, we do not think that our manufactures will ever arrive to that degree of excellence which is to be met with in the fine manufactures from wool in England, so that unless in friezes and coarse stuffs it does not seem that the liberty to export would interfere with Great Britain.

Finally, in order to round off their argument in favor of a freeing of trade, the commissioners said that any wealth made by Ireland must

ultimately circulate through London; which being the resort of amusement and fashion, the residence of Art and Science, the center of Trade and the Seat of Government, will necessarily attract all ranks of people to answer the calls of business or pleasure.

Then comes the third group of opinions—those of Pery, Hussey Burgh, Foster, and Hely Hutchinson. They regarded the commercial restraints as the great cause of the distress. Foster considered the war as having caused a great deal of poverty because it stopped the illegal export of raw wool to France. He thought that smuggling had formerly done much to keep up the country's prosperity, because if the restrictions on trade had operated effectively, "we should long since have been an undone country." Both he and Hely Hutchinson regarded the smuggling of raw wool to France as a great encouragement to the latter's woollen industry, enabling her to compete with British manufacturers.

Pery saw the absentee rents and the payments to creditors outside the country, together with a lack of internal regulations and proper execution of the laws, as additional causes of the economic depression. He did not explain what he meant by "internal regulations," but he was doubtless referring to injurious practices such as the combinations which Annaly and O'Brien appeared to have had in mind. Foster seems to have held the same view since he said that Ireland lacked "the settled habits of industry, the knack of manufacture." But neither man pursued these points or made them major causes of distress in the way O'Brien and Annaly did. By combinations, as described in Chapter IX, was usually meant the equivalent of modern labor unions. These were composed of skilled workmen (journeymen) and exercised a control in many branches of manufacture. Employers condemned them as injurious to the economy.

In general, these opinions, particularly those of Pery and Hely Hutchinson, reflected the doctrines of Adam Smith to a very noticeable extent. Concerning the British manufacturers' fear of Irish competition, Pery held that "the objects of industry are not to be exhausted, and . . . there are markets for more manufactures than both countries can possibly supply, provided they sell cheaper than other nations." Hely Hutchinson's *"Commercial Restraints"* abounds with references to the *Wealth of Nations*. He argued that "with the increase of manufactures, agriculture and commerce in Ireland, the demand for labour and consequently its price, would increase," and thus that there was no need for the British to fear that the lower wages in Ireland would enable Irish manufacturers to undersell English. He expressed one of Smith's ideas in his contention that the wealth of a state derives more from the middle classes than from the nobility and gentry. *"Commercial Restraints"* is written with a scientific footnoting that is almost modern and shows that Hely Hutchinson was a man of knowledge and intellect.

Finally, Lifford reviewed the opinions proffered by all the others and then stated his own. He felt that all agreed that the economic depression was a reality, that there was widespread discontent with the restraints (which all considered the main cause of the distress). There was also general agreement that the economy suffered from the flow of money to England in rents, interest and annuities. Other causes, he continued, mentioned in some of the reports were the licentiousness of the people and the laxity of the laws. There was also agreement that both kingdoms had the same interests, so that relief for Ireland would redound to England's benefit.

Lifford's own view was that the greatest cause of distress was the commercial restrictions, but that other causes also had importance. These were: defective policeing of the country, the drain of money from Ireland in rents, interest and annuities, a government establishment overloaded with expenses not contributing to the public service, and the high rate of interest which hampered trade and economic development. He saw the immediate cause of the depression as the American war, which cut off the clandestine trade with America, combined with the war with France and Spain, all of which made and continued to make it

too dangerous for men ,of small capitals and traders upon a small scale who can't bear the expense of insurance to trade at all and which . . . stops or greatly diminishes those channels by which property used to flow into the kingdom, and which greatly affects public and private credit.

Lifford asked that Ireland be given freedom in trade, but did not commit himself to the view that this alone would cure her economic ills. It would alleviate discontent and reduce future emigration, and would, he felt sure, redound to the honor of Great Britain and the general good of both kingdoms. If a full freedom could not be granted, he pleaded that at least the following measures be enacted: the right to export raw wool, coarse woollens, printed linens (the freedom to export linen had not applied to all forms of linen,) and goods composed of a mixture of wool, linen, or cotton; an encouragement of the growth of corn and its import into England so as to make Ireland "one of the great granaries of Europe;" a free import from the West Indies, Spain, and Portugal; an encouragement of Irish brewing by restoring the drawback on hops reexported from Britain to Ireland; the making of economic regulations such as O'Brien suggested; the establishment of a national bank and an absentee land tax.

Heron agreed with the view that the American war was a major factor in the crisis when he wrote:

Ireland always had a great export; they smuggled their coarse woollens to America, and they will be smuggled there again whenever we are so happy as to have a peace. Nothing less than the navy of England, so is this country [Ireland] situated, could prevent it—the war does, which is one great cause of distress.[50]

The Attorney-General, Scott, paid a like tribute to the importance of illicit trading: "The laws which the Irish complain of, counteracted by smuggling, did not operate here with any effect until the American troubles." [51]

III

All the opinions except those of Lifford had been sent to London by Buckinghamshire before the middle of July, but the British Government made no effort to work out a policy for dealing with Irish discontents. Much blame was laid at the Viceroy's door for his handling of affairs, but he was not responsible for the failure to meet the on-coming crisis. Responsibility for this rests partly on the shoulders of Lord North, who was reduced in the summer and fall of 1779 to a state bordering on melancholia. His sufferings, according to Professor Butterfield, "almost per-suades us to think of him as a dumb animal." [52] He would neither examine the opinions from Ireland nor appoint anyone else to do so. In August, John Robinson wrote in despair to his friend and colleague, Charles Jenkinson, at the War Office:

Ireland is getting very bad and, indeed, I fear much confusion everywhere. . . . I shall not be surprised if the whole ad-ministration blows up even before the meeting of [the British] Parliament. It can't last after that, for in the manner of going on, it is impossible—nothing done, or attempting to be done, no attention to the necessary arrangements at home, none to Ireland, nothing to India . . . a Cabinet totally disjointed and hating I may say, but I am sure not loving, each other, never acting with union, even when they meet . . . can never direct the great affairs of this kingdom, scarce at any time, much less at this critical moment. . . . I know you and I differ in opinion about Lord North, indeed he is the most altered man I ever saw in my life. He has not spirits to set to anything, they are quite gone as to business, tho' well and full as to the Table and Amusements, and his judgement still good when you can fix his attention, but that is most difficult to do. He writes to me from Kent that "nothing can be more miserable than I am" are his words.[53]

North's conduct drove the King almost frantic, but the latter showed much patience and his letter to Robinson indicates that he had to accept much from his prime minister and to accept it with forbearance:

I had again this day pressed Lord North to have the papers from Ireland digested and such papers as may be necessary on the part of this country to be drawn up; ten days [ago] he thought no man so fit to be employed in this business as Mr. Jenkinson. Last Friday he was quite hurt when pressed and said it had originated [i.e. the demand for the investigation] in the House of Lords and that he would not take any part in it; to-day he wants to employ the Attorney-General; to be explicit I am greatly vexed at his frequent changes of opinion which stop all business.[54]

After much haggling, Jenkinson, who at first refused to take up the subject as he considered himself unqualified was induced to study the papers and prepare a statement.[55] But even as late as the end of September it was still difficult to prod North into properly tackling the Irish difficulties, and the exasperated Robinson wrote:

I can't rouse him to an attention to Ireland, and indeed, and most truly, that is a most serious business, and before the next month if there is no instruction sent to the Lord Lieutenant how to conduct himself at the meeting of [the Irish]

Parliament in certain events and propositions by opposition he will be overturned himself, the country will be in confusion, English Government disgraced, if not ruined, and he will overturn with him, perhaps, the King's Government here.[56]

This letter was written a bare two weeks before the Irish Parliament was due to meet. Ten days later, Robinson mentions that he had just written to Ireland for papers to assist Jenkinson in his investigations into Irish trade, which information the latter had requested.[57] This meant, of course, that there was no hope of the British Cabinet's coming to a decision on Ireland until well after the Irish Parliament had met. London did not see the desperate need for haste and expected that the situation could be kept under control until the British Parliament should meet in late November.

Before condemning North, it is important to remember that the failure of London to grapple with Irish affairs partly arose from the belief that British opinion would never condone the granting of full-scale concessions. The Heron Papers show that North did not neglect Ireland as completely as Robinson's correspondence would lead one to believe (or as Professor Butterfield has thought). During the summer of 1779, he wrote several times to the Lord-Lieutenant. In a long letter on July 30, he defended his Irish policy on the ground that more had been done to placate Ireland in the past ten years than in the previous hundred. Granting favors had merely encouraged the Irish to increase their demands. He considered their complaints "both unseasonable and unjust." [58]

The Lord-Lieutenant had certainly given due warning to London of the need for getting down to work on the problem of the commercial restraints, and Heron spent the first half of 1779 in England for this very purpose. In early June he informed Buckinghamshire that he could get no definite assurances from North on trade concessions for Ireland.[59] The Lord-Lieutenant received the news with dismay, regarding it as leaving "little expectation of my carrying His Majesty's business through the next sessions [of the Irish Parliament] with satisfaction to him, credit to myself, or utility to the Publick." [60] Shortly after the British House of Lords had made their request for information on May 11, he had asked Weymouth to inform the King of the urgency of the matter.[61] In July he wrote: "I have repeatedly mentioned how very necessary it was to give some satisfaction to this kingdom upon commercial points." [62] When sending the draft for the Speech from the Throne to Weymouth on September 16, he referred to the present as "a crisis when the difficulties of Irish government hourly multiply." [63]

In July both Heron and Beresford warned North and Robinson of the gravity of Irish affairs.[64] After his return to Ireland, Beresford again pleaded with Robinson for action:

When [the Irish] Parliament shall meet, you are to expect great violence, and, unless something shall be settled beforehand, I fear it will be too late to enter into the subject at such a time, and that guided, in many instances, by the various influences of a popular assembly. The country is arming from one end to the other; . . . I tell you fairly . . . that unless your Administration will turn your most serious attention to this country . . . the consequences will go further than you may possibly imagine.[65]

The situation was deteriorating so rapidly that by the end of September the Lord-Lieutenant was just as pessimistic as Beresford had been two months earlier, and expressed his fears to Germain:

The desire of unlimited commerce will be the unanimous language of this [Irish] House of Commons. The few moderate men will either be awed by national clamour into silence or their voice will be lost amidst the general cry. Nor can anything much short of this be expected in England when the Cabinet considers the stile of the several confidential servants of the Crown in the letters which have been transmitted. An address to his Majesty of this tenor will undoubtedly be introduced. The directly resisting it would be the attempting to stop the ocean with a hurdle, but my best efforts shall be exerted, tho' perhaps in vain, to reduce the terms and temperate the expectations.[66]

It is only a further sign of the ineffectiveness of the British Cabinet at this time that it should have sounded Buckinghamshire on the feasibility of a union between Britain and Ireland as a means of solving the problem of the commercial restrictions.[67] One could hardly imagine a more disastrous time for bringing up such a proposal—the country excited by the non-importation movement and exhilarated by the fears expressed in the British Parliament about the menace of the Volunteers. Buckinghamshire considered that a union would be "an arduous undertaking" as "so many prejudices and local and individual interests must be surmounted"[68] and became alarmed when he learned towards the end of September that information about the plan had leaked out and was being received with hostility in Ireland. He therefore recommended that the matter be dropped for the present.[69] The newspaper attacked the proposal vehemently.[70] The *Hibernian Journal,* on October 4, asked sarcastically whether Ireland, which had refused a union when England was powerful, was likely to accept one now that the English "are deprived of most of their possessions, insulted on their very coast, and drove defeated from visionary Empire of the Sea." Little more was heard of the plan.

Dublin Castle received a jolt towards the end of July when Walter Hussey Burgh, the Prime Serjeant, served

notice that he would not lead the government forces in
the forthcoming session of the House of Commons, and
offered to resign his legal appointment. He said that he
would feel himself obliged to oppose the Government if
commercial concessions were refused, though on all other
issues he seems to have assured Buckinghamshire and
Heron that he would continue to support the government.
They regarded his statement with surprising complacency,
attributing it in part to disappointment in matters of
patronage and emolument, Buckinghamshire even considering that Burgh would shortly return to full support.
Beresford saw it in a more serious light and exulted in
the news as a confirmation of his prophecies:

You may remember that I told you that His Excellency's
Ministers would forsake him: last Thursday Mr. Burgh waited
upon him, and desired not to be any longer considered as
being *confidential,* and he now everywhere declares opposition.[71]

Just before the meeting of the Irish Parliament, North
informed the Lord-Lieutenant that he had heard two
rumors of the intentions of the Irish House of Commons which, if true, could do "infinite mischief both to
Great Britain and Ireland." The first rumor was that the
Commons had decided to demand "the most free and unlimited trade." Should the Irish Administration be unable
to prevent such a motion being made, "everybody will
think that the authority of British Government in Ireland
is nearly overturned." The other rumor was that the Irish
Commons intended to grant "their additional duties for
six months only." Such an action would be likely to "lead
directly to a quarrel between the two countries" and
would almost certainly fail to intimidate the British Parliament. North expressed the hope that those who had

enjoyed Buckinghamshire's confidence and favor would now stand forth and resist "every offensive and virulent motion . . . and every measure which may tend to . . . create jealousy and ill-humour between Great Britain and Ireland." [72]

Buckinghamshire realized that the meeting of the Irish Parliament would witness an outburst of indignant demands for major concessions from Britain. In a letter to Germain two days before the opening of the sessions, he said that

the passions of so many individuals are in the most exalted state of fermentation, and even the discreet and well-disposed must in many instances be warned by the rash judgments of their wild constituents . . . the licentiousness ot the publick prints increases daily, and there is evidently an intention that the agitation of business should be disturbed by mobs. . . . the idea of a projected union is industriously circulated as the best calculated to excite the indignation of the Dublin rioters. . . .

And then with a flash of humor quite out of keeping with his usual character, he added that "as Ireland was formerly stiled the land of saints, it has now full as good pretensions to the denomination of the Kingdom of Patriots." [73]

Arrangements for the opening of Parliament were decided by a Privy Council meeting of the more confidential servants and advisers of the Irish Government on October 9, and again on the 11th. It was agreed that Foster, in speaking on the Address to the King (it had been taken for granted that the Parliament would address the King on the gravity of the economic situation and that it would be folly for the Administration to oppose it), [74] should move in the Commons for a committee to enquire into the "distressed and impoverished state of the nation" and that a similar motion should be proposed in the Lords. By procuring the passing of these motions, the Government hoped to gain a breathing space and retain the political initiative.[75]

NOTES TO CHAPTER VI

1 *Parl. Hist.*, XX, 111–112; DEP, January 26, 1779.

2 FJ, January 2, p. 28; DEP, January 19, 26, 30, 1779.

3 *Parl. Hist.*, XX, 136–38; FJ, February 23, 1779.

4 *Parl. Hist.*, XX, 248–50; FJ, March 18, 1779.

5 *Parl. Hist.*, XX, 269–71; FJ, March 20, 1779.

6 *British Commons Journal*, XXXVII, 275–76; Buckinghamshire to Heron (in London), January 19, March 6, 1779, Heron Papers; Buckinghamshire to Germain, March 31, 1779, HMC, Lothian Papers, pp. 349–50.

7 DEP, April 6, 1779.

8 Heron to Buckinghamshire, March 20, 22, 1779; Buckinghamshire to Heron, March 27, 1779, Heron Papers.

9 Heron to Buckinghamshire, March 20; Buckinghamshire to Heron, March 10, 29, 1779, Heron Papers.

10 DEP, April 8, 1779.

11 FJ, April 20; DEP, April 29, May 1, 1779.

12 DEP, April 29; DEP, June 12, 1779.

13 This was an act (19 Geo. III, c. 35), passed by the British Parliament in the spring of 1779, permitting the growing of tobacco in Ireland.

14 HJ, April 28, 1779.

15 Buckinghamshire to Weymouth, April 29, 1779, *Grattan Memoirs*, I, 345–46.

16 Weymouth to Buckinghamshire, May 7, 1779, *Grattan Memoirs*, I, 346–47.

17 Buckinghamshire to Weymouth, May 13, 1779, SP 63/464, f. 345.

18 Buckinghamshire to Weymouth, May 29, 1779, *Grattan Memoirs*, I, 353–54.

19 *Ibid.*

20 HJ, June 4, 1779.

21 HJ, December 31, 1779.

22 HJ, November 8, 1779.

23 FJ, June 2, 1779; Buckinghamshire to Germain, June 2, 1779, HMC, Stopford-Sackville Papers, I, 255–56.

24 HJ, August 30, 1779.

25 DEP, July 20, 31, 1779; DEP, August 21, 1779; DEP, September 4, 1779.

26 TJ, October 4, 1779; HJ, October 6, 1779.

27 HJ, October 20, 1779.

28 HJ, October 11, 1779.

29 Heron to John Robinson, August 20, 1779, *Beresford Corr.*, I, 46–51.

30 Buckinghamshire to Germain, September 24, 1779, HMC, Stopford-Sackville Papers, I, 256–57.

31 HMC, Charlemont Papers, I, 50.

32 Lecky, *History*, II, 226.

33 Herbert Butterfield, *George III, Lord North and the People, 1779–1780* (London, 1949), p. 84.

34 These newspapers published many letters from writers with country addresses. More important is the fact that many country meetings of various kinds had their resolutions inserted in the Dublin papers. The *Dublin Evening Journal,* which commenced publication in February, 1778, and its successor, the *Dublin Evening Post* (it was just a change of name), often advised its readers on its arrangements for the distribution of copies to provincial centers.

35 This description of the debate is taken from the *Parliamentary History* (XX, 635–57) as it is more comprehensive than the accounts published in the Irish newspapers.

36 This estimate does not agree with the official figure (see Appendix A), but possibly Rockingham was referring to some period other than the year ending March 25, 1778.

37 Buckinghamshire to Heron, May 12, 1779, Heron Papers.

38 Buckinghamshire to Heron, June 3, 1779, Heron Papers.

39 Barrington to Buckinghamshire, May 11, 1779, Heron Papers.

40 Buckinghamshire to Weymouth, May 23, 1779, *Grattan Memoirs*, I, 347–49. The date is erroneously published as May 24, but the original (SP 63/464, ff. 361–62) is dated May 23.

41 Buckinghamshire to Germain, May 29, 1779, HMC, Stopford-Sackville Papers, I, 255.

42 Buckinghamshire to Weymouth, June 12, 1779, *Grattan Memoirs*, I, 358–60.

43 DEP, July 29 and September 7, 1779; Beresford to Robinson, October 24, 1779, *Beresford Corr.*, I, 67–73.

44 DEP, July 29, September 7, 1779.

45 Beresford to Robinson, August 2, 1779, *Beresford Corr.*, I, 43–46.

46 Weymouth to Buckinghamshire, May 18, 1779, SP 63/464, f. 343.

47 *Parl. Hist.*, XX, 661–63.

48 *Parl. Hist.*, XX, 661–75; DEP, June 8, 1779.

49 These opinions (with the exception of Hely Hutchinson's) are published in the *English Historical Review*, XXXVIII (October, 1923), 564–81 and XXXIX (January, 1924), 95–109. Hely Hutchinson's views were published by him anonymously in 1779 in a pamphlet entitled *The Commercial Restraints of Ireland* (Dublin, 1779).

50 Heron to Robinson, August 20, 1779, *Beresford Corr.*, I, 46–51.

51 Scott to Robinson, October 20, 1779, *Beresford Corr.*, I, 64–47.

52 Butterfield, *George III, Lord North and . . .* ,p. 60.

53 Add Mss., 38212, ff. 56–59.

54 August 13, 1779, Add. Mss., 37834, f. 133.

55 Robinson to Jenkinson, August 16, 1779; Jenkinson to Robinson, August 17, 1779; Robinson to Jenkinson, September 27, and October 9, 1779 (Add. Mss., 38212, ff. 61–62; 38307, f. 19; 38212, ff. 115–117, 140–41).

56 September 30, 1779, Add. Mss., 38212, ff. 126–27.

57 Robinson to Jenkinson, October 9, 1779, Add. Mss., 38212, ff. 140–41.

58 North to Buckinghamshire, July 30, 1779, Heron Papers.

59 Heron to Buckinghamshire, June 4, 1779, Heron Papers.

60 Buckinghamshire to Heron, June 9, 1779, Heron Papers.

61 Buckinghamshire to Weymouth, May 24, 1779, tSP 63/464, f. 359.

62 Buckinghamshire to Weymouth, July 12, 1779, SP 63/465, f. 367.

63 *Grattan Memoirs*, I, 379–81.

64 Heron to Robinson, August 20, 1779, *Beresford Corr.*, I, 46–51; Robinson to George III, July 12, 1779, Add. Mss., 37834, f. 119.

65 August 2, 1779, *Beresford Corr.*, I, 43–46.

66 September 30, 1779, HMC, Stopford-Sackville Papers, I, 258–59.

67 Buckinghamshire to Germain, August 20, 1779, HMC, Stopford-Sackville Papers, I, 256; Lord Lucan to Pery, August 21, 1779, HMC, Smly Papers, I, 202.

68 Ibid.

69 Buckinghamshire to Germain, September 30, 1779, HMC, Stopford-Sackville Papers, I, 258–59.

70 FJ, October 3; DEP, October 7, HJ, October 25, 1779.

71 Beresford to Robinson, August 2, 1779, *Beresford Corr.*, I, 43–46.

72 North to Buckinghamshire, October 5, 1779, Heron Papers.

73 Buckinghamshire to Germain, October 10, 1779, Heron Papers.

74 Buckinghamshire to Weymouth, September 16, 1779, *Grattan Memoirs*, I, 379–81; Buckinghamshire to Germain, September 16, 1779; HMC, Lothian Papers, pp. 356–57; Buckinghamshire to Germain, September 30, 1779, HMC, Stopford-Sackville Papers, I, 258–59.

75 Buckinghamshire to Weymouth, October 13, 1779, *Grattan Memoirs*, I, 391–94; Beresford to Robinson, October 11, 13, 1779, *Beresford Corr.*, I, 52–60.

VII

The Success of Radicalism

I

The advisers in the Irish Privy Council had been unanimous in agreeing on the manner in which the opening
session of the House of Commons should be conducted,
and even the pessimistic Beresford was confident of success.[1] When the Speech from the Throne had been read,
Sir Robert Tilson Deane, a pro-Government member, proposed an Address to the King of an innocuous nature
which was duly seconded, and then the blow fell; Grattan
rose to his feet and with all the great oratorical power at
his command, poured forth the violence that had been
building up for a year.

He demanded to know why the Speech from the Throne
was intended to quiet the minds of the people, why did
it not make a declaration in answer to the addresses of
the people demanding a free trade? Were the people of
Ireland undeserving of the notice of British Ministers?

Why didn't the servants of the Crown in Ireland speak out? Were the distresses of Ireland of so private a nature as not to be mentioned?

After this rhetorical outburst, Grattan went on to describe the distresses as two-fold—the poverty and wretchedness of the people, and the bankruptcy of the state. The former was the result of an unfavorable balance of trade and the drain of absentees, but was caused, above all, by the commercial restrictions, particularly the prohibition on the export of woollen cloth. The country owed its present existence to the non-importation associations, but something more permanent and effectual was needed. The bankruptcy of the state was the result of a "system of boundless prodigality, profligacy and violence." The peace establishment of Ireland amounted to one-sixth that of England, but was much too extravagant for her resources—an establishment that consisted of "infamous pensions to infamous men" (here, we are informed by the newspapers, Grattan "launched into personalities," though the reports do not mention the names of the victims). He had already declared that the servants of the Crown were the representatives of the people, and now, after the attack on the "infamous pensions to infamous men," he demanded to know: "Will those men whom we pay, vote against an extension of our trade?"

Ireland then, he concluded, had nothing to expect—no redress of grievances, no extension of trade—but from the efforts and spirit of her own people. Why had the House of Commons less courage than the people? Would it be wise or politic for the Government to oppose the people here or elsewhere, "Will it be SAFE?"

In a House that was electrified by this direct appeal to the populace, to opinion outside parliament, he proposed an amendment to the Address to the King to the effect that the only cure for the wretchedness and misery of Ireland was "to open a free trade, and let your Irish subjects enjoy their natural birthright." [2]

Grattan's speech was dynamic. Never before had the members likely to have voted with the Government been told to their faces that they were cowards and hacks, for that is what, in reality, he was saying. The appeal to the people over the head of the Parliament was something which this assembly of landed gentlemen had not heard before. It meant bringing into the House the non-importation associations and the other public meetings, and, above all, the armed Volunteers. Grattan knew where the power now lay and he had the courage and the ability to mass it against the Parliament. He had unleashed great force and was determined to ride roughshod over all opposition.

The reports of the debate in the newspapers are, of course, inadequate—reports in the eighteenth century were not verbatim and one can grasp the power of the speech only by comparing it with similar reports of other great parliamentary efforts. Beresford's description helps us to understand:

Mr. Grattan arose and made a most violent speech, in which he drew a deplorable picture of the miseries of this country, which he attributed wholly to the tyranny of England, against which country, without descending to particular persons, he made a most violent invective; he then abused Ministers here, excepting in some degree his Excellency; he next abused the House, called upon the mob to do themselves justice; then praised the armed associations, in one of which he is captain; and called upon them to destroy such Members as should oppose his motion, and in short said everything he could to inflame people both within and without the House.[3]

In the shocked atmosphere Foster made a brave attempt to carry through the Government's plan of having a committee appointed, and was supported by Hely Hutchinson and Scott, but their efforts could effect nothing.

The Prime Serjeant, Hussey Burgh, now showed his opposition to the Government by sponsoring an amendment (in concurring with Burgh's amendment, Grattan withdrew his own) for inserting into the Address to the King the clause that "it is not by temporary expedients, but by a free trade alone, that this nation is now to be saved from impending ruin." The entry into the contest of the Prime Serjeant, supported by the Vice-Treasurer, Henry Flood, completed the rout of the Administration, so that the Lord Lieutenant could write:

The impression made by the Prime Serjeant and Mr. Flood, high in office, gave resolution and strength to many of their inferiors; and the very strong terms in which Mr. Conolly supported the Prime Serjeant's amendment, drew after them the whole body of country gentlemen, who used to support the Government.[4]

Heron made a brave stand which won the grudging admiration of the critical Beresford but when Hely Hutchinson, Foster, and other government supporters went with the tide, and Shannon, Scott, and Beresford, though offering full support to the Government, advised against continuing the struggle, the Secretary yielded and allowed the amendment to pass.

All was not yet done. The Lords on the following day adopted a similar address to the king couched in somewhat more respectful terms.[5] On the same day, October 13, the House of Commons, on the proposal of Thomas Conolly, passed a vote of thanks to the Volunteers which simply stated: "That the thanks of this House be given to the Volunteer Companies, for their spirited, and at this time, necessary exertions, for the defence of this country." [6] The next day the House of Lords did likewise.[7]

In the Lords the motion met with a rigid legal opposition from the Lord Chancellor, Lifford, and the Chief
Justice of the King's Bench, Annaly. They argued that
the Volunteers had no legal existence, since they had not
been established by an act of parliament, but Lifford took
the sting out of this very legal disapproval by expressing
his "high esteem of the persons who compose these Associations." Annaly added the point that it was illegal for
Catholics to bear arms, and since he understood there
were several Catholics in the companies, he could not
concur in the motion.[8] Whatever the legal arguments
against the constitutional standing of the Volunteers, the
vote of thanks by both Houses of Parliament could only
mean that, henceforth, the charges of illegality need not
be taken seriously.

In addition to the addresses to the King, both Houses
passed the customary addresses of appreciation to the
Viceroy, but in its case the Commons expressed approval
of his wise and thrifty administration, and gratitude for
having informed England of the country's distresses. The
leading Patriots supported this address with lavish com-
pliments. Grattan described Buckinghamshire's handling of
the revenue in the most laudatory terms, and Yelverton
eulogised a viceroy under whose rule "ministers might
truly be called the ministers of the people." [9] The poor
Lord-Lieutenant had usually been regarded by the Patriots
and radical press as a man of integrity, but now the com-
pliments were an embarrassment since they laid him open
to the charge in England that he had courted "popularity"
at the expense of firm government.

A further humiliation was to follow. On October 14,
the Lord Chancellor and the Speaker of the Commons
went to Dublin Castle to present their respective addresses
to the Lord Lieutenant. It was the usual custom, but on

this occasion there was a difference; the Volunteers made it the opportunity for a great demonstration. The route taken by the two ministers was lined by six companies under the command of Leinster, consisting of 800 men who "For elegance of appearance, steadiness under arms, and military discipline, could scarcely be equalled by any troops in Europe." [10] This flight of fancy was surpassed by the *Hibernian Journal* in regarding the sight as "novel indeed, to a people emerging from slavery." Realizing the political significance of this demonstration, Buckingham-shire tried to have it called off, but finally yielded to Pery's advice that since it could not be prevented, any exhibition of disapproval would only lend it greater importance. The Lord-Lieutenant blamed Leinster who, he said, had de-liberately organized it. [11] The addresses presented, the Irish Parliament in accordance with custom adjourned for two weeks to await the king's reply.

Within three days Grattan's onslaught had reduced the Irish Government to pulp, and the ball was now at the feet of the Patriots. It remained to see how they would follow up their victory and what effect it would have on the British Cabinet.

Foolishly, as time was to show, the British Government refused to alter its policy. The King considered that Buck-inghamshire was more concerned with his own political position in Ireland than with his duty to his native land. North took the view that pressure of this kind from the Irish legislature would be strenuously opposed by the in-habitants of Great Britain. Weymouth informed the Lord-Lieutenant that the King could not "pledge himself to grant what does not depend on him and which must be left to [the British] Parliament to determine." [12] This concern for parliamentary approval before announcing ex-plicit concessions was unnecessary, and a more resolute

government would have committed itself in order to evade
a crisis. The Whig leaders—Rockingham, Manchester,
Richmond, Shelburne, Camden, Burke, and Thomas
Townshend—had publicly demanded a policy of concession, so that by announcing definite measures, the
Cabinet had little to fear from its parliamentary opponents.

The King's reply to the addresses contained little more
than platitudes. The attack was therefore resumed. On
November 1 in a very determined oration in the Commons, Yelverton declared that nothing but a short money
bill would force London to attend to Irish needs.[13] By
such a measure was meant the granting of supplies for
six months instead of two years—the traditional way of
bringing an administration to its knees. On the following
day, he denounced the extravagance of the Government
in its salaries and pensions to office-holders and placemen,
"those reptiles of the State and vermin of the Constitution." [14] Beresford did not appear to think that the passing
of a short money bill was likely, but the Lord-Lieutenant
was less sanguine and nervously commented: "Many of
the old tried friends of Government speak doubtfully of
what will be their conduct respecting the question of a
short money bill, and the very few who will engage to
resist, deem the opposing it a lost cause." [15]

That the Patriots had no intention of allowing the iron
to cool became apparent a few days later. The occasion
was the anniversary of the birthday of William III, November 4, when it was traditional for the viceroy to make
a ceremonial tour of the city. In 1778 this was the occasion
for a modest and uneventful parade of the newly formed
Volunteers under the Duke of Leinster. The celebration
of the glorious birth was such a big affair in 1779 that it
has gone down in history as one of the most dramatic

events in eighteenth-century Ireland. In the morning, some half-dozen corps of Volunteers marched through the center of the city to College Green where they paraded around the statue of William and, according to the eulogistic press, fired several vollies with due attention to "the strictest rules of military discipline" and performed their exercises "with an ease and exactness that would do honor to veteran troops." The meaning of all this was that around the pedestal of the statue, hung in large letters, were the inscriptions, one on each side of the monument:

"Relief to Ireland"
"Short Money Bill—A Free Trade—Or else!"
"The Glorious Revolution"
"The Volunteers of Ireland. Quinquaginta millia juncta. Parati pro patria mori."

Later, the Lord Lieutenant and his equipage made the customary tour. The day concluded "with that happy good order and unanimity, which should ever attend the firm resolve of a PEOPLE ENGAGED IN THE REDEMPTION OF THEIR FREEDOM." [16]

A week later Grattan again entered the fray and showed that his appeal to extra-parliamentary opinion on October 12 was not part of the drama of the moment, but deliberate policy. Now, on November 10, he enunciated the principle that it was the duty of members of the Commons to obey the instructions of their constituents. He said that associations had been formed all over Ireland and had decided never to vote again for any representative who should accede to the grant of new taxes before Free Trade was obtained. The first sign that some Patriots were becoming uneasy at the vigor of the radical tide, occurred when William Brownlow, a leading Patriot, said that Grattan's idea was incompatible with the dignity of Parliament.

This objection provoked from Grattan an even clearer
definition of the member of the Commons as

the servant of his constituents, whose commands he was as
much bound to obey, as the servants of the Crown were the
Royal Authority. If a member deviates from the intentions
of his constituents, they were authorized to associate against
him to reprobate his proceedings—and never trust him with
their rights again.

To this dogma, Brownlow replied that members should
pay every deference to their constituents' advice but
should retain their freedom of action. Otherwise, members
would be the "slaves and not the Trustees in whom the
People confided their liberties."

With his usual hardihood Scott, the Attorney-General,
stated his opinion as a lawyer that participation in such
associations should render the constituents disqualified
from voting. Grattan now went further along the radical
path by justifying his support of a short money bill on
the grounds that he was acting on the instructions of
his constituents: The Voice of the People, and not the
Voice of the House of Commons, must be followed. It was
the people who had compelled Parliament to "emerge
from the stupefaction of slavery, and address the Sovereign
for a Free Trade." Three million people were now to
direct the conduct of three hundred (the House of Commons) ; "the tide of corruption" could be met by the "tide
of the people." And he then reduced his doctrine to an
epigram: "I respect the Gentry of this country much but
I respect the people more." [17]

The associations of which the House of Commons was
now being informed were meetings in counties and towns
of a kind similar to those which had passed resolutions to
form Volunteer corps, or enter into non-importation

agreements. They now demanded a short money bill until Free Trade should be gained, but showed a much more radical spirit by demanding that their representatives in the House of Commons should act in accordance with their instructions. These efforts were encouraged shortly after Grattan's speech of October 12 by such newspaper editorials as that of the *Dublin Evening Post* on October 21 which hailed "the several cities and counties, now about to instruct their representatives, relative to their parliamentary conduct and suffrages" and stated that restricting supplies to six months would be the indispensable duty of the Commons. As in the non-importation movement, Co. Galway led the way as early as October 8 by holding a county meeting of the "Gentlemen, Clergy and Freeholders" which was assembled by the High Sheriff. The official account of this meeting, inserted in the *Dublin Evening Post* of October 12, states that it was decided to

address our representatives in Parliament [Denis Daly and W. P. K. Trench] and to instruct them as to the conduct we wish them to pursue in the present most alarming situation of the affairs of this country.

There followed an exhortation to restrict the supplies to six months for the purpose of obtaining Free Trade, and the address concluded with:

. . . we are firmly persuaded you will conduct yourselves like honest men, . . . and [we] think this address less necessary as a direction for your future conduct, than as an example which we hope, the rest of the Kingdom will follow.

The insertion stated that the signatories to the declaration totalled more than seven hundred.

Daly and Trench did not take too kindly to the address:

their joint answer was an implicit refusal to accept orders (it was inserted with the official account of the meeting) :

We will pay the strictest attention to those points, upon which you have given us your opinion and advice, as it is our sincere wish to act in such a manner, as may obtain your approbation. . . . And we look upon those, who uniformly vote either for or against Government, to be stimulated more by interested motives, than by the true spirit of patriotism.

In the ensuing two months, some twenty counties and many cities and towns held similar meetings which were reported in the press, usually in the form of official insertions. They varied in the politeness of their approach, some using the term "instruct" or even "insist" while others limited themselves to "recommend" or "desire and expect," but all implying a degree of compulsion in addressing their representatives.

The replies are of great interest. In most cases the members addressed did respond, thus showing that the meetings were important and representative. A majority of the members were careful to show some measure of agreement with the recommendations or instructions given but many omitted—and the omission is highly significant —to use any such term as "instructions." The more radical Patriots were only too glad to express obedience, but some Patriots such as Brownlow and Denis Daly (the latter's reply has just been quoted) tactfully disobeyed.

The Co. Dublin meeting pulled no punches in declaring "we deem it our indispensable duty to instruct you *not to vote* for any Money Bill of a longer continuation than *six months,* until this important object [Free Trade] shall be obtained." [18]

The representatives concerned were the independent supporter of the Government, Luke Gardiner, and the radical Patriot, Sir Edward Newenham. The former avoided all reference in his reply to being instructed and reserved the right to use his own judgment:

Whether the limitation of the grants of the Commons to the space of six months, be, or be not, productive of that great object [Free Trade], I cannot at present determine, as I have not heard the subject fully debated. . . .

Newenham, on the other hand, encouraged his constituents by replying: "I have received your instructions and advice, to which I shall pay due respect and regard by adhering to them." He went even further by stating that anyone deserting the interests of Ireland "must be deemed a National Traitor."

John Foster, the firm supporter of the Government and chairman of the Commons' Committee of Supply, was polite, but made it clear that he had no intention of taking orders from Co. Louth. The stand taken in the Commons by William Brownlow, the Patriot member for County Armagh, in opposing Grattan on the subject of a member's duty, has already been described. His reply to his constituents was a careful declaration that he would always take pleasure in receiving their *advice*, and "I shall be particularly happy, when I can frame my conduct to coincide with your wishes." The snub was obvious.

Three Patriots, whose replies were important, were Robert Stewart (the father of the celebrated Castlereagh), Sir Vesey Colclough, and George Ogle. To a very peremptory address from the freeholders of Co. Down who stated their number to be 1663, Stewart made a reply which showed that his thinking coincided with that of Grattan in regard to parliamentary representation:

With peculiar pleasure I find you, as well as most other bodies of electors through this kingdom, have adopted the constitutional mode of addressing and instructing your repre-

sentatives. . . . Much and great good will result . . . from
this communication with representatives; it will not only
evince that they are acting under the general sense of their
constituents, but must give vast confidence and solemnity to
the resolves of Parliament, as well as teach the people at
large to feel and to understand their own weight and significance, when the very salvation of the state is in question.[19]

The address which the voters of Co. Wexford sent to
Ogle and Colclough was merely advisory, but the two
representatives joyfully announced their servitude. Ogle
replied that "I have had the honor to receive your instructions which I shall most faithfully and implicitly obey."
Colclough went one better:

Your orders shall be implicitly obeyed . . . no consideration
would ever make me put my private opinion in competition
with that of the spirited Gentlemen and Freeholders of the
County of Wexford. . . . I am, and always was of opinion,
that the people are not truly represented in Parliament except their instructions are obeyed by their representatives;
or, to use the language of Elizabeth's days, if the representative in Parliament do not implicitly follow the instructions
of those that sent him there.

His sense of history induced him to include the following:

Shall we, born and educated in revolution principles, the
warm friends and steady assertors of the illustrious House of
Hanover, hesitate to demand from his Majesty, and from
the people of England, a Free Trade, our natural right? [20]

Hely Hutchinson's handling of the peremptory Cork
address was a model of tact. He was notorious for his
nepotism and greed for sinecures and pensions, and, as a
member for the very important trading city of Cork, had

spent the past three years skating on thin ice. The embargo on the export of provisions and now the movement for a free trade were very delicate subjects for a representative who happened to be a member of the Government. But he was equal to the situation:

The instructions of Constituents are always entitled to great respect, but when given without a negative voice, on subjects in which they are particularly conversant . . . their sentiments ought to be received with reverence—they are truly the Voice of the People.[21]

He then made an implied reference to his (anonymously published) *Commercial Restraints* which of course had placed him in the advantageous position of being known as an authority on free trade and an eager supporter of it. In discreet terms he implied that he would undertake the support of the short money bill. It is a measure of his ability that he saw the need for candor when he added that he had not participated in the attempt to have the embargo repealed because he had considered it necessary for the public safety. What he really thought of his constituents' address is indicated in a letter he received from Welbore Ellis in January, when Free Trade had been granted:

"I congratulate you on resuming your proper position, that of leading and not being led by the City of Cork." [22] His co-representative, Richard Longfield, had sent a diplomatic answer implying that he had no intention of accepting instructions.

It is not known whether the remaining members of the Dublin Castle administration who sat for counties or important cities—John Beresford and Speaker Pery, who represented Waterford County and Limerick City, respectively—were faced with the embarrassment of addresses from their constituents. The newspapers examined give no clue, so it is probable that no addresses were presented and no meetings held. Their political prestige and influence would probably have been sufficient to prevent such occurrences. The fact that Hely Hutchinson was obliged to receive instructions does not mean that he lacked a large political following. Cork was the Bristol of Ireland and no amount of political influence could have induced its merchants to remain silent.

The popular discontent which had been stimulated over the previous months by Volunteer parades, non-importation agreements, and now the demand for a short money bill, boiled over into riots in Dublin on November 15.[23] A mob of three or four thousand assembled about midday in College Green before the Parliament building and kept shouting such slogans as "A Free Trade," "A Short Money Bill," and "The Rights of Ireland." Each member of the Commons was accosted on trying to enter the building, and if he was believed likely to vote against the short money bill, he was forced to declare his support for the measure. Known supporters were cheered. Scott, the Attorney-General whose audacious defense of the Administration had been so noted of late, was subjected to special attention. A part of the mob tried to find him at the Four Courts, but he had been warned and was able to find refuge in Dublin Castle. Others attacked his home in Harcourt St. and smashed its windows.

The mob came from the Liberties, a working class part of Dublin, and were instigated, according to Beresford, by an inflammatory pamphlet. When a popular member of parliament asked one of the crowd for an explanation of the riots, he received the reply, "If you do not want us, why did you send for us?" That these accusations of incitement to riot were not without foundation is borne out by a letter to the press on behalf of the Journeymen in connection with the Combinations Act of 1780, which appears, because of the circumstances under which it was written, to lay responsibility at the door of manufacturing employers:

I am happy to find that the journeymen are preparing . . . to discover to the world who were the persons that bribed them to the burning Lord Townshend's effigy, who instigated the unfortunate muslin riot . . . and also who it was that equipped them with arms for the late attack on his Majesty's Attorney-General.[24]

A group of soldiers had been sent to College Green, but the Lord Mayor and the magistrates had decided against using force since the rioters did little injury even to unpopular members of parliament. The Dublin newspapers, except for the pro-Government *Faulkner's Dublin Journal* which virtually ignored the commotion, reported on the riots with a measure of approval and praised the humanity of the magistrates in dealing with the occurrence. The Lawyers corps did make a limited effort to control the riots.[25] This is what one would expect from members of the legal profession since the Four Courts' buildings and the Attorney-General's house were being attacked. Otherwise, there is no mention of the Volunteers taking the field as they were usually so ready to do when the lower orders got out of hand. One is left with the impression that the outbreaks were fomented by employers and countenanced, if not encouraged, by the Patriots.

In the Commons on the following day, Pery and Hely Hutchinson denounced the riots. The Attorney-General delivered an angry castigation not so much of the rioters as of Grattan because of the provocative effect of Grattan's attack on him in the debate of November 10. Though

Grattan took the reprimand lying down, Yelverton delivered an opinion on the riots that was more laudatory than disapproving. Scott lost his temper and accused Yelverton of being the "seneschal of sedition," and received in retort the title of "uniform drudge of Administration." The House was reduced to an unroar, but order was eventually restored and the two belligerents apologized to each other. Both Houses of Parliament passed resolutions calling on the viceroy to issue a proclamation offering rewards for the capture of anyone involved in the attempt to intimidate members during the riot.[26] Buckinghamshire described Scott's speech as spoken "with great ability and animation . . . and what he delivered was received by the House with the utmost attention and approbation." [27] The riots seem to have had a big effect on the British Cabinet in inducing them to grant Free Trade, but they clearly only consolidated opposition in the Irish Parliament to the radical turn which events had taken since October 12. Grattan's silence under Scott's reprimand suggests that he felt that events had outrun prudence, and that a tactical withdrawal was the better policy.

Dublin Castle became more despondent about the chances of preventing the passing of a short money bill as November wore on. Beresford now saw no hope at all of staving it off, and Thomas Waite, the Viceroy's Under-Secretary, was not optimistic.[28] Buckinghamshire had no illusions left; he realized that Scott, Foster, and Beresford were the only important props which his government still possessed. In a last appeal for a decision on Free Trade before the advent of the short money proposition, he showed his exasperation with the indolence of London:

Three most important dispatches remain unnoticed, and a letter this morning received, mentions that Lord North and

Mr. Robinson were both in the country upon the 13th. If within two days no instructions are sent me, it will become necessary to form some decision with the best advice I can obtain.[29]

But no word came from London, and Dublin Castle had to make its own plans for meeting the crisis. However, North did send word giving Dublin Castle a degree of freedom in arranging its parliamentary tactics.[30] Two meetings of the confidential servants of the Crown were held. As a result, it was decided not to oppose the popular feeling and to seek only a six months supply for ordinary expenses, but a two-year one for the interest on the national debt, or, as it was called, the Loan Fund. This plan was adopted partly because it was considered impossible to prevent a short money bill being passed, but also in order to save the supporters of the Government from popular anger and resentment.[31] In accordance with the plan, Heron rose in the Commons on November 23 and announced that the Government would ask a six months supply for ordinary expenses and a two-year one for interest on the Loan Fund. Then the onslaught commenced —Daly, Bushe, Ogle, Brownlow, Yelverton, and Grattan entered the lists, and it soon became obvious that even the capitulation of the Government on the ordinary revenue issue was not enough. Heron's request for new duties to meet the payments on the Loan Fund merely added fuel to the flames. Hussey Burgh maintained that the Commons had already stated in its address to the king that nothing but a free trade could save Ireland from ruin. Therefore, he said, let no new taxes be granted until Free Trade had been gained.[32]

On the resumption of the debate on the following day, November 24, Grattan took the initiative by proposing that "At this time, it would be inexpedient to grant new taxes." Daly, Yelverton, and Henry Flood, the Vice-Treasurer, supported the motion while Conolly made an ineffective plea for moderation.[33] Scott was the champion of the Government's cause, but he could effect nothing against the landslide vote of 170 to 47 in favor of Grattan's proposal. It would have been wiser if Heron had not insisted on a vote, since a graceful retreat would have been less humiliating. The only comfort to be gained from the rout was the fact that Thomas Conolly had exerted himself on the Government's side.[34] On November 25, in an attempt to refute Grattan's radical outburst of November 10, he appealed to the more sober sentiments of the House:

Three millions without doors making 300 do what they please within, is contrary to the principles of the House of Commons, to the principles of Representation. Who have the power of voting for Members to serve in Parliament? It is those who have property. You represent property, not numbers.[35]

Grattan renewed the attack by engaging Conolly in a tussle, and by stating that, though there were many men of great property in the Commons, they were of little consequence and ruled the House by "a contemptible aristocracy."

Then came Hussey Burgh's famous declamation. He entreated the House to be firm; the bonds of slavery imposed on Ireland by a foreign parliament must be broken and she must be brought out from her Egyptian bondage. He gave full vent to his flair for dramatic metaphor and ended on the note that caught the popular imagination:

Talk not to me of peace; Ireland is not in a state of peace; it is smothered war. England has sown her laws like dragon's teeth, and they have sprung up in armed men.[36]

According to the *Grattan Memoirs,* the Commons "rose in a mass and cheered him repeatedly." [37]

The limitation of the Loan Fund supply to six months was carried by a vote of 138 to 100. Though it was some small consolation to have the Government's minority raised from 47 to 100, the vote completed the rout of the Administration. Buckinghamshire stood naked before his enemies; all the resources of government had gone down before the united onslaught of the Patriots, backed up and, perhaps, pushed by the Volunteers, by the non-importation agreements and by the meetings of constituents. The revolution had won.

II

The Dublin riots seem to have galvanized Lord North into action. He informed the King that "the mob are the masters of [the Irish] Parliament" and that matters there appeared to have got out of the control of the Patriots.[38] Robinson informed Jenkinson on November 20: "Tomorrow I am trying to work on Ireland. Lord North is now in a hurry about it." [39] On the opening of the British Parliament on November 25, the newly appointed Secretary for the Southern Department, Lord Hillsborough, stated in the House of Lords that he had accepted the seals of office on being satisfied that Ireland would be granted an "equal trade." [40] Dublin Castle had not known the good news on November 25, and it is obvious from Buckinghamshire's letter to Weymouth of November 26 that he was not yet aware that the great decision had been made.

In the British Commons on November 25, Lord North said that Ireland would be placed on an equal footing with England: to grant a completely free trade would be unfair, since it would put Ireland in a more advantageous position than that of England.[41]

The choice of the term "equal trade" instead of "free trade" was no mere quibble. A complete removal of restrictions by Britain without the enactment by the Irish Parliament of equalizing duties would give Ireland the benefits without the disadvantages of the imperial system: the whole structure of British duties and drawbacks would be upset. Thomas Allan, a commissioner of the English customs, expressed the confusion in a letter to Beresford: "You say a free trade, without defining what you want; we say, you shall have a free trade, without specifying what we mean to give; between the two, public confusion ensues." [42]

Lord Townshend was equally puzzled:

Pray write write me word . . . how far you think, confidentially (if it is not asking too much), the establishing an equal trade is practicable, and in what manner, whether by our or your Parliament. [43]

The difficulty involved in loose terminology, and in the attempt to forecast the Irish Parliament's reaction to concessions, had been described by North in a letter to Buckinghamshire two weeks previously, on November 14:

Those two words [free trade], unexplained and unaccompanied as they are, seem calculated to throw the two nations into a flame. To ask a free trade, without any limitations, conditions, or regulations, is to ask that Great Britain shall consent to put Ireland on a better footing with respect to trade than herself. . . . But no person can as yet say with certainty whether Ireland will submit willingly to any limitations or regulation of their trade whatever.

North added that Britain was well disposed, but

instead of the necessary information as to the most probable manner of giving it [we] receive only a vague and unexplained demand, which, in its full extent, will revolt the whole kingdom of Great Britain.[44]

The Prime Minister's statement shows that the problem was a thorny one, but does not excuse his dallying with it over most of the summer and his delay in giving notice that substantial concessions would be made. As already pointed out, the leading Whigs had committed themselves to a policy of major concessions so that the Cabinet had little to fear from the British Parliament by announcing some radical slashing of the commercial restrictions. North's sincere desire to placate Ireland cannot be doubted, but the difficulties of arriving at the decision to announce an equal trade should have been investigated by him at a much earlier date.

The British Government's decision was the signal for a rash of denunciations by the Opposition of the Cabinet's inept handling of the Irish grievances.[45] The English Whigs went out of their way to flatter the Volunteers by praising their virtues and attributing to their power the major reason for the grant of Free Trade; 42,000 armed men in Ireland were demanding it, and English government would be foolish to trifle with them. Shelburne praised the police work of the Volunteers in making property more secure, and, as a result, his own rents had been paid more punctually than for years past. Camden accused the Government of neglecting Ireland's grievances, and of distributing arms which the Volunteers were now using to obtain a redress of those grievances. Rockingham considered that the armed associations (in the British Parliament the Volunteers were always referred to as "armed associations" or "armed men," but never Volunteers) looked to their strength as the means of compelling the British Government to grant relief. Charles James Fox was of the opinion that the American war, which produced the war with France and Spain, had enabled Ireland to establish a powerful and illegal army which he took care to praise.

Burke made comparisons between Ireland and America. A mob had arisen in Dublin and non-importation agreements had been entered into. Why not, as in the case of ill-fated Boston, shut up the port of Dublin, burn Cork and reduce Waterford to ashes? Why not alter the usual mode of striking juries as was done with the Massachusetts Bay Charter Bill? Why not declare the whole Kingdom of Ireland in rebellion? The answer was plain and direct; ministers dare not. Their insolence and arrogance had given way to fear and humiliation.

North, in his usual cool and good-natured manner, pointed to the justice of Irish claims. The commercial restraints were of long standing and should not be laid at the door of the present government. From it Ireland had received more benefits than from any other administration over the previous forty years. Ireland needed England more than England needed Ireland, and he considered that the Irish were opposed to violent measures. Henry Dundas, the Lord Advocate for Scotland, made the interesting anti-mercantilist statement that "the age was liberal, and a liberality, and unrestrained or at least an unclogged system of commerce, was of its very essence." He said that he had been strongly prejudiced against granting commercial relief to Ireland, but had been converted by Burke during the previous session to the opposite view.

Shelburne described the addresses of the Irish Parliament as the voice of the whole country—Church of England men and Roman Catholics, Dissenters and sectaries, Whigs and Tories, placemen, pensioners, country gentlemen, and English residents. A free trade meant "an un-restrained trade to every part of the world independent of the control, regulation, or interference of the British legislature." The people of Ireland had made that clear. He had received information that a trade had opened between northern Ireland and the American colonies, and that Dr. Franklin, the American minister at Paris, had been given full power to treat with Ireland on commerce and matters of mutual interest and support. As if he had not said enough to provoke the Irish into fresh demands, Shelburne now added that Ireland labored under one grave defect, namely, the Crown's control of its hereditary revenue which amounted to fully two-thirds of the total taxation. This could be disposed of at the king's pleasure; it provided both governments with the means of corruption, impoverished the Irish people and furnished ways by which they could be oppressed in the future.

In short, the English Whigs were continuing their denunciation of Lord North's ministry, and, in doing so, were quite willing to provoke further unrest in Ireland. Their flattery of the Volunteers, which the Tories were obliged to condone and even to imitate, could only have a disastrous effect on the Irish Government's attempt to regain proper control of the country.

The debates were of course primarily concerned with trade, but some references were made to the legislative independence of the Parliament of Ireland. Lyttelton considered that the Irish were now demanding not only a free trade, but a free constitution. Hillsborough retorted by saying that the English connection was necessary to Irish freedom and independence, and he was quite sure that the Irish did not think otherwise. In his usual passionate manner Fox defended himself against the charge that his inflammatory speeches had helped to give strength to the discontent in Ireland; the Volunteers had been called illegal, but whether that charge was true or not, he approved of them. When the last particle of good faith in men would be exhausted, the Irish would seek in themselves the means of redress; they would recur to first principles, to the spirit as well as the letter of the constitution. Such a power was inherent in men as a sacred trust, as a defense against the actual or possible abuse of power, political treachery, and the intrigues of government. When all other means failed, he would ever hold resistance as perfectly just. Considering the provocative effect that such a speech was likely to have in Ireland, one can only smile at his bland denial that he was contributing to Irish discontent. It is significant that Burke said nothing likely to further provoke indignation in Ireland. He always avoided matters of a constitutional nature as he well knew his countrymen's propensity for politics as opposed to economics. It was one of the themes of his letters over the years that Irish and English interests were compatible and could best be served by friendship between the two countries.

It was only on December 5 that the Cabinet made the *formal* decision to grant Free Trade to Ireland.[46] On December 9 Lord North proposed three resolutions in the Commons. They amounted to giving Ireland the right to export glass, wool, and woollen goods, and to trade freely with the British plantations. He felt that this would give satisfaction to Ireland. Nowhere, he continued, either in Britain or Ireland, had it been suggested that a free trade meant a free, untaxed, and unlimited trade. He then traced (according to the newspaper report of the debate) the history of the commercial restraints of which, he said, the wool restrictions were the result of a compact whereby Ireland was promised a linen industry as compensation for having her woollen manufacture restricted. This compact had not been kept since Britain now had her own linen industry. Thus, Ireland was entitled to participation in the woollen trade. Permission to trade with the empire would be a boon to Ireland and a gift to which she had no rightful claim, because the British colonies and settlements were Britain's own and had been gained by her effort and sacrifice. It would be unfair to give Ireland such rights without equalizing restrictions so that she should not be put on a better footing than Britain. Such restrictions should be left to the consideration and decision of the Irish Parliament. On December 13 Fox said he would not take up any position, for or against the concessions, since he had said all he wished to say in previous debates. He approved of them, of course, but the subject was no longer a commercial question but a political one, and could not be called a parliamentary one.[47]. He obviously meant that the matter was now closed and any further debate would be redundant. Unfortunately, the Whig silence was interpreted in Ireland as hostility, but this aspect of the matter will be considered later.

The resolutions were passed on December 14.[48] There was virtually no attempt to oppose them.[49] The first implementation of Free Trade—a bill to allow the free export of wool, woollen goods, and glass—was rushed through Parliament and received the royal assent on December 23. [50] Hillsborough wrote to Pery with glee:

It is a very agreeable circumstance in the passing this Bill that there was not the least opposition in either House of Parliament, and that his Majesty . . . was pleased to say he would go to the House in person, upon an occasion of so much importance to his faithful kingdom of Ireland.[51]

Having conceded Free Trade, the British Government waited anxiously for the Irish reaction. Obviously, the Cabinet would look foolish if Free Trade didn't satisfy

Ireland. On December 4 North pleaded with Buckinghamshire:

For God's sake . . . prepare the gentlemen of Ireland to
receive the concessions of England with reciprocal marks of
kindness and affection . . . to oppose that wicked spirit
which is growing daily in the country, and which aims . . .
to dissolve all political ties between the two kingdoms.[52]

On December 9 when he introduced the three resolutions
to the Commons, he again made the same appeal to the
Lord-Lieutenant "for upon the temper with which these
propositions are received, depends the salvation of the
Empire." Unless the Irish exhibited satisfaction, he added,
the British Government would encounter much opposition in Great Britain.[53]

Four days later he stated that if the concessions

should miss of their desired effect, I am undone, the Ministry
are undone, and the two kingdoms are undone, for, in that
case, a quarrel will probably ensue which may prove the
destruction of both.[54]

The Prime Minister made similar appeals to Scott and
Pery.[55] George III considered that if the resolutions "have
the effect they ought on the Irish [they] may do good; but,
if not, will only raise their demands."[56] Welbore Ellis
informed Hely Hutchinson that if the concession did not
procure satisfaction in Ireland, it would simply mean that
the demand for Free Trade had been merely a pretense.[57]

After months of comparative complacency about Irish
affairs, North seems to have gone to the opposite extreme.
His fear that some men in Ireland might induce the country to separate from England found expressions among
politicians in both countries, but the King, Hillsborough,
and Germain took a more moderate line.

The first reaction in Irish parliamentary circles to the announcement of Free Trade was mixed but, on the whole, favorable. Beresford wrote that Hillsborough's speech had been interpreted as contemplating a union between the two kingdoms, and Lord North's as seeking a *quid-pro-quo* for the concessions.[58] But Buckinghamshire thought differently and wrote that the news "has given very general satisfaction here." A week later, he considered that "all moderate men" were content.[59] However, until the Irish understood what an "equal trade" really meant, that is, until North's three resolutions of December 9 were known in Ireland, opinion there could not take definite form. When this news was received on December 12, the Irish Privy Council were asked for their opinions. Most agreed that the concessions would satisfy Irish demands, but Pery, Hely Hutchinson, and the unpredictable Vice-Treasurer, Henry Flood, hesitated to commit themselves to such an opinion, though they seem to have been reasonably satisfied themselves with what was granted.[60] On December 17, Pery informed Lord North that he found "the temper and disposition of the leading men in this Kingdom such as you could wish." [61]

In the Irish Parliament resolutions of gratitude were passed in both Houses. Both the Lord-Lieutenant and his Secretary were delighted with the debates in both assemblies, the former describing several of the speeches as "capital performances." The Patriots—Grattan, Bushe, Yelverton, and Hussey Burgh—expressed themselves as well satisfied, the utterances of Daly and Ogle coming in for special praise by the Viceroy. Buckinghamshire was widely commended for his representations to Britain on the distressed state of Ireland, and North received many bouquets.[62] Grattan praised the efforts Ireland had made, and Bushe paid a tribute to the Volunteers who had "enabled" Lord North to carry out his wish to help Ireland. Henry Flood and Scott also praised the Volunteers enthusiastically, the latter describing them as the salvation of Ireland.[63] In London, Robinson was jubilant because of the good effect the concessions had on leading Patriots.[64]

The Dublin newspapers were not so ready to rejoice. The *Dublin Evening Post* considered that the proposed concessions would be so hedged about with qualifications that as a remedy they would be worse than the disease. The *Freeman's Journal* thought that "an equal privilege of commerce with England" would be useless, and was an example of governmental treachery, since Ireland, because of the long restrictions on its manufactures, could not compete with England on an equal basis. Even after members of parliament had declared themselves satisfied, the press was slow to be anything but skeptical and hostile. It was only in the last week of December that it applauded the concessions. The *Hibernian Journal* then made up for lost time by bestowing the title of viper on anyone not content, and the *Freeman's Journal* hailed the news of British victories in America and the West Indies as a sign that St. Patrick's malediction had been removed.[65]

The newspapers' hostility, which had continued until well into the second half of December, was part of a vigorous opposition in radical circles outside parliament. On December 19 a public meeting addressed by Napper Tandy, and two Volunteer corps, the Lawyers and the Merchants, passed resolutions to the effect that any rejoicing would be premature because the proposed concessions were either insufficient or not properly known. Illuminations ordered by the authorities for the city had to be postponed or abandoned for fear of mob riots. On December 20 a printed notice was distributed: "No illuminations, no rejoicings, until the English Parliament shall do away all its acts that in any manner affect this country, and our constitution made free."

However, radical sentiment was eventually conciliated by the act when it received the royal assent on December 23. After news of the event had reached Dublin, the Lord-Lieutenant was able to write:

The passing a bill so favourable to Ireland's objects, and the various important and most favourable intelligence, seems to have created universal good humour. Even the Patriotic newspapers have adopted a favourable cast.[66]

The reaction in Dublin shows that the more radical elements were not acting in harmony with the parliamentary Patriots. Furthermore, it is clear from one of Heron's letters that the Patriots neither condoned nor approved of this continued discontent.[67]

And now there took place the same praise of the Tories that had followed the passing of the Catholic Relief Act in 1778, but this time there also occurred a denunciation of their opponents. It started in the Irish Lords on December 17 when Bellamont delivered an oration on the iniquity of the Whigs. Who were the friends of Ireland in Britain, were they the parliamentary Whigs or were they the Ministers? The former, he contended, had represented the Irish as rebellious and in correspondence with the Americans. They also had maintained that the Irish had made a treaty with the "Arch-Rebel Franklin." They were supposedly urging Britain to grant favors by proving that the Irish deserved none. The radical Mountmorres replied to this harangue of Bellamont by praising Rockingham and Hillsborough as the authors of Free Trade, the enactment of which North had tried to delay.[68] Four days later, Bellamont renewed the attack by charging that the English Whigs were using Irish problems merely to unhorse the present government in London. He added, however, that he based his opinion on the press reports of a British Commons' debate. Irnham, a radically anti-government peer, supported this castigation of the English Opposition. Leinster parried by saying that the English Whigs were merely waiting to see whether the concessions would be considered satisfactory in Ireland before speaking on them. He then made disparaging remarks about Hillsborough.[69] On December 9 Leinster had spoken quite bitterly of the new Secretary for the Southern Department and had accused Lord Buckinghamshire's administration of not consulting the proper people in Ireland.[70]

In the Irish Commons Scott denounced the English Whigs for having deserted Ireland on Free Trade. Their purpose, he said, was polititcal and selfish and they were using Irish grievances to embarrass North's ministry. Scott threatened them with the vengeance of Heaven if they should persist in their treachery. Toler and Ogle agreed.[71] Grattan appears to have been silent, which is surprising since Leinster had come out so strongly on the Whig side, but he may have been waiting until he knew what their attitude was.

The sudden bitterness with the unfortunate parliamentary opposition in England infected the press: the *Dublin Evening Post* of December 23, 1779, condemned

the *almost unaccountable* conduct of Opposition upon that day [December 15, the day on which Lord North introduced into the British Commons the bill to give freedom to export wool and glass]—our Countryman Burke endeavoured to raise every obstacle to prevent their being carried through the House—but finding every means ineffectual, stole away *mute*, and was followed by the whole *squad*.

On that day Burke had been involved in angry altercations with North over English and not Irish issues.

The decision of the English Whigs not to speak on the trade issue once North had introduced his resolutions was a mistake as it undoubtedly led to serious misunderstanding in Ireland. Naturally, the Irish expected that their friends in England would be the first to celebrate, and the latter's silence was disconcerting. As in 1778, there was the fact that the concessions came from a Tory ministry and this produced a sudden change in favor of North. In the ensuing year gratitude to Buckinghamshire for his earnest representation to London of Irish distress was a constant theme in public meetings, parliamentary debates, and newspaper columns. Needless to say, he was delighted at seeing the English Whigs attacked in Ireland since their parliamentary conduct had been so provocative. In a letter to Germain on December 21 he said: "The triumph of Lord North and the disgrace of his English opponents were equally complete." [72]

Again, as in 1778, Burke was indignant with this change of front and on January 1, 1780, wrote a semi-public letter to Thomas Burgh, a member of the Irish Commons.[73] As much in sorrow as in anger, the letter laments the Irish "liberality of invective on the Whigs of this kingdom [England] as I find has been the fashion . . . both in and out of Parliament." He explains his own silence when the resolutions were introduced by North:

Why, what had I to say? If I had thought them too much, I should have been accused of an endeavour to inflame England. If I should represent them as too little, I should have been charged with a design of fomenting the discontent of Ireland into actual rebellion.

He added that the efforts of the English Whigs to fight for liberty and against the tyranny of government in England would be weakened if Ireland were to combine with the Tories: if liberty were lost in England, it would also be lost in Ireland. Burke implied that even Grattan seemed to have misunderstood the attitude of the Whigs.[74]

Burke's concern for the good name of the English Whigs was shared by Thomas Townshend and Charles James Fox. Townshend assured Charlemont that the silence on the passing of the Free Trade legislation was intended as a help rather than a hindrance; the Whigs had done all in their power to hasten the measure.[75] Fox wrote in the same vein to Leinster, asking him to show the letter to Charlemont, Grattan, Daly, and others. He added that

Ireland ought not to forget that Lord Rockingham was the first person who stirred the affairs of Ireland here, and at a time when we were not forced to it in the manner we are now; that having stirred it, it was impossible not to leave the business in the hands of ministry, who had means of treating with Ireland which we had not.[76]

III

Buckinghamshire had felt particularly hurt because the shattering defeat of the Administration on the first days of the parliamentary session had been "supported and in a great measure produced by persons whom from the earliest days of my appointment it has been my study to please and oblige." He took comfort, however, from the fact that though "the clamors of the lower orders continue . . . the alarm of men of judgment and property, increases." [77] To the charge that his neglect of the friends of the Townshend and Harcourt Administrations had been the cause of the present catastrophe (even his close friend, Germain, stated now that he had never thought the "alliance" with Hussey Burgh was wise),[78] Buckinghamshire made a vigorous defense. One should be in Ireland, he said, to understand the course of events, particularly over the past twelve months. The appointment of Hussey Burgh as Prime Serjeant, continued the Lord-Lieutenant, had been made on the advice of Tisdale, the attorney-general at that time, and had then been considered a wise move.

Tho' it has generally been thought in England that . . . [my] favours . . . have been withheld from the old friends of Government, it is the contrary conduct which has contributed to produce the present difficulty. . . . [appointments calculated to please Scott, Perry and Beresford have] in my opinion determined the cast of all the late proceedings. A free trade would certainly have been pressed for, but in a very different mode, and with a very different temper.[79]

As a major cause of his difficulties, including the growth in strength of the Volunteers, Buckinghamshire singled out the debates on Irish affairs in the British legislature. He felt that

the frequent unsuccessful agitation of commercial topics in the British Parliament at the same time [that] that Parliament acknowledged the distress of this kingdom [Ireland] have stimulated the resentment of the nation at large. . . .[80]

The Viceroy now set about winning back the members of the Commons to the support of the Administration. He considered that many were ready (since the address on Free Trade had been passed) to return to the governmental fold, though he added the comment that "it will be difficult to resist popular motions, which, I understand, are already in contemplation." [81] Among others, the Duke of Leinster, John Fitzgibbon, and James Browne were contacted, but only the last of these three seems to have accepted the advances, since he became Prime Serjeant some time later in succession to Hussey Burgh.[82] The latter tendered his resignation on December 2, but it was not formally accepted until the following year, 1780, since Buckinghamshire was undecided as to whom he should nominate as the new incumbent.[83]

The effect of the Free Trade agitation and Grattan's radical speeches could not so easily be overcome by bargaining, and this was to become very clear over the succeeding six months. In mid-November Buckinghamshire expressed his inability to build up a governmental block in order to defeat the short money measure.[84] He realized that he was living in an entirely new Ireland, and in February, 1780, informed Hillsborough of the extreme difficulty of his position:

The late distressed state of this kingdom, which has furnished an apology to those by office and inclination attached to government to adopt a different line of conduct has diffused a spirit unknown before; at this time the attention of the whole nation is fixed upon Parliamentary proceedings, and not only the electors but even the mob are instructed that their opinions are to determine the suffrages of members, whose sentiments cannot be so openly canvassed as formerly when the contest was merely between different factions. Beyond a certain line you cannot press for the intended conduct of Independent Gentlemen; and even positive assurances may not be able to resist popular clamor and intestine connection. A promise therefore from those in certain predicaments must be deemed rather equivocal.[85]

A few days later he wrote: "Every informed person with whom I converse assures me that there is well founded reason to depend upon a decided majority yet none of them advise me to engage positively for it."

And then he added the meaningful comment:

"No retrospective knowledge of Ireland can enable any man to form a judgment of the present situation."[86] With this letter he had enclosed a list of the members of the Irish House of Commons, and had divided the names into those supporting government, those hostile, and those doubtful.[87] The respective numbers were 153, 68, and 63, while the remainder are listed as "absent." The Administration had an overall majority—153, and an opposition of only 68. Yet the Lord-Lieutenant admitted that the precise information sought by London could not be obtained:

A set of those who are marked adverse will I think be with us, and so large a proportion of the doubtful as may compensate for the desertion of some expected friends. It pains me to repeat that I cannot make myself responsible for the conduct of a popular assembly, or answer for the effects of Faction, timidity and the train of insidious arts universally exerted to distress the British Empire.[88]

It was a sign of the weakness of the Administration and the political flux in parliament that Hely Hutchinson (the Provost and Secretary of State), Henry Flood (one of the Vice Treasurers), and Luke Gardiner should have been listed among the doubtful. On the other hand, it signified the withdrawal from radicalism of some Patriots since Denis Daly and William Brownlow were also placed in that category.

Buckinghamshire's trials were bad enough but were made much worse by the lack of understanding in London of the Irish situation and the blame which was consequently laid at his door. Nor was it merely the ministers in England who misjudged the situation. As already pointed out, two of the leading officials in Dublin—John Beresford and Attorney-General Scott—heaped abuse on both the Viceroy and the Secretary as being the prime causes of the calamities. Beresford had visited London in July, 1779 and from then at least until the summer of 1780 kept up a stream of correspondence with John Robinson, Lord North's secretary, and sent him Irish newspapers regularly as evidence of the course of events in Ireland. Scott also wrote frequently to Robinson in a like vein. In October, 1779, Beresford blamed the Lord-Lieutenant for having imagined he could run the administration in a different way than his predecessors:

His private connections led him to other men. . . . They persuaded him that the majority obtained by Lords Townshend and Harcourt . . . had cost the nation an immense sum, that it was to be governed by . . . cheaper means . . . that every dependence was to be had upon men of virtue and integrity; and that . . . Parliament . . . to be governed by the appearance of public economy . . . and every man left to himself.[89]

A month later Beresford warned Robinson that "the whole system of Government is over, if these people [Buckinghamshire and Heron] are left here in their *present situation*." [90] Scott expressed an identical opinion of the Administration and made the same plea for new appointments:

The causes that have co-operated to render Government so weak for the last two years, are . . . the omitting America in His Excellency's speech on his arrival . . . and a foolish rhapsody of Mr. Conolly's . . . insulting every former administration, and announcing that this Administration was to be a system of retrenchment.[91]

Buckinghamshire and Heron, Scott continued, had believed this advice, but retrenchment involved disappointing the unrewarded, and the latter "sought their strength in the volunteers, the mob, free trade, and a short Money Bill."

A more moderate and charitable criticism of the Viceroy's policy came in the form of friendly advice from Germain. He said that London opinion considered that

Your letters are vague, inexplicit, and leave Administration to rest upon general assurances without . . . a satisfactory account of the measures you are pursuing, or of the persons upon whom you depend for carrying on the King's Government, that your favor and partiality incline you to listen to Mr. Conolly and more new acquired friends who lately deserted you, and that those who formerly supported Government were slighted . . . that whatever is resolved is immediately communicated to Mr. Conolly.[92]

For all their ability and practical intelligence, Beresford and Scott lacked the vision to see that the Irish situation was a revolutionary one and could not be controlled by a mere change of tactics. They managed to convince Robinson, Jenkinson, and the King that Buckinghamshire should be recalled.[93] Hillsborough appears to have concurred somewhat reluctantly with this decision [94] and his correspondence with Buckinghamshire at this time exhibits a carping attitude. About the middle of December the Cabinet had almost decided that the recall of the Viceroy was necessary, but before taking any irrevocable step, they sent Lord Macartney, a former secretary to an Irish viceroy, to Dublin to investigate the political situation.[95] His report was certainly unfavorable to the poor Lord-Lieutenant since he informed North that "a majority in Parliament might be got but Government here does not know how to get it," [96] and, after his return to London, wrote a harsh letter to Buckinghamshire on the need to repair the errors in his policy.[97] North, however, seems to have never consented to the recall of the Lord-Lieutenant. He was reluctant to agree on the choice of a successor, and felt that the Irish situation was so perilous that a change of viceroys would achieve no useful purpose.[98] And he did not fall into the error of thinking that the solution lay in mere parliamentary arrangements.

The weakness of the Irish Administration in 1779–1780, and the great increase in extra-parliamentary force, can be seen in one very interesting piece of legislation during this session. It was the repeal of the Test Act, or, to be more precise, the repeal of the clause directed against the Presbyterians in the Act "to prevent the further growth of Popery" of 1704. As explained in the account of the Catholic Relief Act of 1778, the English Privy Council had excised the repeal of the sacramental test from this relief measure. On the first day of the new session, October 12, 1779, Sir Edward Newenham, the sponsor of the effort in 1778, obtained permission from the Irish Commons to introduce the heads of a bill for the repeal. He stated that his attempt in the previous session had met with the approval of all the members, but that some had objected to its mode of introduction. The manner in which he was now introducing it would, he felt, ensure its success. He was supported by Yelverton, Sir Richard Johnston, and very warmly by Thomas Conolly, all three of whom were closely connected with the north of Ireland.[99] Newenham considered that since the Government had granted relief to the Catholics, it would be ridiculous to deny relief to those [the Protestant Dissenters] who had placed the crown on the head of the present royal family, and he warned the Administration not to insult the Presbyterians again, as times had changed since 1778.[100] There was no opposition, and in due course the heads were transmitted to London. Nearly thirty members of the Commons (most of them representatives of northern constituencies), including Newenham (described by the *Hibernian Journal* as "the father of the bill"), Grattan, Conolly, Yelverton, and Bushe, accompanied the heads as they were carried from the Parliament house to Dublin Castle.[101] The only opposition in Ireland to the measure came from the Protestant bishops, but this seems to have had little effect on the Irish Privy Council.[102] Buckinghamshire repeatedly advised London to allow the bill's enactment due to the importance of conciliating the Presbyterians.[103] Pery added his plea for the bill's success in a letter to North, saying that the repeal would "certainly produce much good humour amongst people who are perhaps too much disposed to complain without reason, and deprive men of ill intentions of an instrument with which they may do much mischief."[104]

The Prime Minister asked the Viceroy to oppose or at least delay the transmission of the measure to London for as long as possible. A repeal in Ireland would encourage the same demand by Dissenters in England and

We cannot gratify them without running the risk of displeasing our best, most zealous and steady friend, the Church of England. . . . This I write to your Excellency upon the supposition that we cannot refuse to English what we grant to Irish Dissenters, which I fear, will certainly be the case.[105]

The Archbishop of Dublin, Dr. Fowler, on behalf of a meeting of the hierarchy, wrote to Germain the recommendation that in the event of the repeal being enacted, all candidates for office be compelled to make the declaration:

I, A. B., do solemnly profess and declare that I do not believe that the public worship of the Church of Ireland as by law established is sinful or idolatrous, and that I do not hold myself bound in conscience to use any endeavours to introduce any other form of public worship which in some respects I may conceive to be more expedient.

The prelates felt, continued the archbishop, that, should the test be repealed, "our religion would not remain many years the Established one in Ireland, and if they [the Presbyterians] adhere to their ancient tenets will not even be tolerated." [106]

On March 1, 1780, the English Privy Council passed the heads, much to the delight of the Lord-Lieutenant who considered that the measure would give satisfaction to both the Presbyterians and the Irish House of Commons, the latter being "extremely anxious for its return." [107] The Commons passed the bill speedily, but in the Lords a protest was registered by four prelates—the archbishops of Cashel and Tuam, and the bishops of Kildare and Limerick:

Because this Bill makes a most material alteration in the Constitution of this Kingdom, the consequences whereof are much to be apprehended, tho' possibly they may not all be foreseen in their full extent.[108]

The Archbishop of Cashel went even further with his own declaration:

That the same attachment to the Constitution of this country, in all its parts, which induced me, in the course of debate, to offer at large my reasons for opposing the progress of this bill, has determined me to leave my dissent against the passing of it on record to posterity.[109]

The same prelate had opposed the bill in the debate in the Lords of April 27 and said that he regretted doing so since it had passed the Commons unanimously. He was, he said, a friend to toleration when it did not interfere with the principles of the constitution in Church and State, but the removal of the sacramental test left the first offices of the state open to Turk, Jew, Infidel, and Papist. Every country, he continued, had some established religion, and it was the custom for a state, however tolerant, to confine its positions of honor and trust to those of the established religion. Should the Irish Parliament, added the archbishop, set itself against the wisdom of the ages and enlightened nations? The Bishop of Waterford, William Newcombe, defended the bill on the ground that its rejection would antagonize the numerous and respectable Protestant Dissenters and sow jealousies among his Majesty's subjects; and over so unimportant a matter as the way in which a Protestant should receive communion. Furthermore, he continued, because of the test, the sacrament had to be tendered to any scoundrel wishing to qualify for political office, and thus it did not serve as a barrier against the unscrupulous. Besides, its removal would not affect the position of Catholics since they were debarred by the oath and declaration which would still be required.[110]

The Dublin newspapers paid little attention to the repeal, but their comparative silence did not indicate a lack of interest, but rather exemplified the confidence in Ireland that the repeal would be enacted. Since it was unlikely that the borough corporations would admit Presbyterians (nearly all Ireland's Protestant Dissenters were Presbyterians), and as both boroughs and counties were largely controlled by the Anglican landlords, it is unlikely that the removal of the Test made any real difference in parliamentary representation. Likewise, an administration virtually limited to Anglicans would be slow to admit

Presbyterians to office. It is difficult to say how successful
the measure was in allaying discontent, but it may well
have helped towards weakening the radicalism which had
been building up through 1779, and which was to show in
the summer of 1780 a notable decline.

NOTES FOR CHAPTER VII

1 Beresford to Heron, October 7, 1779, Heron Papers; to Robinson, October 11, 1779, *Beresford Corr.*, I 52–53.

2 The debate of this day, October 12, 1779, is reported in the
newspapers. The above description is based on the *Hibernian Journal* of October 13 and the *Dublin Evening Post* of October 14, as
well as the letters of Buckinghamshire and Beresford of October
13 to which reference has been made in the preceding chapter, as
well as in the *Irish Commons Journal*, X, 9–12.

3 Beresford to Robinson, October 13, 1779, *Beresford Corr.*, I,
53–60.

4 Buckinghamshire to Weymouth, October 13, 1779, *Grattan
Memoirs*, I, 391–94.

5 *Irish Lords Journal*, V, 130–31; Heron to Robinson, October
13, 1779, *Beresford Corr.*, I, 60–61.

6 *Irish Common Journal*, X, 13.

7 *Irish Lords Journal*, V, 130–33; *Irish Commons Journal*, X 13;
Heron to Robinson, October 13, 1779, *Beresford Corr.*, I, 60–61.

8 FDJ, October 21, 1779.

9 *Irish Commons Journal*, X, 13; *Irish Lords Journal*, V, 131–32;
DEP, October 14, 1779.

10 DEP, October 14, 1779.

11 Buckinghamshire to Weymouth, October 14, 1779, *Grattan
Memoirs*, I, 395–96.

12 George III to North, October 23, 1779, *The Correspondence
of George III 1760–83*, ed. Sir John Fortescue (London, 1928), IV,
469; North to Buckinghamshire, October 23, 1779, Heron Papers;
Weymouth to Buckinghamshire, October 24, 1779, SP 63/471, ff.
210–211 (if kept in strict chronological order, this letter should
appear in SP 63/467).

13 HJ, November 3, 1779.

14 *Ibid.*

15 Beresford to Robinson, November 5, 1779, *Beresford Corr.*, I,
73–75; Buckinghamshire to Hillsborough, November 8, 1779, SP
63/467, ff. 101–102.

16 HJ, November 5, 1779; DEP, November 4, 1779.

17 Irish House of Commons, November 10, 1779 (HJ, November 12, 1779).

18 The report of the meeting and the representatives' replies were published in the *Faulkner's Dublin Journal* of November 13, 1779.

19 DEP, November 25, 1779.

20 DEP, November 22, 1779.

21 DEP, November 22, 1779.

22 HMC, Donoughmore Papers, p. 295.

23 The account of the riot is taken from four newspapers (DEP, FJ, and FDJ of November 16, 1779 and HJ of November 17, 1779) and three letters (Buckinghamshire to Weymouth, November 15, 1779, SP 63/467, ff.106–107; Beresford to Robinson, November 16, 1779, *Beresford Corr.*, I, 75–81; Monck Mason to Pery, November 16, 1779, HMC, Emly Papers, I, 205). Beresford estimated the mob at three or four thousand while the newspapers' estimate is slightly higher. His would probably be the more realistic calculation.

24 FJ, April 1, 1779.

25 IPD, November 17, 1779.

26 DEP, November 18, 1779.

27 Buckinghamshire to Weymouth, November 17, 1779, SP 63/467, f. 117.

28 Beresford to Robinson, November 5, 18, 1779, *Beresford Corr.*, I, 73–75, 77–81; Waite to Germain, November 11, 1779, HMC, Stopford-Sackville Papers, I, 260.

29 Buckinghamshire to Germain, November 18, 1779, HMC, Lothian Papers, pp. 358–59.

30 North to Buckinghamshire, November 15, 1779, Heron Papers.

31 Scott to Robinson, November 21, 1779, *Beresford Corr.*, I, 81–84; Beresford to Robinson, November 22, 1779, *Beresford Corr.*, I, 85–91; Buckinghamshire to Weymouth, November 25, 1779, *Grattan Memoirs*, II, 5–10.

32 HJ, November 24, 1779.

33 IPD, November 24, 1779.

34 Commons debate, DEP, November 24, 25, 1779; Buckinghamshire to Weymouth, November 25, 1779, *Grattan Memoirs*, II, 5–10; Beresford to Robinson, November 26, 1779, *Beresford Corr.*, I, 91–94.

35 IPD, November 25, 1779.

36 This quotation is taken from the *Grattan Memoirs*, I, 403. The newspapers give a slightly different rendering.

37 *Grattan Memoirs*, I, 403.

38 November 19 or 20, 1779, *George III*, ed. J. Fortescue, IV, 491.

39 Add. Mss., 38212, ff. 227–32.

40 DEP, December 2, 1779.

41 DEP, December 2, 1779.

42 November 27, 1779, *Beresford Corr.*, I, 97–98.

43 Townshend to Beresford, November 27, 1779, *Beresford Corr.*, I, 96–97.

44 HMC, Emly Papers, I, 205–206.

45 These debates were: British Lords of November 25 and December 1, 1779; British Commons of November 25 and 26, and December 1 and 6. The description is taken, unless otherwise indicated, from the *Parliamentary History*, Vol. XX.

46 Minute of Cabinet meeting, December 5, 1779, *George III*, ed. J. Fortescue, IV, 509.

47 HJ, December 17, 1779; *Par. Hist.*, XX, 1284–85; FDJ, December 21, 1779.

48 See Appendix B for a transcription of the resolutions.

49 Hertford wrote to Hely Hutchinson on December 29: "Here we have done all we can to relieve Ireland and we have overcome prejudices of such long standing and such deep root that I am surprised at our success. Sir R. Walpole would have been stoned for naming what we have carried without a dissentient voice in either house, I do not say, a dissentient heart. . . ." (HMC, Donoughmore Papers, p. 295.

50 20 Geo., III, c. 6.

51 HMC, Emly Papers, I, 208.

52 North to Buckinghamshire, December 4, 1779, eron Papers.

53 *Ibid.*, December 9, 1779.

54 *Ibid.*, December 13, 1779.

55 *Beresford Corr.*, I, 109; HMC, Emly Papers, I, 207.

56 George III to Robinson, December 9, 1779, Add. Mss., 37835, f. 57.

57 December 16, 1779, HMC, Donoughmore Papers, pp. 293–94.

58 Beresford to Robinson, December 3, 1779, *Beresford Corr.*, I, 102–105.

59 Buckinghamshire to Hillsborough, December 2, 1779, SP 63/467, ff. 198–99; to Germain, December 9, 1779, HMC, Stopford-Sackville Papers, I, 263.

60 Buckinghamshire to North, December 14, 1779, SP 63/467, ff. 247–248.

61 HMC, Emly Papers, I, 207.

62 HJ, December 22, FJ, December 24, 1779: Beresford to Robinson, December 20, 1779, *Beresford Corr.*, I, 120; Heron to Anthony Chamier, December 20, 1779, SP 63/467, f. 267; Buckinghamshire to Germain, December 21, 1779, HMC, Stopford-Sackville Papers, I,

264–65; Buckinghamshire to Hillsborough, December 22, 1779, SP 63/467, ff. 299–300.

63 FJ, December 24, 1779.

64 Robinson to Jenkinson, December 20, 1779, Add. Mss., 38212, ff. 299–300.

65 DEP, December 4, 16; FJ, December 4, 18, 23, 28; HJ, December 15, 27, 1779.

66 HJ, December 20, 1779; FJ, December 21, 1779; Buckinghamshire to Germain, December 21, 1779, HMC, Stopford-Sackville Papers, I, 264–65; Buckinghamshire to Hillsborough, December 28, 1779, SP 63/467, ff. 297–98.

67 Heron to Anthony Chamier, December 20, 1779, SP 63/467, f. 267.

68 HJ, December 20, 1779.

69 FJ, December 24, 1779; HJ, December 22, 1779.

70 Irish Lords, December 9, 1779 (HJ, December 13, 1779).

71 FJ, December 24, 1779; FDJ, December 21, 1779.

72 HMC, Stopford-Sackville Papers, I, 264–65.

73 *The Writings and Speeches of Edmund Burke,* VI, 209–234.

74 *Ibid.* A footnote to the letter in this edition indicates that Burke was referring to Grattan.

75 HMC, Charlemont Papers, I, 367–69.

76 HMC, Charlemont Papers, I, 369–70.

77 Buckinghamshire to Germain, October —, 1779, Heron Papers; Buckinghamshire to Weymouth, October 14, 1779, *Grattan Memoirs,* I, 395–96.

78 Germain to Buckinghamshire, October 21, 1779, Heron Papers.

79 Buckinghamshire to Germain, October 28, 1779, HMC, Stopford-Sackville Papers, I, 259–60.

80 November 4 or 8, 1779, Heron Papers.

81 Buckinghamshire to Weymouth, October 18, 1779, SP 63/467, ff. 44–46.

82 *Ibid.;* Buckinghamshire to Germain, October 28, 1779, HMC, Stopford-Sackville Papers, I, 259–60; Scott to Robinson, October 15, 20, 1779, *Beresford Corr.,* I, 64–67; Beresford to Robinson, October 24, 1779, *Beresford Corr.,* I, 67–73.

83 Hussey Burgh to Buckinghamshire, December 2, 1779, Heron Papers; Buckinghamshire to Hillsborough, December 2, 1779, SP 63/467, ff. 198–99.

84 Buckinghamshire to Germain, November 18, 1779, HMC, Lothian Papers, pp. 358–59.

85 February 6, 1780, SP 63/468, ff. 180–81.

86 Buckinghamshire to Hillsborough, February 9, 1780, SP 63/468, ff. 205–208.

87 SP 63/468, ff. 210–20.

88 Buckinghamshire to Hillsborough, February 9, 1780, SP 63/468, ff. 205–208.

89 Beresford to Robinson, October 13, 1779, *Beresford Corr.*, I, 53–60.

90 November 5, 1780, *Beresford Corr.*, I, 73–75.

91 Scott to Robinson, October 15, 20, 1779, *Beresford Corr.*, I, 61–67; November 21, 1779, *Beresford Corr.*, I, 81–84.

92 January 31, 1780, Heron Papers.

93 George III to Robinson, November 13, 1779, December 23, 1779, Add. Mss., 37835, ff. 15, 81; Jenkinson to Thurlow, November 17, 1779, Add. Mss., 38307, ff. 82–83.

94 Robinson to Jenkinson, January 31, 1780, February 2, 1780, Add. Mss. 38213, ff. 99–104, 110–113.

95 Robinson to Jenkinson, December 20 (two letters), 1779, Add. Mss., 38212, ff. 299–300, 301; North to Buckinghamshire, December 19, 1779, Heron Papers.

96 Macartney to North, January 9, 1780, HMC, Abergavenny Papers, pp. 27–28.

97 Macartney to Buckinghamshire, January 21, 1780, HMC, Lothian Papers, p. 361.

98 Robinson to Jenkinson, December 20, 1779, January 31, 1780, Add. Mss., 38212, ff. 299–300, 38213, ff. 99–104.

99 FJ, October 14, 1779; DEP, October 16, 1779.

100 Irish House of Commons, November 26, 1779 (FJ, November 29, 1779).

101 HJ, December 3, 1779.

102 Buckinghamshire to Hillsborough, December 21, 1779, SP 63/467, ff. 295–96.

103 Buckinghamshire to Hillsborough, December 21, 1779, January 8, 1780, SP 63/467, ff. 295–96, 63–468, f. 15; to Germain, January 10, 1780, HMC Lothian Papers, pp. 356–60.

104 December 17, 1779, HMC, Emly Papers, I, 207.

105 January 16, 1780, Heron Papers.

106 February 5, 1780, HMC, Stopford-Sackville Papers, I, 267–68.

107 Hillsborough to Buckinghamshire, March 4, 1780, SP 63/468, f. 320; Buckinghamshire to Hillsborough, March 9, 1780, SP 63/468, f. 373.

108 *Irish Lords Journal*, V, 171.

109 *Ibid.*

110 DEP, April 29, 1780.

VIII

The Assault on Imperial Control

I

Fresh from their victory on Free Trade, the Patriots now moved on to their next objective. Their aim—to free the Irish Parliament from British control and make it more responsive to Irish public opinion—involved a two-fold struggle. The first struggle was the repeal of Poyning's Law and the Declaratory Act of 1719 which together had the effect of making the Irish legislature a subordinate one, and Ireland subject to the acts of the British Parliament. The second struggle consisted in freeing to some extent the representation from the aristocratic borough-owners by whom, in large measure, the British government controlled the Irish House of Commons. The Patriots decided to concentrate in 1780 on the first part of their aim, that is, the removal of the constitutional supremacy of Britain over Ireland and the Irish Parliament. Their efforts involved the introduction of three measures: a resolution declaring that only the King, Lords and Commons of Ireland could legislate for Ireland; a bill for the partial repeal of Poyning's Law; and an Irish Mutiny bill, the passing of which would implicitly invalidate the British Mutiny Act which had always been accepted as binding for the armed forces in Ireland.

Before dealing with these constitutional matters, it is necessary to first consider the completion of the Free Trade concession. The right to export freely had been only one leg of Free Trade: the other was the right to import direct from the colonies, a measure which was passed by the British Parliament in February of 1780 and was known as the Plantations Act. This would have to be balanced by passing equalizing duties in Ireland so that Irish external commerce would be placed under the same burdens and restrictions as British. The enactment of these duties involved no difficulty except for a tariff on the import of refined sugar; and it was found that sugar could create, politically as well as chemically, what the eighteenth century called a "ferment."

The completion of the concession was launched in the British Commons by Lord North on January 24, 1780, when he introduced a bill

to allow the trade between Ireland and the British Colonies and Plantations in America and the West Indies, and the British Settlements on the coast of Africa, to be carried on in like manner as it is now carried on between Great Britain and the said Colonies and Settlements.[1]

The bill met with little difficulty in either house of parliament and received the royal assent on February 24. Sir Thomas Egerton made the interesting point that because the trade issue was now one of great national importance and no longer merely one of commerce, the manufacturing towns of Britain had desisted from petitioning and had trusted, instead, to the wisdom and justice of Parliament.[2] In response to a query, Lord North said it was clearly understood that the Irish Parliament would be required to lay the same duties on imported sugar as Britain did.[3] It was feared that the Irish Parliament might try to protect the sugar refining industry with a prohibitive import duty injurious to the English refiners.

Dublin Castle waited impatiently for news of the passing of the Plantations Act so that addresses of thanks to the king could be put through the Irish Parliament before the spring recess. Their passing would enable supporters of the Government to procure expressions of gratitude from meetings at the assizes, and thus spike the guns of the parliamentary opposition.[4] In the nick of time, the good news was received from London and delighted the Lord-Lieutenant: "The proceedings in consequence will, I flatter myself, evince the gratitude of both Houses of Parliament."[5] In the Commons Denis Daly introduced the address to the king in a speech that flowed over with feeling, and Ogle urged that every aid be given to England in her desperate war, so that her position of eminence among the kingdoms of the world might be restored. Brownlow and Conolly eagerly concurred, and the address was voted for unanimously.[6] The address, obviously with one eye on the agitation over Poyning's Law, assured the king that

on our part, our utmost endeavours shall never be wanting to maintain that intimate connection between both kingdoms which we are most firmly persuaded is inseparable from their happiness and prosperity.[7]

Leinster proposed the corresponding address in the Lords, thereby showing that he had divested himself of his radical tinge, and was now working in harmony with the Administration. After the usual plaudits, the Lords' address reached the core of current political problems by expressing a determination to

discourage and defeat every attempt which misguided men may make towards raising groundless jealousies in the mind of his Majesty's people, or diverting their attention from the commercial advantages, so extensively held out to them.[8]

Lord Carysfort objected strongly to what, in his view, amounted to a false admission that faction and sedition existed. The legislature had become for the first time the Voice of the People; and he would enter a protest if the address were insisted upon. Mountmorres supported Carysfort and referred to the constitutional restrictions under which the Irish Parliament lay. He held that the Parliament would be respected and revered as long as it attended to the rights of the people and took the lead in affairs, but if it rejected this role, men of desperate fortune outside the legislature would assume that leadership, and a new Cromwell might arise. In reply, Leinster said that there was too much idle dispute which turned the minds of the people away from industry and labor; formerly, the commercial restrictions had rendered labor unprofitable, but now the country should desist from faction and trade combinations, and instead make use of the new freedom. Constitutional questions were not involved here and there would be time enough to discuss them on an appropriate occasion.[9]

Leinster's motion was passed by a large majority, the minority consisting of seven—Moira and Irnham by proxy, and Carysfort, Mountmorres, Eyre, Arran, and Charlemont in person. These five peers then entered a resolution of dissent, stating that the denunciation of "misguided men" in the address would do harm by showing the people that their

legal and temperate proceedings are beheld by Government with a jealous eye; and may tend to create a suspicion, that such extensive commercial advantages have been held out to them with an intention to seduce them into a dereliction of the Constitutional Claims.

The radical peers ranged themselves further on the Patriot side by adding

. . . If the insinuation that groundless jealousies have been raised in the minds of the people is founded, as it was thrown out in the debate, upon the resolutions which have been entered into in different parts of the kingdom, we conceive that it is the undoubted right of the electors to instruct their Representatives.

They concluded by denying that there was any evidence of groundless jealousies in the popular mind.[10]

At the end of February the Lord-Lieutenant asked Pery to go to London since he considered Pery "without comparison the person who, of all others, best understands the situation of Ireland and whose sentiments would be attended to in England with the greatest deference. . . ." [11] An important part of Pery's work in England was, of course, to discuss the equalizing measures which would need London's approval before being introduced into the Irish Parliament.

The passing of all but one of the equalizing acts through the Irish legislature entailed no major difficulty, and they do not need any special consideration. The exception was the tariff which the Irish Government was expected to

place on the import of refined sugar, or, to be more precise, the altering of the existing tariff so as to meet the new
conditions brought about by the grant of Free Trade. The
Irish refiners sought a very high tariff, but the London
Government, under pressure from British refiners, wanted
the new duty kept as low as possible.[12]

Buckinghamshire feared that the British claim in regard
to the sugar duties would raise a great deal of excitement.
He wrote to North:

The accounts which reach me from every quarter, evidently
demonstrate that unless the duty of one pound eight shillings
(as stated by Sir Richard Heron) is allowed to be laid upon
British refined sugars, the indulgence of trade to the West
Indies will be esteemed by Ireland as nothing.[13]

He added that the matter was of considerable importance
to the Irish revenue.

As time wore on and no decision came from London,
Buckinghamshire began to get worried.[14] Even so friendly
a Patriot as Daly was showing a determined attitude on
this problem which boded ill if London should set the
tariff too low.[15] The Lord-Lieutenant continued to tug
at Hillsborough's sleeve,[16] and finally on May 17 the decision arrived on the very day on which the sugar question
was due to be raised in the Commons.[17]

In consequence of the English Government's decision,
the Attorney-General moved for an addition of 5/10¼d.
per cwt. (five shillings and ten pence farthing sterling per
hundred weight) to the present duty on the import of
refined sugar. Opposition immediately showed itself with
amendments that the additional duty be raised to much
higher levels, but these amendments were all defeated. Sir
Lucius O'Brien complained that only the sugar bakers'
side of the case had been heard, and that other interests

should be consulted. When all opposition to the original motion of 5/10¼d. was seen to be hopeless, it passed without a division (the taking of a vote). This motion was only passed in committee and was not yet formally a part of the heads of a revenue bill.[18]

In the debate Grattan, Hussey Burgh, Metge, Bushe, Brownlow, Ogle, Newenham, Yelverton, and Hely Hutchinson spoke against the Government. The Provost was not forgetting that he represented Cork. Bushe delivered an indignant attack on a Free Trade that did not allow the Irish to tax goods they themselves consumed.

From the middle of February until August, some twenty petitions from ten towns against a low additional duty were presented to the Irish Commons.[19] Only one of them, a petition of Merchants and Grocers, favored the low duty. It maintained that a high duty would hurt the consumer; the Dublin sugar-bakers were prospering and were unable to supply the needs of the city.[20]

On May 18 Yelverton delivered a stinging attack on the additional duty of 5/10¼ per cwt. and demanded that the motion concerning it be sent back into committee. He said that such a duty would produce a non-importation movement, and he even hinted at violence. Grattan supported him but in a milder strain. Others, including Sir Lucius O'Brien and Hugh Carleton, one of the law serjeants, added their voices, and the Government was forced to allow its motion to be recommitted.[21] The next day Yelverton again took up the cudgels, and showed by his detailed knowledge and by his constant attention to the subject that he was the parliamentary spokesman of the refiners. Beresford and Scott held to the Government's line, but Foster and Sir Hercules Langrishe, a Commissioner of the Revenue, compromised, and thus showed how delicate and embarrassing the Government's position really was. The Administration opposed the recommittal but was defeated by 130 to 55. The followers of Leinster, Shannon and Ely as well as two other Commissioners of the Revenue, Monk Mason and Townshend, supported the motion for recommittal.[22] Mason's and Townshend's support indicates the refining industry's importance as a source of revenue.

An amusing diversion occurred after Yelverton had presented a petition in favor of the sugar-bakers from the Corporation of Weavers. Scott expressed his astonishment that the weavers should have been brought into the matter: when the barbers petitioned the king to wear a wig they had at least their own interests in mind, but the Corporation of Weavers had no right to thrust themselves into Parliament on behalf of the sugar refiners: "Such unconstitutional irruptions of the populace should not be a guiding principle in politics."

As soon as the subject had been recommitted, David Latouche proposed an additional duty of 16/7½d. per cwt. which was defeated without a division; then Peter Metge's motion for one of 12s. (12 shillings) per cwt. was passed by a vote of 106 to 71.[23] The large numbers in all the divisions indicate the importance which the Commons attached to the matter. Since there was no popular pressure exerted—the newspapers were virtually silent and all the petitions came from employers rather than from any section that could be called a "mob" [24]—the defeat of the Government must, in large measure, be attributed to the wealth and influence of the sugar refiners. However, the refiners did have a case. Heron obviously sympathized and explained to Robinson that the grocers, in whose interest it was to have a low duty, considered 9/2d. per cwt. a suitable figure. Therefore, continued Heron, the Commons' opposition to 5/10¼d. per cwt. was understandable,

especially since it was generally considered that the plantation trade, now granted by Britain, "depends much on the
preservation of the Irish refinery." [25] In due course the
heads were transmitted to London, and the matter rested
for the time being.

II

The constitutional struggle was much more important
than the sugar tariff as a subject of public interest. As with
so many agitations, it was the debates in the British Parliament during November and December, 1779 which helped
to spark the campaign for the independence of the Irish
Parliament.[26] It was obviously in reference to these
speeches (some of which had been made by members of
the Government in rebuttal of Whig statements) that Pery
expressed regret when writing to Lord North on December 17, 1779:

I must, however, acknowledge to your Lordship that there is
nothing I dread so much as stirring any question relative to
constitutional powers. . . . It is unfortunate that the extent
of the sovereignty of Great Britain has ever been defined. It
should have remained a mystery, and never called forth but
upon the utmose necessity to save the empire, and then it
would have been submitted to without reluctance. Upon less
occasions I am certain it never will.[27]

In a letter to the King on December 4, Robinson had said
that his Irish friends were convinced of the "absolute
necessity of keeping from discussion those great constitutional questions relating to the superiority of Great
Britain." [28]

In Ireland the matter was by the end of the year

becoming one of practical politics. On December 6 the
Bandon Independent Company of Volunteers demanded

a bill declarative of the rights of this oppressed kingdom,
and asserting the legislative authority of this nation to be
vested solely in the King, Lords and Commons of Ireland.[29]

On December 26 the Cork Union Volunteers decided on
an address to the Lord-Lieutenant. In it they thanked him
for his representations to London of Irish distress which
were in great measure responsible for obtaining Free
Trade. This expression was innocuous, but then they trod
on delicate ground:

We entreat your Excellency to assure his Majesty that as we
have armed ourselves at our own expense in defense of his
Majesty and of our constitutional rights as *Irishmen*. . . .

The emphasis on constitutional rights was meaningful and
it is not surprising that Buckinghamshire refused to accept
the address. The sentiments implicit in it came into the
open when a meeting of the corps on January 10 declared:

We earnestly regret that a system of politics should now
prevail, which seems to discriminate between loyalty to government, and zeal for the *constitutional* rights of our
country. . . .

Buckinghamshire informed Hillsborough of the occurrence and said that several other addresses from Volunteers, though not objectionable in themselves, had been
similarly refused.[30]
    On December 11 there appeared in the *Dublin Evening
Post* a letter which, because of its determined tone and

the eloquence with which it called for action, could be regarded as a "kick-off" in the constitutional struggle:

You now have an opportunity of asserting your natural, unalienable rights, which if you let slip, may, nay probably, never will come again. The present hour is big with the fate of Ireland. The question is whether Ireland shall enjoy the very best constitution that ever was established, I mean the English constitution, or the very worst that any people pretending to freedom ever had, that constitution, if it can be called one, by which Ireland is at present governed? Do not imagine, my friends, that I mean either a Union with England, or a separation from her.

In the Irish Commons Thomas Conolly made the foolish and unnecessary statement that though he would support the repeal of Poyning's Law, he did not think such a measure should be brought forward while England was at war. This drew from Grattan the angry retort that war was the only time for obtaining concessions from England: it was while she was weak that she would grant Ireland her freedom. He wished to "hear the public speak . . . to hear the Voice of the Nation—he is a hot-headed man who would anticipate that Voice—he is a bold man who would resist it." [31]

It can be seen in his parliamentary speeches since October 12, 1779 how Grattan came to the fore in Irish politics. His speeches show a power and aggressiveness, and a deliberate appeal to extra-parliamentary opinion and to the country as a whole, which was not found to the same extent in those of the other Patriots.

A letter to the *Dublin Evening Post* of January 15 hailed the "glorious spirit now prevailing among our Volunteers, with their resolutions to preserve our legal rights, and . . .

to have certain enslaving statutes repealed." The following months saw in the press, either as news items or inserted addresses, declarations from thirteen corps. Some
of these declarations were addresses to Grattan and, often,
Yelverton, Ogle, and Hussey Burgh for their parliamentary activity on the Declaratory issue and Poyning's
issue. Probably dozens of other corps passed similar resolutions, but mention of them did not find its way into the
press. In the eighteenth century newspapers devoted little
space to news items, and there was no pressing reason why
corps should have had addresses inserted.

More important for any such agitation were the county
meetings. Most of these were held during the assizes, and
great importance was attached to them by the Government. Buckinghamshire had been most anxious that news
of the passing of the Plantations Act should be received so
that loyal addresses could be passed in the Irish Parliament. These would be "the most likely means of stopping
inflammatory instructions and addresses at the assizes and
may enable the Friends of Government to procure addresses of thanks to his Majesty." [32] The Patriots were also
very active, and the result of the campaigning by both
sides showed itself in declarations from the majority of the
counties.

Some eighteen counties held meetings where they declared their support of the repeal of Poyning's Law and
instructed their parliamentary representatives accordingly.[33] In addition, similar action was taken by the cities
and towns of Dublin, Cork, Drogheda, Lisburn, and
Newry. Opposing action (addresses of loyalty and gratitude
for the grant of Free Trade) came from six counties—
Cavan, Cork, Limerick, Longford, Tipperary, and Westmeath, and the city of Cork. It is significant that of the
loyal addresses only two came from meetings composed of

more than the Grand Jury. This meant that the loyal addresses were not receiving wide public support. Two counties, Cork and Longford, and Cork city held separate meetings, and from each meeting an address was sent, one loyal, and the other in support of the repeal of Poyning's law.

The number of replies published was somewhat less than in the previous November on the Short Money issue, and tended to be less obedient to the constituents' instructions. Foster apparently did not receive any address from Co. Louth this time, and Hely Hutchinson's reply to Cork city was the diplomatic statement that he would use his judgment. Robert Stewart replied with a long letter on the rights of the Irish Parliament which showed he was still a radical. In general, there was a small but noticeable change to greater independence on the part of representatives towards their constituents than in November. As in November, Co. Waterford and Limerick city were quiescent, a tribute to the respective influence of Beresford and Pery.

The British Government was of one mind about the attempt to make any change in the constitutional relationship between the two kingdoms: no alteration would be countenanced. For once, Dublin Castle was given a clear line to follow and given it in good time. Buckinghamshire was ordered to "oppose and resist any such attacks in every stage of their progress." [34] Pery wrote from England that he had been told by North that the Cabinet had resolved "not to admit of any innovation in the constitution of Ireland, and this is the public language of all persons connected with the [London] administration." [35]

The attack was planned to take place in two stages: the first would be the moving by Grattan of a resolution declaring that only the King, Lords, and Commons of Ireland were competent to make laws for Ireland; the second, a motion by Yelverton for regulating the transmission of bills to England. The latter would necessarily involve the partial repeal of Poyning's Law by freeing the Irish Parliament from the necessity of passing the heads of bills.

The big day for Grattan came on April 19 when at the conclusion of one of his great speeches he moved "that the King's most excellent Majesty, Lords and Commons of Ireland, are the only Powers competent to make laws to bind this Kingdom." [36]

He protested vigorously against the "usurpations of the Parliament of Great Britain" and declared that had he a son, he would, like Hamilcar, bring him to the altar to swear to the "sacred maintenance of the People's rights." Again and again he stressed this appeal to the people outside parliament. Constitutional freedom would be the completion of Free Trade:

It is not in the power of England to resist. Can she war against ten millions of French, eight millions of Spaniards, three millions of Americans, three millions of Irish . . . with her [England's] ten millions; with a national debt of 200 millions, a peace establishment of 14 millions, and a war establishment of 21 millions, can she pretend to dictate terms?

He said that everything short of total independence had been offered to the Americans, and he asked the Irish people, "will she yield that to their arms and refuse it to your loyalty?"

But the real target of the speech, the real object of the menaces and vituperation and the reason for the appeals directed to the "Voice of the People," was not the British Government or even the Dublin Administration, but the

Irish House of Commons. In other words, the target was those members (and they were a majority) likely to side with the Government and oppose Grattan's aim. He addressed the Commons as the "Guardians of the Public Liberty" whose duty it was to restore their country's freedom. Their former servility and corruption had led to a situation in which the people could see nothing but starving manufacturers and a "corrupt Senate." Eighteen counties, he continued, deserving of freedom, who are "Your legal Constituents, have petitioned for this redemption . . . your Constituents have instructed, and they will support you." He continued to lash the members with the words: "No man in this House dare defend the claims of the English." The speech came to its climax with:

. . . let nobody say the Parliament was bought by a broken Ministry and an empty Treasury. That having made a God of Self-Interest, you kneeled down to worship the Idol of Corruption. . . . assert and maintain the Liberties of your country.

This oration was reported in the press in the unusual form of separate phrases joined by hyphens, indicating that these potent expressions had been taken down verbatim and one can sense the bursting forth of phrases fine in form and pregnant with menace. It is much more than the ebullient eloquence of Hussey Burgh's high-flown metaphors about dragons' teeth and armed men. Grattan meant what he said; his figures of speech showed the discipline of cold deliberation. He was not trying to win the House of Commons, but rather to frighten it into the same submission that it had known on October 12. Grattan knew that the achievement of his aim—the independence of the Irish Parliament—necessitated the breaking of the governmental majority in the Commons. He was bringing the people into politics and, in a sense, into parliament for the purpose of bearing down on the patronage and "corruption" of the Administration.

The debate which followed showed that the Patriots lacked unity. Grattan was opposed by Denis Daly and Gervaise Bushe who in spite of his present attitude was planning at this time to introduce an Irish mutiny bill which the Government greatly feared. He considered Grattan's motion ungrateful to England because of her recent concessions, and likely to endanger the success of other measures. Also, it would lead to the recall of Buckinghamshire and the appointment of a viceroy who would resort to the former system of corruption. He knew that his opposition to Grattan's motion "will be the most censured action of my life," but was conscious that "it is the most meritorious." Daly emphasized a point raised by Scott, namely, that such a resolution implicitly cast doubt on the legality of many titles to land in Ireland which depended on English acts of parliament. He attacked even more vigorously than Bushe the designing men who sought to create hostility between England and Ireland. It was a novel thing, he added, for him to support the Administration, but he believed he was doing right.

Fitzgibbon denounced the instructing of members of parliament and maintained that only the "imbecility or incapability" of the Administration would have allowed these instructions to have been drawn up.

Opposition to the motion, whether by Government supporters or by others, rested primarily on its inexpediency —it could do no good and would only antagonize England, but it was freely admitted that England had no right to legislate for Ireland. Hussey Burgh, Newenham, Yelverton, and Ogle supported Grattan. Flood played his usual part of pricking the Administration and showing his independence; after some truculent references to England's having no right to legislate for Ireland, he came down on the Government's side. However, he asked the Attorney-General to state the grounds on which he had asserted that England had such a right. Scott denied that he had said so and maintained that he had said only that an English act of parliament had disposed of vast quantities of Irish land. The introduction of the question of title to land was a very telling one in an assembly in which many, if not the majority, owned land from which some owner in the past had been dispossessed. Scott seems to have got over the problem of explicitly denying England's legislative right with the qualification that he reprobated "as a man" all such English legislation which was not approved by the Irish Parliament. This qualification enabled him to have his cake and eat it since he could still say that English legislation was binding on Ireland if it was approved by the Irish Parliament.

As the leader of the Government's team, Scott proposed as an amendment that consideration of the motion be postponed to September 1—the accepted way of killing a proposal. Later, Foster, moved an amendment to Scott's proposal, and it was this later amendment designed to have Grattan's motion rejected on which the vote was taken, 136 to 97. This meant defeat for Grattan and brought the debate to an end.[37] On this occasion he had failed to overawe the Commons.

Grattan's motion was a clever one since no member of the Irish Parliament would want to deny or limit its legislative power. Thus, it could be defeated only by the argument that such a motion was inexpedient. The Dublin "mob" showed no sign of becoming excited over the debate, but the addresses passed by so many county meetings and Volunteer corps prove that the constitutional issue did provoke widespread interest at least among the more politically conscious sections of the community.

In reporting the debate the Lord-Lieutenant expressed concern over the fact that the members were almost unanimously hostile to any admission that the British Parliament had the right to legislate for Ireland.[38] Lieut-General Robert Cuninghame informed Germain that "there was not a single member that spoke who did not declare that Ireland was not bound by British Acts of Parliament in any cases whatsoever. . . ."[39] Nevertheless, the vote was a victory for the Government or, at least, a defeat for the Opposition. It was a sign that the Administration was beginning to regain its power and prestige which had been so rudely shaken by the Free Trade agitation. This much was appreciated by the *Hibernian Journal* which stated (admittedly with a certain exaggeration):

The Servants of the Crown begin to look up with some degree of confidence in Parliament, since the victory they obtained over the Constitution on Thursday morning [i.e. on Grattan's motion]. The supplicating tone of humiliation is no longer used; Sir Richard Wigblock [Heron] is often on his legs, and as he enters into no other argumene but to give a flat negative to every motion he does not like, he delivers himself without his natural confusion. Large majorities make everything flow in its old channel, and the business of corruption goes on as usual.[40]

The opposition of Daly and Bushe to Grattan on this issue shows how weak the Patriots were when it came to pursuing a consistent policy. As will be shown,[41] Daly had found the tendency to radicalism not to his liking and was now attempting to apply the brakes; yet he supported Yelverton's proposal on Poyning's Law a week later. What exactly was Bushe's motive, if he had any other than those he expressed in the debate, is difficult to say, but he may have shared Daly's hostility to the radical tide. He certainly was not under the influence of the Government, since he was at this time preparing his mutiny measure. This disinclination to follow what today would be called a "party line" shows how difficult it was for even a leader like Grattan to mount a strong offensive against the Government, however effective he was in seizing opportunities and exciting public opinion. Only the Administration could hold to a policy which, with the aid of patronage and pensions, was likely to win in the end provided no extraordinary circumstances intervened. That Grattan did achieve so much is a tribute to his ability.

The next hurdle that Buckinghamshire had to surmount was Yelverton's motion on the partial repeal of Poyning's Law which came a week after Grattan's Declaratory resolution. Since several members of the Commons who had pledged themselves to support the Government on the Declaratory motion had then voted with the Patriots, the Lord-Lieutenant saw the prospect of the coming struggle with anxiety: "How can the Lord-Lieutenant speak with confidence upon any point at a period when no fixed principle directs, no obligations attach and no assurances can bind." [42] He complained to Hillsborough that the Administration should have a majority on Yelverton's coming motion if members would be mindful of their assurances, or grateful for favors conferred on condition of giving support, but "the behavior indeed of some has lately led me to doubt whether I fully understand the force of the English language. . . ." [43]

On April 26 Yelverton asked the House of Commons for leave to introduce heads of a bill for regulating the transmission of bills to Great Britain. In his speech he went into the history of Poyning's Law which he considered placed a tyrannical power in the hands of the Crown. This power was an abuse of the constitution: it did not exist in the English constitution which had won the admiration of the world. The constitutional bodies of France and Spain had been abolished, but Britain had retained her parliament. She had the substance of freedom but Ireland had only the shadow. He had no objection to bills being transmitted to England, but the Irish Parliament must have the right to initiate bills. Thus, he was not aiming at a complete repeal of Poyning's Law.

Yelverton's speech had little of the striking metaphor or cadence of Grattan's orations, but it had a certain simple directness which was appealing. He described the members of the Commons as representatives of the people, but does not appear to have made that appeal to extra-parliamentary opinion with anything approaching the fire and forcefulness of Grattan. The motion was supported in the debate not only by Grattan but by Ogle, Brownlow, Daly, Henry Flood, and Newenham. Grattan again emphasized the support which had been received from eighteen counties and three millions of people, and again struck the popular note with his question: "What answer, in the name of God, Gentlemen, do you mean to return to your constituents?" The Government's side was led by Heron and Scott and pointed to the radical nature of the motion, its inexpediency, and the danger of alienating an English administration which had conferred such benefits on Ireland. Despite the country and town addresses and all the vigor of the Opposition, the motion was defeated by 130 to 105—a serious defeat for the Patriots, but the smallness of the majority meant that it could scarcely be regarded as a complete victory for the Government.[44] However, the pressures exerted by the Patriots were still sufficiently effective to force many members committed to

the support of the Administration to vote with the Opposition.[45]

But the strength of the Government was reviving and
this can be seen in the bitter comment of Newenham in
the debate that there was possibly a need to redress the
influence of the rotten boroughs by the addition of 100
members to the counties and cities. Poor Buckinghamshire had at last achieved some substantial success. Hillsborough, with his usual irritating condescension and lack
of grace, congratulated the Lord-Lieutenant, but added
the comment that his success "was not so clear and direct
as might have been expected." [46] Nevertheless, the tide had
begun to flow in favor of the Government.

The *Dublin Evening Post* carried the editorial:

The wonder of wonders! That, notwithstanding the sense of
the nation, the voice of our Volunteers, and the instructions
of the principal counties in Ireland to their representatives,
there should have been 130 senators, who voted lately [on
Yelverton's resolution] against their country's independence.[47]

III

Chastened by defeat, the Patriots were now to launch
their third attack. It consisted of an attempt to have the
Irish Parliament pass its own Mutiny Act, thus implicitly
denying the validity of the British Act in Ireland. Vigorous opposition by the British Government was a foregone
conclusion, and now that Dublin Castle had been able
to procure the defeat of Grattan's and Yelverton's measures, it might seem that there would be comparatively
little difficulty in killing the Mutiny motion. Unfortunately for Buckinghamshire's peace of mind, this measure
was attended by an important factor—the dangers to
which the country would be exposed once there was any

tampering with army discipline. To question the legality of military law was no light matter in any European country in the eighteenth century when government rested on a much narrower base than do most Western European administrations today. It had frightening possibilities in Ireland, a land rent by deep hostilities and traditional prejudices. It involved a risk which few Irish landlords could view with equanimity. The attempt to pass an Irish Mutiny Act was therefore a political stroke of almost Machiavellian cleverness. The British Government would be obliged to oppose it, but pro-government members of parliament might easily find themselves torn between their obligations to Dublin Castle and their fear of having to rely on the protection of an army no longer under martial law.

On April 18, Gervaise Bushe obtained leave from the Commons to introduce the heads of a Mutiny Bill. He argued that domination by a foreign legislature was universally condemned in the country, yet 12,000 men were subject to a British law. Hussey Burgh argued in support that it was a matter of Ireland's being bound by British legislation. Richard Hely Hutchinson, the Provost's son, and others stated that the internal peace of the country demanded this measure since magistrates might be unwilling to enforce the British act. Denis Daly and Fitzgibbon spoke in support but obviously with some reluctance. Scott led the supporters of the Administration and rested his case on the doubtful ground that the army was the king's and the motion was an attack on the power of the Crown. He then crossed to safe constitutional ground with the argument that it was a most dangerous measure and might lead to bloodshed between the two kingdoms. Conolly spoke against the motion; and it was temporarily frustrated by Foster's amendment that the matter be adjourned.

Lieut-General Cuninghame, the Deputy Commander-in-Chief of the army in Ireland, asked that the measure should be the same as the British act so as to avoid confusion when troops were moved from one country to the other. Such difficulties had been experienced in America in the different provinces. Bushe replied that he intended proposing the same bill as the British one.[48]

The subject was very delicate since magistrates had in at least two cases refused to recognize the legality of the British act; [49] and in the debate on Grattan's Declaratory resolution on April 19, several members who were magistrates declared they would "never execute for the future any part of the British Act of Mutiny." Buckinghamshire reported that the leading members of the Administration considered that "few magistrates or juries, grand or petit, would enforce the Mutiny Act, even if Grattan's declaration had not been made." [50] The Viceroy informed Hillsborough that many Government supporters were likely to vote for the motion if it were to come up again in the Commons. He added that many persons, including Lieut-General Cuninghame, considered an Irish act advisable as a provision against "doubts in the army, and the disinclination in magistrates' to enforce the British law. The Lord-Lieutenant was careful to add that he would oppose the motion all along the line if such were the policy of the London government, but he doubted if he would succeed.[51] The Irish Privy Council had advised that the enactment of the measure would be necessary in order to preserve military discipline. Consequently, Buckinghamshire pleaded for an early decision from London.[52] Lifford, the English Lord Chancellor of Ireland, stated as his official opinion that the British act applied to the army wherever it might be, and thus the whole question at issue was constitutionally irrelevant,[53] but he shared the general view that a special act for Ireland was, in practice, necessary.[54]

London's decision, transmitted to Buckinghamshire on May 7, was very definite: the measure must be opposed.[55] On May 8 before he knew of the Cabinet's decision, the Lord-Lieutenant held a meeting of the Privy Council, and those who attended included Leinster, Ely, and Shannon. The Council advised strongly against opposing Bushe's motion when it would come up again in about two weeks. Foster, according to the Lord-Lieutenant, advised that opposition would not only be futile but would "weaken the future ability of every man appearing in such a division, not only to support this, but every future administration, so long as his vote on that occasion should be remembered." [56] Buckinghamshire warned Hillsborough that if the discipline of the army were to break down, any members disliked because of their support of the Government would find themselves at the mercy of the people. The situation looked black, and the Viceroy added that he would not oppose the motion unless explicitly instructed to do so.[57] This last appeal had its effect as the instruction of May 7 to oppose firmly was qualified on May 14 by another letter which granted Buckinghamshire permission, should the Irish Commons pass the heads of the bill, not to veto them (in Council) if the Irish Privy Council wished them to be transmitted to London.[58]

On May 22 Bushe again moved for leave to introduce the heads of his Mutiny bill. Heron opposed him on the ground that his proposal denied, in principle, that British acts of parliament were valid in Ireland. Sure of their strength, the Patriots insisted on a division, and Bushe had his way by 140 votes to 18. Only three of the principal servants of the Crown voted in the minority—Scott, Toler, and Monck Mason. The discomfiture of the Administration was made worse by Bushe's contemptuous assertion that Heron's opposition was purely formal and not really intended to oppose "the necessities of the times, and the just demands of a united people." [59]

On May 25 the heads were introduced and committed, but the Government managed to have their further consideration postponed with the view of procuring some modification.[60] During the discussion Grattan launched a furious attack on Scott for having played, as an Irishman, a contemptuous part in opposing every constitutional question which had arisen in the current session of parliament. Scott retorted by accusing Grattan of having "unlocked the springs of opposition and disorder" (a more hurtful charge in the eighteenth century than it would be in the twentieth). He maintained he had consistently supported Lord Buckinghamshire's government, which had won praise all over Ireland. Grattan admitted that the praise of the Lord-Lieutenant was just but insisted that Scott was "the uniform enemy of every measure proposed for the good of the country." [61]

And now, after many months of seeing the Patriots hold the initiative, Dublin Castle played a clever game. The British Cabinet had relented somewhat in its instructions to resist the mutiny heads four-square. The letter from Hillsborough of May 14 had given Buckinghamshire permission not to veto them if they were allowed to pass by the Irish Privy Council, but this letter provided a second loophole which Dublin Castle seems to have been quick to seize upon. It was the instruction to oppose if the motion contained anything suggesting that British acts were not binding in Ireland. On May 28, the day before the big debate, Buckinghamshire sent Hillsborough the heads of a bill designed to render less obvious any implication that they were a challenge to the validity of British legislation. Apparently this draft contained no reference to the British Mutiny Act. He asked for permission to accept it.[62]

What was in the Viceroy's mind became clear on the following day, May 29, when Foster proposed as an amendment to Bushe's motion "That his Majesty's Army in this Country should be regulated by such Laws as the King had made or may make. . . ." [63] This clause would radically alter Bushe's heads which had been drafted along the lines of the British act. The latter started with the statement:

Whereas the raising or keeping a standing army within this kingdom in time of peace, unless it be with the consent of Parliament, is against Law: and whereas it is judged necessary by his Majesty, and this present Parliament, that a body of forces should be continued for the safety of this kingdom. . . .[64]

Foster's motion, however, placed the army in Ireland directly and solely under the king. The Patriots attacked the amendment violently. Grattan said that "if the King was to govern the Army of Ireland, he must govern it by the Law of Ireland," and that the amendment was "dangerous to the Freedom of this country." Hely Hutchinson, the Provost, supported Bushe's heads and opposed Foster's proposal. Heron opposed both. On a division the amendment passed by 117 votes to 80.[65]

Through Foster's amendment the aim of the Patriots— to pass an act implicitly denying the validity of British legislation in Ireland—was being frustrated. The Commons wanted a mutiny act and now they were going to get it, but in a form that conflicted as little as possible with the British constitutional claim. Naturally, the British Government would much prefer to see no mutiny measure whatever enacted, but it was a consolation to have one that would not please the Opposition in Ireland. By having Heron resist both motion and amendment, Buckinghamshire was sticking to the letter of his instructions. A broad hint as to how Dublin Castle was handling the mutiny crisis is conveyed in a letter from William Knox, who was visiting Ireland at this time:

Firmness and temperance, with a readiness at expedients, will do here yet, but you [the British Cabinet] must be sparing of your instructions, for it is much better people here should use their discretion without pledging administration, and then your judgement has free scope to operate afterwards.[66]

The Commons passed the mutiny heads without further difficulty on June 2. The Irish Privy Council did likewise but refused to accept Heron's proposal that it be made perpetual. On July 3 it was transmitted by the Viceroy to London.[67] The delay of a month between its passage by the Commons and its submission to the Irish Privy Council on July 3 (it was transmitted to London the same day) is curious, but was probably due to business pressures which were fairly acute at that time.[68]

Until late in July of this year, 1780, the mutiny measure does not seen to have created much of a stir outside parliament, except among the magistrates. It was reported in the *Dublin Evening Post* of May 27 that army recruiting had ceased in Dublin because magistrates were refusing to swear in recruits. This report was not without foundation as was proved by the Lord-Lieutenant's letter to Hillsborough of June 5.[69] The Volunteers gave no sign that they were unduly disturbed. The lack of any frequent mention of the mutiny issue in the newspapers before July suggests that it had caused more concern inside parliament than outside. The prospect of an army not subject to martial law was probably too frightening to an assembly of propertied men, whether Patriots or "Courtiers," to want to make of it a "popular" issue. A widespread agitation might have very unpleasant consequences if common soldiers were to get the idea that they need not obey their officers.

The support which the mutiny proposal obtained through all its stages, whether before or after it had been amended by Foster, was undoubtedly due to the fear of anarchy once the legality of the British Mutiny Act had been seriously questioned. Virtually every servant and adviser of the Crown considered the enactment of an Irish measure a necessity. The fear of many members and supporters of the Administration was described bluntly by General Irvine, Commander-in-Chief of the army in Ireland:

The fact is they . . . are afraid of their popularity and of the Volunteers, and it seems not unreasonable for men under these impressions to wish the Mutiny Bill to pass in a manner which will be agreeable here [Ireland], because if the army were to be disbanded, or not kept under discipline, the only sort of support they can have will be their popularity, and their only protection the Volunteers. . . .[70]

Irvine added that Buckinghamshire feared that if the Mutiny heads were materially altered in London they would very probably be rejected by the Irish Parliament. This statement is surprising since the willingness of a majority in the Commons to accept the heads as amended by Foster suggests that they would accept *any* measure designed to stabilize the military position; and the above quotation from Irvine's letter would bear out this contention.

NOTES FOR CHAPTER VIII

1 *British Commons Journal*, XXXVII, 532.

2 *Parl. Hist.*, XX, 1307–1315.

3 HJ, February 7, 1780.

4 Heron to Porten, February 26, 1780 SP 63/468, f. 316; Buckinghamshire to Hillsborough, February 28, 1780, SP 63/468, ff. 328–29.

5 Buckinghamshire to Hillsborough, March 1, 1780, SP 63/468, ff. 330–31.

6 Irish Commons debate of March 1 (HJ, Mar. 3, 1780).

7 *Irish Commons Journal*, X, 81.

8 *Irish Lords Journal*, V, 162.

9 HJ, March 6; FDJ and FJ, March 7, 1780.

10 *Irish Lords Journal*, V. 162.

11 Buckinghamshire to Pery, February 29, 1780, HMC, Emly Papers, II, 157.

12 This oversimplified and inadequate statement of the position is all that one can derive from the various debates, letters, and editorials on the subject. Only a most intensive investigation could possibly yield a really adequate understanding of the technicalities involved. However, the above explanation enables one to appreciate the political aspect of the matter.

13 April 2, 1780, SP 63/469, f. 15.

14 Buckinghamshire to Hillsborough, April 28, 1780, SP 63/469, f. 126.

15 Irish Commons debate of April 28, 1780, HJ, May 1, 1780.

16 Buckinghamshire to Hillsborough, May 2, 1780, SP 63/469, f. 153.

17 Heron to Robinson, May 18, 1780, SP 63/469, ff. 256–57. The letter is published in the *Grattan Memoirs*, II, 422–24 under the date, May 13, 1780, but internal evidence proves that this is an error.

18 *Ibid*: HJ, May 19, FDJ, May 18, 1780.

19 *Irish Commons Journal*, X, 72 *et seq*.

20 *Ibid*. pp. 86–87.

21 HJ, May 19, 1780.

22 HJ, May 22, 1780; Heron to Robinson, May 20, 1780, *Grattan Memoirs*, II, 428–30.

23 HJ, May 22, 1780.

24 All the petitions but two came from refiners and other merchants. The two exceptions were from the "Freemen and Freeholders of Dublin" and the "Inhabitants of Newry."

25 Heron to Robinson, May 20, 1780, *Grattan Memoirs*, II, 428–30.

26 These debates are described in Chapter VI.

27 HMC, Emly Papers, I, 207.

28 Add. Mss., 37835, ff. 85–87.

29 DEP, January 4, 1780.

30 *Hibernian Chronicle* (Cork), January 10, 1780; Buckinghamshire to Hillsborough, January 12, 1780, *Grattan Memoirs*, II, 410.

31 HJ, February 18, 1780.

32 Buckinghamshire to Hillsborough, February 28, 1780, SP 63/468, ff. 328–29.

33 Between February 19 and April 27 twelve of the county meetings were recorded in the *Dublin Evening Post*, usually in the form of official insertions. The remainder were recorded during the same period in one of the other of the following papers: *Faulkner's Dublin Journal, Freeman's Journal, Hibernian Journal* and *Hibernian Chronicle* (Cork).

34 Hillsborough to Buckinghamshire, March 28, 1780, *Grattan Memoirs*, II, 31.

35 Pery to Buckinghamshire, March 28, 1780, HMC, Emly Papers, II, 157.

36 This account of the debate is taken from the *Hibernian Journal* of April 21, 1780.

37 The various accounts of the debate, whether in newspapers or correspondence, are ambiguous and vague in regard to the amendments proposed, but it is perfectly clear that Foster's proposal was designed to kill Grattan's motion and succeeded in its purpose. Buckinghamshire's letter to Hillsborough of April 20, as published in the *Grattan Memoirs* (II, 51–52), erroneously gives the Opposition's vote as 79. The newspapers and Cuninghame's letter to Germain give the figure as 97 which is obviously the correct one.

38 Buckinghamshire to Hillsborough, April 21, 1780, *Grattan Memoirs*, II, 52–54.

39 April 20, 1780, HMC, Stopford-Sackville Papers, pp. 269–70.

40 HJ, April 26, 1780.

41 See p. 316.

42 Buckinghamshire to Germain, April 22, 1780, HMC, Lothian Papers, 363–64.

43 April 23, 1780, SP 63/469, ff. 116–17.

44 This description of the debate is taken from: DEP, April 28, 1780; HJ, April 28, 1780; Buckinghamshire to Hillsborough, April 27, 1780, *Grattan Memoirs*, II, 78–80. The date of the letter is erroneously published in the *Grattan Memoirs* as April 29 but the

original (SP 63/469, ff. 134–35) is dated April 27 and the accuracy of the date in the original is supported by internal evidence.

45 In his letter to Hillsborough of April 27, Buckinghamshire wrote: "The majority of last night would have been far more considerable, if many members under obligations to government had not very unexpectedly deserted, and several independent gentlemen acted contrary to assurances which might have been deemed binding."

46 Hillsborough to Buckinghamshire, May 7, 1780, SP 63/469, ff. 165–67.

47 DEP, May 6, 1780.

48 HJ, April 19, 1780; FJ, April 20, 1780.

49 Heron to Porten, April 8, 1780, Grattan Memoirs, II, 71–73.

50 Buckinghamshire to Hillsborough, April 22, 1780, Grattan Memoirs, II, 73–75.

51 Buckinghamshire to Hillsborough, April 19, 1780, Grattan Memoirs, II, 45–47.

52 Buckinghamshire to Hillsborough, April 22, 1780, Grattan Memoirs, II, 73–75.

53 SP 63/469, ff. 173–76. Lifford's opinion, dated April 29, 1780, was forwarded to Hillsborough by the Lord-Lieutenant on May 1 (SP 63/469, f. 171).

54 In the Irish House of Lords on April 25, Lifford said he would like to see a special act passed for Ireland (DEP, April 27, 1780; HJ, April 28, 1780).

55 Hillsborough to Buckinghamshire, May 7, 1780, SP 63/469, ff. 165–67.

56 Grattan Memoirs, II, 85–89.

57. Ibid.

58 SP 63/469, ff. 205–206. This permission suggests that a viceroy could veto the heads even after the Irish Privy Council had passed them. Buckinghamshire states in letter of May 18 to Hillsborough (SP 63/469, f. 247) that there is no precedent for such an action, at least since 1711, the books of the Privy Council for the period prior to that having been burned.

59 Buckinghamshire to Hillsborough, May 22, 1780, SP 63/469, f. 266; DEP, May 23, 1780, HJ, May 24, 1780.

60 Buckinghamshire to Hillsborough, May 26, 1780, Grattan Memoirs, II, 430–31.

61 DEP, May 27, 1780; HJ, May 29, 1780.

62 Buckinghamshire to Hillsborough, May 28, 1780, Grattan Memoirs, II, 93–95.

63 HJ, May 31, 1780.

64 This quotation happens to be taken from the British Mutiny Act of 1779 (19 Geo. III, c. XVI).

65 DEP, May 30, 1780; HJ, May 31, 1780.

66 Knox To Germain, May 26, 1780, HMC, Stopford-Sackville Papers, I, 270.

67 Buckinghamshire to Hillsborough, July 3, 1780, SP 63/470, ff. 48–49.

68 Heron to Porten, June 29, 1780, SP 63/470, f. 5.

69 SP 63/469, f. 314.

70 Irvine to Germain, July 11, 1780, HMC, Stopford-Sackville Papers, I, 270–71.

IX

The Collapse of Radicalism

The failure of the Patriots in the case of the Declaratory Act and Poyning's Law was an indication that the Government was beginning to recover its control of the legislature. The fact that both measures were opposed by the pro-government members only on ground of expediency, and not on any admission of the supremacy of the British Parliament, proved that the situation was still one of flux, and that the victory of the Administration was far from being decisive. It was not until August, when the Mutiny Bill and the sugar tariff came up for final discussion in the Commons, that the victory of the Administration was clearly established.

On August 11 the sugar measure was received from London. The additional duty of 12 shillings per cwt. had been lowered by the Cabinet to 9/3d.,[1] as opposed to its original figure of 5/10¼d., a compromise that showed awareness of the determined attitude of the Irish Commons. In accordance with custom the Commons could not accept an altered money bill, so it was formally defeated and a new heads, identical with the bill returned from England, was introduced and passed. The vote on it was 119 to 38, a satisfactory result for Dublin Castle.[2] In due course these heads were received back from London and went through the Irish Parliament without opposition (the Patriots had accepted defeat), and received the royal assent from the Lord-Lieutenant on September 2, the day on which the parliamentary session of 1779–1780 came to an end.

In the debate on August 15 Langrishe, one of the revenue commissioners, had described the sugar tariff as

a bill . . . of regulation . . . not an act of taxation, but an article of prohibition. . . . I know the whole importance of the Trade to the Colonies does depend upon the operation of this bill, and we must protect our trade.

Foster, one of the government's most reliable supporters in all matters but the sugar issue, had then summed up the position with the rhetorical question: "Does the duty of 9/2 guard the Refiners . . . or does it not? Policy requires it should, and justice requires we should not go beyond it." [3]

The sugar tariff was one of the more important issues of 1780. It was the only equalizing duty arising from the grant of Free Trade that caused major difficulty, and the solution was a compromise between London and the Irish House of Commons. Dublin Castle clearly had no objection to a substantial tariff because of the importance of the refining industry, but London had ordered otherwise. The matter shows how great the marginal effect of mercantile wealth could be. The sugar refiners were able to make of an unpopular case a parliamentary issue serious enough to defeat the Administration and to force the British Government to compromise.

Of more urgent political importance was the Mutiny bill, which was received by Dublin Castle from London on August 11. It had been altered to a perpetual one.[4] By passing the altered bill the Irish Parliament would give the king the right to maintain an army in Ireland forever. In theory at least, this bill would grant the king a right denied him by the British Parliament since the Glorious Revolution. The rumor of this change had already reached Ireland, and on August 8 Grattan showed his chagrin by denouncing the alteration as "a mortal stab to the Constitution." It would produce a rebellion and if it was accepted by the Parliament, he would secede and appeal to the people. He was supported in his fury by Forbes, Fitzgibbon, Yelverton, and Ogle, though Ogle said he would not go so far as secession. Grattan even threatened that such a measure would "endanger the safety of the King's Servants" in Ireland.[5] Rage at seeing the tables turned was probably responsible for this outburst. The House not only failed to support Grattan but did not seem to like his harangue.[6] The renewed strength of the Administration is seen in Heron's letter to Porten of August 14:

I hope a few days will finish our business here for altho' it may be necessary to send the altered money bill the business of the session will I conclude be understood to be over.[7]

In the Commons on August 16 the Patriots attacked the mutiny bill, but there was no attempt to repeat the fire-eating of the previous week. Bushe stated that the purpose of his bill had been to negate the validity of English law in Ireland, which would be more efficacious than merely passing a declaratory resolution. Grattan spoke bitterly of the power which the perpetual bill would place in the hands of the Government; it would enable the Administration to suppress the Volunteers if the war should end soon. The speeches were those of men who knew they were defeated: they proposed a motion designed to destroy the perpetual clause in the bill but its rejection (114 votes to 62) was a foregone conclusion.[8] The measure went speedily through all its stages and received the royal assent on August 19. The victory of the Administration was so complete that Scott and Foster, who had been ready for action, did not have to speak.[9] The tone of the debate, as well as the embittered resignation in the speeches of Grattan and Bushe, indicates that the Patriots took no part in fomenting the radical disturbances of the next few days. It was too obvious that they had accepted defeat.

It was only in July that the press began to take a real interest in the sugar and mutiny issues, and it was only in August that that interest turned into excitement. On August 1 the *Dublin Evening Post* in a long editorial on the two topics considered that the Commons could no longer be depended upon and called for a non-importation movement. A week later the *Hibernian Journal* reproached the members of parliament who were absent, since they were thus leaving both measures to the

Band of Castlemen, &c., who compose the present scandalous Majority; and . . . the late patriotic efforts, which reflected such glory on the present session of Parliament, if not strongly seconded at this period, will but confirm our bondage, and heighten the disgrace of our situation.

The *Dublin Evening Post,* in reference to the altered bill, said on August 8:

By this manoevre the Parliament of Ireland will have no more control over their own army, paid and supported by

the people, than they can have over the Irish brigades in
the service of France.

Dublin radicals had no intention of accepting the victory of the Administration in silence. On August 17 the
Merchants Corps of Volunteers passed two violent resolutions:

That we consider their [the Irish Parliament's] consent to
the mandate of the British Minister, by which the Bill for
the regulation of the Army, is made perpetual, and the
control thereof for ever vested in the hands of the Crown,
as a subversion of the Constitution, and a stab to the Liberty
of the Subject.

and,

That, considering the Army of this Kingdom . . . we cannot
but feel for their situation, who, by this Law, are 'in danger
of being made at a future day the unwilling Instruments of
Despotism, to violate the Liberties of Ireland.

They then called for the support of the "Volunteer Corps
of this Kingdom, and the rest of our fellow-subjects, in
every effort, which may tend to avert the dangers we are
threatened with." [10] Over the next two days the Independent Dublin and the Liberty Volunteers followed
suit.[11] The *Freeman's Journal* on August 19 went even
further with the editorial:

We are happy to find that a general meeting of the independent merchants and Volunteers of this city is fixed for Tuesday
evening next. . . . It is hoped that their spirit and example
may animate the Kingdom to rise in support of the violated
Rights of Ireland, and that the Nation may be restored by
their means to those inherent privileges which their treacher-

ous Representatives have basely sold to the infamous Ar-
ministration of Great Britain.

The opportunity was too good to miss, and the opponents
of radicalism grasped it with both hands. In the Commons
on August 21 Thomas Conolly, having observed that the
House was sparsely attended with none of the "members
styled Patriots" present, denounced the addresses of the
three corps as an evil that must be nipped in the bud. He
praised the Volunteers as a whole but moved that the
House, in order to prevent the spread of the seditious activities of these three corps, express its abhorrence and ask
for a state prosecution.[12] Accordingly, the House passed
two resolutions *nem. con.* The first condemned the three
addresses published in the *Hiberian Journal* and the editorial in the *Freeman's Journal,* which were described as
containing matters

that are false, scandalous, seditious and libellous, grossly as-
persing the Proceedings of Parliament, and most manifestly
tending to create discontents amongst his Majesty's subjects,
to withdraw them from their obedience to the Laws of the
Realm, and to subvert the Authority of the Legislature of
this Kingdom.

The second resolution, also voted *nem. con.,* called on the
Government to prosecute the "Printers and publishers and
authors and contrivers thereof." [13]

The same resolutions were passed *nem. con.* on
Leinster's proposal, in the Lords a few days later.[14]

The Patriots were placed in an embarrassing position.
They clearly took no part in this outburst of radicalism
since in the debate on the Mutiny Bill on August 16 their
attitude had been a chagrined acceptance of defeat. Had

they any plan in mind for extra-parliamentary activities they would have given some indication of being ready to continue the fight. In the Commons Sir Samuel Bradstreet was the only Patriot to say anything on behalf of the offending corps.[15] In the Lords the two radical peers, Carysfort and Mountmorres, admitted the justification of the first resolution but considered a prosecution unnecessary.[16]

The Merchants Corps of Volunteers were concerned not merely with the Mutiny Act, but also with the sugar tariff which they considered "an overthrow to the refinery of this kingdom," and a negation of the freedom to trade with the plantations. The Liberty Volunteers on August 19 also expressed indignation over the tariff and called for a non-importation movement. On August 24 the sugar refiners of Dublin protested against the low tariff and suggested by implication the adoption of non-importation agreements.[17] The idea was taken up by the radical County of Galway, which had been the first county to adopt a non-importation agreement in 1779. The High Sheriff and Grand Jury passed resolutions to refuse to consume any British refined sugars and to boycott any merchant who imported them.[18] Three days later, on September 5, the Freemen and Freeholders of Dublin City, convened by the high sheriffs, called on the whole country to enter into such agreements.[19] On September 24, the Galway Volunteers decided not to purchase any British goods until the sugar act had been repealed.[20]

Dublin Castle was not worried. Heron considered that the resolutions adopted by the Merchants Corps of Volunteers on August 17 had been "framed at the instigation of some sugar bakers" and he expressed the opinion that the attempts to rouse the country would fail.[21] In October the

Lord-Lieutenant reported that the non-importation movement had not materialized. He added that the refiners' efforts to prevent the importation of British sugars was unlikely to succeed because their purpose

is generally seen through, and it is contrary to the interests of the grocers and every consumer of sugar, it is believed that it cannot be brought to bear, and that the design will of itself fall to the ground from the impracticability of carrying it into universal execution.[22]

After the middle of September the newspapers made only occasional references to a non-importation movement, and by late October the whole idea had died a natural death.

So complete was the failure of radicals to muster a following that the Administration did not prosecute the offending Volunteers and the *Freeman's Journal* for sedition. It was considered that these efforts had produced no effect and would best be ignored.[23] Radicalism had had its day and the Government could now settle down to peace and quiet.

It remained for the Viceroy to have his promises of "pensions, peerages and places" implemented. In September he sent applications for preferment to London. These were the engagements he had entered into in order to build up a pro-government majority in the Commons after the Patriots had grasped the initiative in October, 1779. He introduced the subject in his letter to North with the statement:

Nothing could be more against my inclinations than the yielding to solicitations of gentlemen upon the line of peerage; but without engagements strongly to recommend several . . . it would have been impossible for me in any sort to have surmounted the various difficulties which have lately attended Government.[24]

Two months lated he added:

I had not contracted any absolute engagements of recommendation either to peerage or pension, till difficulties arose which necessarily occasioned so much and so forcibly communicated anxiety in His Majesty's Cabinet, that I must have been culpable in neglecting any possible means of securing a majority in the house of commons.[25]

In October, 1780, a new viceroy and secretary were appointed [26]—the Earl of Carlisle and William Eden (later Lord Auckland)—and they arrived in Ireland in the latter part of December. Having handed over the cares of office, Buckinghamshire spent Christmas with the Conolly family at Castletown before embarking for England.[27] For reasons of political discretion, he declined a Volunteer escort for his departure.[28]

His bestowal at the end of his viceroyalty of "pensions, peerages and places" led to his being castigated by Lecky who wrote:

In the last months of his administration Buckingham [shire] had been reduced to the necessity of opposing the overwhelming preponderance of national sentiment and nearly all honest men in Parliament, by the most flagrant and overwhelming bribery.[29]

The comment is scarcely fair. Buckinghamshire had wanted to rule without "corruption" and had resorted to time-honored practices only when his administration faced shipwreck. The Patriots and the radical press consistently showed some appreciation of his good intentions and the practical efforts he made to implement them. But Lecky's statement is unfair on quite a different count; that is, in its implication that the parliamentary supporters of the Government were dishonest. He overlooks the fact that a very large proportion was compelled to go along with the radical tide on Free Trade and the constitutional issues due to the enthusiasm of the middle classes. As soon as this enthusiasm began to diminish in 1780, the pro-government members were only too glad to revert to their former role as supporters of Dublin Castle. What Lecky describes as "flagrant and overwhelming bribery" merely encouraged them to draw away from a radicalism which they feared and disliked. To regard these recipients of governmental "favors" as necessarily dishonest is to view them from the standpoint of the bourgeois nineteenth century.

NOTES FOR CHAPTER IX

1 Heron to Porten, August 14, 1780, SP 63/470, f. 271.

2 HJ, August 16, 1780; Buckinghamshire to Hillsborough, August 16, 1780, SP 63/470, f. 258. The *Grattan Memoirs* (II, 436–37) erroneously gives the Opposition's vote as 88.

3 These two statements are taken from the IPD for August 15, 1780.

4 Heron to Porten, August 11, 1780, SP 63/470, f. 242.

5 HJ, August 9, 1780; FJ, August 10, 1780.

6 Heron to Porten, August 9, 1780, *Grattan Memoirs*, II, 125–26.

7 SP 63/470, ff. 269–70.

8 DEP, August 16, 1780.

9 Buckinghamshire to Hillsborough, August 17, 1780, *Grattan Memoirs*, II, 126–27; Buckinghamshire to Germain, August 17, 1780, HMC, Stopford-Sackville Papers, I, 272.

10 DEP, August 17, 1780.

11 HJ, August 21, 1780.

12 HJ, August 23, 1780.

13 *Irish Commons Journal*, X, 194–95.

14 *Irish Lords Journal*, V, 218.

15 DEP, August 29, 1780.

16 HJ, August 25, 1780.

17 DEP, August 29, 1780.

18 DEP, September 19, 1780.

19 DEP, September 19, 1780.

20 DEP, October 10, 1780.

21 Heron to Porten, August 17, *Grattan Memoirs*, II, 437–38; Heron to Porten, August 30, 1780, SP 63/471. f. 15.

22 Buckinghamshire to Hillsborough, October 16, 1780, SP 63/471, f. 192.

23 Buckinghamshire to Hillsborough, September 1, 1780, SP 63/471, ff. 45–46; Buckinghamshire to Hillsborough, December 11, 1780, *Grattan Memoirs*, II, 444–45; Scott to Buckinghamshire, December 11, 1780 *Grattan Memoirs*, II, 445–46.

24 Buckinghamshire to North, September 8, 1780, *Grattan Memoirs*, II, 163–65.

25 Buckinghamshire to Hillsborough, November 19, 1780, *Grattan Memoirs*, II, 169–71.

26 Hillsborough to Buckinghamshire, October 13, 20, 1780, SP 63/471, ff. 176–88.

27 Buckinghamshire to Hillsborough, December 23, 1780, SP 63/471, f. 465.

28 Buckinghamshire to Germain, November 12, 1780, HMC, Lothian Papers, p. 376; DEP, November 9, 1780.

29 Lecky, *History*, II, 261.

X

Class Conflicts and the Failure of Radicalism in 1780

I

The collapse of radicalism in 1780 has been recorded by historians, but they have not attempted to give an adequate explanation for this surprising reversal of political trends after the great victory of the Patriots on Free Trade. Bribery has been seen as the main reason for the Government's recovery of control of the Parliament. Undoubtedly Buckinghamshire's use of rewards helped, but in itself it was far from being enough. The policy of building up a pro-government majority had commenced in October, 1779, but during the spring of 1780 the Viceroy had repeatedly expressed his exasperation at the virtual impossibility of depending on pledges of support. The reversal of the movement towards radicalism among members of Parliament must be ascribed to one great cause—

the consciousness among landlords that the Free Trade agitation was developing into a demand by the middle classes for a real share in political power. At first this realization could not alter the conduct of the members since they continued to fear the extra-parliamentary forces. Thus, Buckinghamshire's efforts to regain control of the Commons were not successful until the summer of 1780. By that time three factors had made themselves felt: the Combinations Act, the Tenantry Act, and the attempt, in which the middle classes were involved, to strip several aristocratic borough-owners of some of their political importance.

The achievement of Free Trade naturally led to the question as to how manufacturers might best be able to use the new freedom. Much was said of the country being able to attain prosperity if better methods and a new attitude to work were adopted by skilled workmen. The latter problem was a serious one. There existed in Dublin organizations of such workers known as journeymen combinations and for many years these bodies had been at loggerheads with employers in various manufactures. The journeymen were organized in the different types of manufacture in groups that had the elements of modern labor unions. Each was a tightly knit body subject to regulations of its own and the payment of membership fees and able to present a united front to employers.[1]

In these quarrels it is legitimate to use the term class conflict since they denoted a struggle between two economic groups, identifiable as classes and involving harsh and protracted antagonism. These conflicts occurred in an economy that was still pre-industrial, that is before the advent of the Industrial Revolution. Here the concern was with small capital investment and units of production, comparatively inexpensive and simple machinery operated in small workshops or in the home, and the emphasis on *manus* rather than *machina*.

As a solution to this major problem, a parliamentary enquiry under the chairmanship of Sir Lucius O'Brien, was instituted in February, 1780, to investigate the combinations. Evidence was given before this body, the House of Commons Grand Committee for Trade, by nearly twenty masters in a variety of manufactures. The spirit in which the enquiry was set up is suggested by an editorial in a Dublin newspaper on January 22, 1780:

We are informed, that as the most effectual means to promote industry and extend the manufactures of this Kingdom, a bill is intended to be brought into Parliament, to regulate workmen . . . and prevent those destructive combinations which are the source of idleness, drunkenness and cruelty: and as the laws now in being have been found ineffectual . . . such pains and penalties will be inserted in this . . . as must give a new face to business.

The great complaint of the masters was that the journeymen combinations had forced employers to pay wages and remuneration for piece-work at an excessively high level, and, by restricting the entry of apprentices, had ensured a scarcity of skilled labor. Many evils, according to the masters, had resulted from these practices; women and children had been ousted from employment, and the engaging of journeymen from other parts of Ireland had been prevented; work was often inefficient but the scarcity of skilled workmen meant that employers had to tolerate bad workmanship. Strikes had been frequent not merely over wages and prices but, also, when a master engaged more apprentices than the journeymen would allow. The masters were very definitely of the opinion that if Ireland were to benefit from Free Trade, journeymen combinations must be suppressed, and the full vigor of the law must be invoked for that purpose.

These combinations had existed for two decades in some of the manufactures, and the Irish Parliament had passed several acts concerning them, the most recent being that of 1772. Towards the end of 1776 a determined effort in co-operation with the Lord Mayor had been made by masters of the following trades—tailors, cabinetmakers, brewers, tallow chandlers, bakers, cotton printers, cutlers, and carpenters—to break the combinations, but without success.

Having heard the evidence, the Committee adopted a number of resolutions that dealt with the existence of these combinations, their injurious effects, and the need for legislation. The resolutions prove that the substance of the masters' allegations had been accepted. In the succeeding months a measure called the Combinations Act was passed by the Irish Parliament and received the royal assent in August of the same year, 1780.

The journeymen had no intention of going like lambs to the slaughter. They presented five petitions to the House of Commons; and some very able letters and paid insertions were published in the press. These were obviously drafted by educated people hired for the purpose, since they were written in a good literary style and argued cogently and with calculated moderation. A subscription list was opened for the purpose of engaging legal counsel to plead the workmen's cause before parliament.

Most of the journeymen's statements admitted the existence of combinations but described them as a necessary defense against the injustice and deceit of masters. The latter were accused of having broken faith with their workmen on agreements and tables of rates; by fraudulent manufacturing procedures they deceived the public and oppressed their employees. Then came a biting statement with important political implications in a letter to a newspaper:

I am happy to find that the journeymen are preparing their witnesses against the opening of parliament, to discover to the world who were the persons that bribed them to burning Lord Townshend's effigy, who instigated the unfortunate muslin riot, which cost the city so many lives; and also who it was that equipped them with arms for the late attack on his Majesty's Attorney-General [John Scott]. [2]

In their evidence several of the masters described journeymen combinations. There was one in each manufacture or stage of manufacture, and each elected a committee; the committee imposed regulations and levied fees, and refusal to pay could involve unpleasant consequences. The employment by a master of more than the stipulated number of apprentices or journeymen recruited from outside Dublin was considered cause for striking. The candid and vehement manner in which these allegations were made carries conviction. It is significant that the journeymen, though aware of the charges, made no attempt to refute them. Even when allowance has been made for exaggeration in the employers' evidence, it is still safe to conclude that there did exist organizations which were a crude form of modern labor unions.

The Combinations Bill passed through the Commons without any real opposition. Hely Hutchinson, the Provost, procured an amendment favorable to the journeymen. Only one of the Patriots—Sir Samuel Bradstreet, a member for Dublin City—took any noticeable part in the proceedings and that of a nature hostile to the workmen. The Dublin press, for the most part politically radical, showed little concern for the journeymen.

Matters came to a crisis in June when the House of

Commons, having heard legal counsel plead on behalf of the employees, passed the bill. The critical day was June 13 when a large number of journeymen assembled in Phoenix Park outside Dublin for the purpose of drawing up a petition for presentation to the Lord-Lieutenant. They were unarmed and presumably had no thought of violence, but such a gathering a week after the astonishing Gordon riots in London caused great alarm and the military were called out. The crowd dispersed peacefully after signing a petition, which was presented by a deputation to Buckinghamshire.

It is significant that the Volunteers assembled "with an alacrity that must ever do them honour" and remained on duty in the streets till all fear of riots had passed. The Lord Mayor thanked them publicly, and at least four of the corps published statements that they would always defend the public peace. As already described, two of these, the Merchants and the Independent Dublin, were denounced by the Parliament two months later as guilty of seditious libel concerning the Perpetual Mutiny Act. But where labor demands were the issue, these two radical corps were stout upholders of law and order; the former declared their intention to always support "the civil power in the suppression of every unconstitutional measure," while the latter went one better by pledging themselves to defend their "native city against foreign or domestic enemies." That the Volunteers' hostility was not a panic reaction is proved by the fact that six months later three corps, the Dublin, the Liberty, and the Lawyers, passed resolutions of a like kind against journeymen combinations. Events in 1781 showed that they meant what they said. The struggle with the skilled workers was one in which the middle classes stood firmly on the side of the masters.

Journeymen difficulties continued in the Irish economy

until well into the nineteenth century. Moreover, the Combinations Act was not even temporarily successful. During a strike in 1781 a writer in the press described the "force of the Laws and the wisdom of the Legislature being found of little consequence." In 1782 these combinations were denounced as "an evil which hath long existed, and still continues the bane of industry and national prosperity."

In the summer of 1781, James Gandon, the English architect brought to Ireland at the invitation of John Beresford, started work on Dublin's new Custom House, which is considered today perhaps the most graceful public building in Ireland. He had much to say on the journeymen:

Hitherto, none but Dublin masons were employed in the city, but for the expedition of this great work it was found necessary to employ all who would offer. This was opposed by the Dublin fraternity, unless the aliens would take an oath of secrecy, subscribe one guinea each, and submit to their laws of combination.

At first, according to Gandon, the "aliens" were reluctant to obey but eventually yielded, and generally ended up more difficult to deal with than the Dubliners:

It was just the same with English carpenters and stone cutters who were invited over; they were very orderly at first, but in the end more refractory than the natives, more exhorbitant in their demands for increase of wages, and worse by far as to drunkenness.

That the middle classes and especially the more politically radical among them should have been so hostile to the workmen was no accident. A parallel can be drawn with the conduct of the bourgeois French National Assembly when it passed Le Chapelier's Law in June, 1791. Like the Irish Act of 1780, this measure outlawed all combinations of employers as well as employees, as inimical to civic freedom, and its provisions regarding workmen, against whom it was really directed, were even harsher than those of the Irish Act.[3] The latter was the first measure in the British Isles to deal with combinations generally and not just with one segment of the manufacturing economy. In Great Britain it was only in 1799–1800 that legislation of this general kind was passed, and then its enactment arose partly from the fear engendered by the French Revolution.

The Act created or accentuated hostility between the journeymen and both Parliament and Volunteers. The Volunteers's reaction to the Phoenix Park meeting, and the Patriots' neglect of the workmen on the passing of the measure, meant that middle-class political radicalism would have little appeal for Dublin workmen in the future. The agitation for Free Trade directly concerned the journeymen, but under popular Patriot leadership, they might well have supported agitation on more constitutional matters. In the spring of 1780, before the Declaratory and Poyning's measures were debated in the Commons, the workmen must have known that their cause would receive little sympathy from the Patriots. This consideration would explain why the radicals' indignation at the defeat of both measures provoked no riots. The *Dublin Evening Post* of August 14, 1779, described mobs as usually consisting of the "lower artisans." In August, 1780 when Patriots talked belligerently of an appeal to the people, and Volunteers used language considered seditious, it is not surprising that the Dublin "mob" showed no inclination whatever to man the barricades.

This withdrawal into quiescence on political matters

meant a weakening of radicalism in Dublin, though the effect can hardly be considered decisive: Dublin was not Paris. More politically influential was the Tenantry Act, which will now be considered.

II

Throughout the eighteenth century there existed in Ireland the custom of granting land on leases for lives renewable for ever. A *life* meant the life of any person so named in the lease. On the expiry of a life the lessee, in order to have the tenancy renewed, would make a payment called a fine to the landlord who was then obliged to renew the lease and substitute a new life for the deceased. As properties so granted were normally of large acreage, the lessee was usually a man of substance and very often a landlord, himself. He regarded the land as his own in perpetuity, and frequently let all or part of it to under-tenants.

The lessor was known as the superior or head landlord. Once the lease had been executed, he lost control of the property and, unless the lease should expire, became for all practical purposes little more than a *rentier*. In former times, owing to the disturbed and primitive condition of the economy, owners readily granted such leases: the more advanced development, and increase in population and land values, of the second half of the eighteenth century brought about a different situation. Head landlords were now desirous of recovering possession of their estates.[4]

Advertisements for the sale of landed estates occasionally appeared in the Irish newspapers. The acreage of each holding and the name of the tenant were always mentioned. In the case of very long leases, including leases for lives renewable for ever, the land held by a tenant usually ran into a couple of hundred acres or more. In a proportion of these holdings, often as much as one third, the tenant's name was followed by the designation, "Esq.," which indicated that he was, at least socially, of the land-owning classes. Frequently, this form of tenancy was used as a means of handing on family property from an owner to his heirs. It had the advantage of conferring the fran-chise on the lessee, which was not the case with leases for any fixed period however long.

An example of an aristocratic leaseholder is found on the estate of the second Earl of Arran. In July, 1783, Lord Arran advertised in the press the sale of a considerable amount of land "for the discharge of encumbrances." [5] The holdings were all let on leases for lives renewable for ever (this explains why he was such a sturdy opponent of the Tenantry Act of 1780). One of his "tenants" was his close relative, Sir John Evans-Freke, a baronet and the owner of the borough of Baltimore in Co. Cork. Later, this "tenant" became the sixth Lord Carbery.

Any disturbance of the rights of leaseholders necessarily involved a threat to the rights of their undertenants. Since a large part of the land of Ireland was held under these leases, and since many leaseholders had created numerous subtenancies, any tampering with the system was likely to have widespread and serious repercussions.

The traditional legalities of the system were questioned in 1775 when there came before the Irish courts the case of Murray-v-Bateman, in which it was claimed that the failure of a tenant to make known the expiry of a life and to pay the fine to the head landlord at the proper time rendered the lease void. On appeal to the (Irish) Lord Chancellor's Court, the Lord Chancellor, Lifford, gave a judgment upholding the "old Irish equity" and thus in favor of the lessee. The case was then appealed to the

British House of Lords where in 1779 a judgment ,in which Lord Mansfield's opinion appears to have been dominant, was given in favor of the head landlord. The point of legal controversy was the extent to which the leaseholder was liable for making known the expiry of a life. The British judgment laid strict obligations, whereas the "old Irish equity," confirmed by Lifford, had allowed the tenant far greater latitude. Since failure to pay the fine on time was an omission of frequent and easy occurrence, the British Lords' judgment was a threat to the very system itself. The Irish Attorney-General, Scott, expressed anxiety about the position of these leaseholders when he referred in a letter to John Robinson to

. . . property by some late determination of the British House of Lords upon covenants for perpetual renewals of leases very much set at sea, and no means to a great multitude of families to supply its place.[6]

Naturally, the British judgment was welcomed by head landlords since it would enable them in many instances to recover possession of properties where the leaseholder had failed to pay the fine at the proper time. The problem was resolved by an act of the Irish Parliament in 1780 called the Tenantry Act, which explicitly restored the "old Irish equity." [7] The rights of these leaseholders and, consequently, the position of their numerous undertenants and mortgagees were safeguarded to the chagrin of the head landlords. It was a popular measure, and anyone opposing it was likely to provoke widespread resentment.

Despite the importance of the matter, little appeared in public concerning it until the Attorney-General raised the subject in the Irish House of Commons. On February 29, 1780, he announced his intention of introducing legislation immediately after the Spring recess. In a plea for the welfare of leaseholders he said:

There is one class of people that seem to have escaped our recollection, I mean the Tenantry of this Kingdom. . . . I am sure I shall have the assistance of the wise, the benevolent in this House, to carry any scheme into execution that will put the Peasantry of Ireland upon a footing with Great Britain. . . . I have not a foot of land that can be affected by any determination with regard to a clause of renewal. . . . The Yeomen of every country are the first class of men that ought to be looked after.[8]

On May 15 he entered more fully into the matter and described the historical origin of the practice of creating these leases:

When this species of grant took place, the Country was almost in a state of barbarism . . . uncivilized, the soil of little value: it became difficult to get Tenants to occupy, & improve. . . . The species of Tenant for this perpetual renewal are the most useful, the most valuable, and most permanent members of our Nation. . . . Tenants can't renew with ease. They can't understand the necessity of those Grants in Great Britain. . . . the subject is not understood in Great Britain. . . . If you have a number of farmers, of yeomanry, of Gentlemen, the inferior classes of men ought to be the first objects of your affection.[9]

Hely Hutchinson and Fitzgibbon opposed the passing of any legislation on the matter as being unnecessary. In order to show his lack of self-interest the latter said: "I have not an acre of land held [by my tenants] under this tenure. I have a very valuable estate I hold by lease of lives renewable for ever." Sir Lucius O'Brien considered that every county would have instructed their representa-

tives to take up the subject if they thought the House
would not do so. Grattan and James Browne, Hussey
Burgh's successor as Prime Serjeant, supported Scott. At
the latter's suggestion, Grattan agreed to sponsor a measure
designed to clarify the legal position and protect the leaseholders. On June 2 an attempt was made by Fitzgibbon
and Sir Samuel Bradstreet, one of the more radical Patriots, to have the heads of the bill defeated, but it failed
on a division by 60 to 36.[10]

Three hostile petitions were presented to the House of
Commons, the most important being one from four of the
members, Sir Robert Tilson Deane, William Burton,
James C. Ponsonby, and the Patriot, Hercules C. Rowley.
Their petition saw the proposed bill as causing the

greatest injury and losses to them and to many other proprietors of land . . . [and would involve] every person who is
interested in those tenures in tedious, expensive and trouble-
some suits.[11]

In the Commons on June 12 the Attorney-General described the measure as his "favourite bill." The next day
saw further opposition by Fitzgibbon in a vigorous debate.
Scott was apparently not present, but two of the members
of the Administration—Hely Hutchinson (who now an-
nouced his conversion), and Serjeant Fitzgerald, supported
the bill as did Grattan and Hussey Burgh. The heads were
passed but only by a very small majority, 56 to 53, and
Grattan carried them to Dublin Castle for transmission
to London.[12]

It is apparent that in this age of rising land values a
man with money to invest would prefer to acquire a leasehold rather than a head interest in property. As a lessee,
he would have effective control of an estate, while in the

position of head landlord he would be little more than a
rentier. Thus, Crown servants with the emoluments of
office to invest, wealthy merchants and bankers, together
with the holders of mortgages on leasehold interests, had
an economic reason for supporting this measure.

The Dublin newspapers took up the matter early in
June. The *Freeman's Journal* described the heads as intended to "completely secure the property of the tenant
against the fraudulent designs of a rapacious landlord"
and called it the "Attorney-General's Bill." A correspondent maintained that Free Trade and the Poyning's Law
issue were but "trifles when compared with the bill for
easing the minds of four-fifths of the people of Ireland,
and confirming to them the fruits of their industry." Opponents of the bill were "hell-hounds who are hunting
for the property of the widow and the orphan." Another
correspondent maintained that "as leases forever are held
by Protestants only, it [the defeat of the bill] will be attended with the total extirpation of the Protestant religion." He paid a special tribute to Sir Lucius O'Brien
and Luke Gardiner, both of whom, and particularly
Gardiner, were supporters of the Government, for assisting the measure. Still another writer considered that something ought be done so as not to deprive nine-tenths of
the Protestants of Ireland of their just rights: "the liberty,
the property, and the established religion of this country
depend on it." When the heads had passed the Irish Privy
Council, the *Freeman's Journal* commented:

. . . there never was any law agitated in our senate, that hath
so much roused the attention of the people. The gloomy
indications of a smothered resentment . . . foreboded dreadful ills, had this bill miscarried in its progress through the
Privy Council.[13]

Heron, Scott, Hely Hutchinson, and Pery voted for it in the Privy Council, while no prominent member of the Government, except John Beresford, was reported to have voted against it.[14]

On June 16 a committee was formed in Dublin to organize support for the measure. They passed a vote of thanks to Grattan and appointed one of their number— John Keogh, an attorney—to act as their representative in Dublin, while Richard Troward was similarly employed in London. On July 12 Troward wrote (and the letter was published) that he had employed counsel to argue the case before the British Privy Council since he understood that counsel had been retained by Lord Arran and others.[15] Arran was one of the politically radical peers who had opposed the Government on the address of appreciation on March 2. His hostility to the Tenantry bill was likely to bring discredit on the Patriots. Some two weeks later a meeting was held in Dublin, obviously organized by this committee, which passed a vote of gratitude to the Lord-Lieutenant and Secretary (Heron) for their support of the bill. They also passed the resolution:

That the said Bill [strictly speaking it was yet only the heads of a bill] tends to the attaining great national objects, namely the preservation of the Protestant Interest, the settlement and establishment of Property and Yeomanry, the prevention of emigration, the Peace, Prosperity and improvement of the Country, by removing doubts that have alarmed the Kingdom by their tendency to shake the ancient equity in these cases of renewal.[16]

On July 19 a meeting of the Freeholders of Co. Dublin called on their representatives in parliament, Gardiner and Newenham, to support the bill and received affirmative answers.[17] The meeting thanked John Keogh for "his great attention and care in the support of said bill," and appointed him along with the High Sheriff and three others as collectors of subscriptions for the promotion of the enactment.

By July 21 the *Hibernian Journal* saw the Tenantry bill as rescuing two millions of people from slavery and raising from ruin a "starving and naked tenantry." It originated with the Attorney-General "whose life has been devoted to relieve his fellow beings," a description which the much abused Scott would not have dared to hope for a few months previously. The *Dublin Evening Post* of July 22 noted that George Ogle was one of those who had petitioned against the bill in England. The same newspaper on August 1 described the Mutiny and Tenantry measures as "the bills of the people." On August 17 it published "Hints submitted to . . . the Volunteer Corps" by a writer who described the force as consisting of "the Protestant Tenantry of Ireland." He asked:

Can any individual be entitled to the protection, aid, or assistance of any of these corps, who attempts . . . to weaken, break, or destroy that Tenantry? . . . Could the Volunteer Corps more effectually serve themselves, their Country, and posterity, than by an immediate avowal . . . that they would not . . . protect, aid, or assist any individual who has, or may hereafter oppose the passing of such bills into a law?

The resolution of the Dublin meeting in July to induce addresses to parliament for the support of the bill had its effect. At least five counties and three towns held meetings addressed to their parliamentary representatives. They were the counties of Dublin, Waterford, Kilkenny, Wexford, and Armagh, and the towns of Dublin, Dungarvan, and Wexford.[18] The three most interesting reactions were those of John Beresford in Co. Waterford, George Ogle in

Co. Wexford, and Sir Samuel Bradstreet in Dublin. Beresford said he would use his judgment in the matter and act
accordingly, but he took care to say this diplomatically
(he voted against the bill in the critical division of August
11).[19] Ogle, the great Patriot who had been so willing
to obey his constituents on the Short Money and Poyning's
issues, now declared that he would be neutral. His "dis-
obedience" was spotlighted when his co-representative for
the county, Sir Vesey Colclough, replied that he would
obey his electors' "commands." [20] Bradstreet, in a speech
in the Commons on the bill on August 11, admitted that
he had been opposed to the measure, but now that he had
received his constituents' instructions he would vote for
it, which he did.[21]

In due course, the Tenantry heads (it is now technically
permissable to call them a bill) were returned from London with only one serious alteration, and that in favor of
the tenants. The English attorney and solicitor generals
on being consulted by the Cabinet had approved of the
bill.[22] In the great debate that took place on it in the
Commons on August 11, it was partially opposed on the
ground that it would injure the rights of the landlord but
also on the constitutional ground that to accept a bill that
had been altered in England was to accept the supremacy
of the British Parliament. One could hardly imagine a
more convenient and intellectually dishonest use of the
desire for legislative independence. It was further argued
that the bill would strengthen the position of the middle-
man at the expense of the undertenant. Fitzgibbon denied
that the bill would help to establish a yeomanry and saw
the middleman as the great oppressor of the poor. Scott
praised the "middling-man," that is the leaseholder, as
beneficial to the poorer peasantry; the miseries of the
latter were due to rapacious landlords. Grattan emphasized

the importance of the bill as the interests involved were "immense." The section of the community concerned were the "middling class of men, the Yeomanry," and the leases were held by very ancient proprietors and existed before

land jobbing began. . . . The land jobber has nothing to say to the leases for lives renewable for ever . . . you have under deliberation that very property that sends you to Parliament . . . the interest of the most useful part of Society being for the bill.[23]

He considered that the consequence of rejecting the measure would be "beggary in one part of Society, and mischievous accumulation of wealth [in another part]." Hussey Burgh and Lieut-General Cuninghame gave strong support to the bill, Hussey Burgh making the point that the absentee landlords in England had not opposed it. At the end of this stormy debate the critical vote was taken and resulted in the triumph of the measure by 90 to 55.

In the division Beresford was the only prominent member of the Government who voted against the bill. The other Crown servants, at least all those of position, voted for it. Such independent supporters of the Administration as Gardiner, Sir Lucius O'Brien, and John Foster did likewise. The very moderate Patriot, Denis Daly, also gave his support, as did the more confirmed Patriot members— Grattan, Hussey Burgh, Bushe, and Newenham. The actions of two other Patriots call for mention. Brownlow had been instructed by his constituents to vote in favor of the bill, but he desisted from both replying and voting.[24] More important was the abstention of Yelverton from both debate and division. He had, it is true, expressed support before the heads had been formally introduced, but his name was not again mentioned. Considering the leading part he was taking in the constitutional issues, his silence on the Tenantry measure must have been very noticeable. Taking all into consideration, it must be admitted that the "servants" and "courtiers" had at least as popular a record as the Patriots on the Tenantry Bill. But worse was to befall (from the point of view of the parliamentary Opposition) when the measure went to the Lords.

The opponents in the Upper House, particularly the Archbishop of Cashel and the two anti-government radicals, Carysfort and Mountmorres, tried to prevent its committal on August 18, but were defeated by 35 votes to 30. Proxies were used, and it was only their use which enabled the bill to pass, since the peers in attendance on that day, August 18, had shown a slight majority against it. On the following day the Archbishop pressed the issue to a division in committee, a stage in which proxies could not be used, and thus there was every prospect of the measure's being defeated. Aware of the danger, John Keogh made a feverish attempt to round up sufficient peers, which he just succeeded in doing thanks to the intervention of the Duke of Leinster on behalf of the bill. As a result, it passed by a bare majority of one—20 votes to 19. A long and informative letter in the *Hibernian Journal* on August 23 describes the dramatic course of the bill through the House of Lords and ends with the statement:

This great day's [August 19] decision decides probably two thousand suits in Chancery—continues these interests in the hands of Protestants for ever and saves one hundred thousand Protestant families from destruction.

The opposing peers expressed their anger at seeing the bill pass by formally protesting in the *Journal of the Lords*.[25]

They numbered twenty-one, thirteen in person and eight by proxy. They included four (Carysport, Mountmorres, Arran, and Moira) of the seven peers who had been anti-government radicals on March 2 when they opposed the address of loyalty and gratitude which Leinster introduced on the passing of the Plantations Act. Powerscourt, another Patriot peer, was among those signing this protest. In due course the Tenantry Bill received the royal assent.

In the Commons the Government had shown that it was favorable to the leaseholders' interest, while the Patriots had given what could at best be regarded as a very mixed support. In the Lords the Patriots had done their best to oppose that interest. In the latter the only Patriot to support the lessees was Leinster, and in radical circles he was now scarcely considered a Patriot.

The Tenantry issue provided the much maligned members of a "venal" administration and the "corrupt courtiers" with a golden opportunity to even the score with many of the Patriots, and they seized it with both hands. Nor did they neglect to rub salt into the wounds. In the debate of August 11 (the most important Commons' debate on the bill) Sir Boyle Roche, the epitome of courtier-ism, took full advantage of the occasion:

I have heard the strenuous opposers of this bill declare in this House, that they would not be bound by English laws, yet I am sorry to find from some of those gentlemen, a partial preference given in this case [a reference to the opportunist argument that the bill should be opposed because it had been altered in England].

He then proceeded to lavish praise on the Volunteers and made quite certain that they would know who their friends were by describing them as the very persons on whose fate we this day determine, and who will be chiefly injured or assisted by the result of our debates as they are composed in general of the Protestant tenantry of Ireland.[26]

Though the Dublin newspapers supported the Patriots in general political outlook, they could not altogether control their resentment over the Tenantry Act. The *Dublin Evening Post* of August 31 stated editorially:

This great law was opposed in all its stages by some of the persons called patriots, particularly in the House of Lords; a proof that private interest prevails in some minds, over all attachments to the general benefit. Let people therefore beware, when these men cry out, Oh, Liberty! Oh, my country!

The pro-government *Faulkner's Dublin Journal*, which had suffered from anaemia during the previous year while the other newspapers indulged their animal spirits in boisterous opposition, now could join Sir Boyle Roche in having its day:

The Tenantry Bill is of more real benefit to the Nation than any act that has passed since the Revolution. Mr. Keogh, who originally proposed it, and has in the most uniform and spirited manner, supported it through every stage, merits more gratitude and thanks from his country, than all the Patriots, who have gone before him either in England or here.[27]

The much slandered Duke of Leinster came back into his own when the *Dublin Evening Post* of August 31 described him as meriting "the greatest gratitude from all the Protestants of Ireland. His Grace has been ever ready to support what he thinks is for the real and solid advantage of this nation."

Small wonder then that radicalism collapsed in the summer of 1780. Yelverton's thunder on sugar and mutiny in the Commons during August no doubt reverberated throughout the land, but his significant absenteeism, when the rights of leaseholders (and their undertenants) were in the balance, must have been a splash of ice water in the face of many a Volunteer. Numbers of brave Irish farmers, furious with the tyranny of English government, must have experienced a cooling of ardor when confronted by the unexpected withdrawal of such radicals as Carysfort and Ogle from the popular side, and by the sight of the Attorney-General, "the uniform drudge of the administration," laboring on their behalf.

The struggle over the Tenantry Act was not in any immediate sense a class conflict. The leaseholders comprised men from all propertied sections of the community including landlords. The act was a popular measure, since a large number of leaseholders and probably tens of thousands of undertenants were involved. Because it concerned so many people, it obviously produced strong feelings among the middle classes. It will be remembered that the Attorney-General saw it as the means of establishing a "substantial yeomanry" and of curbing the greed of landlords. The newspapers testified to its being the defense of the tenant against "the fraudulent designs of a rapacious landlord;" the raising from ruin of a "starving and naked tenantry;" and the saving of "one hundred thousand Protestant families from destruction." Though the press comments were gross exaggerations, they treated the issue as occurring between the middle classes and a vague landlord power; and the much more sober statements of Scott and Boyle Roche were not of the sort to correct this distortion.

Thus the Tenantry Act took on, quite unjustly, the complexion of a class conflict. Seen in this light, it was a victory for the middle over the upper classes.

The Act has escaped the notice of historians. Lecky makes no mention of it whatever, and neither does Francis Plowden in his *Historical Review*. In the *Grattan Memoirs,* written more than forty years after 1780, it is treated as one of the less important events of that year, and the description shows that Grattan in his old age only vaguely remembered it. The failure of the Tenantry Act to impress itself on historians, contemporary or modern, is not so surprising. The measure was enacted during what seems in retrospect the nadir between the achievement of Free Trade in 1779–1780 and legislative independence in 1782. The only events in between that seem to be of any importance (and since they failed from the Patriot point of view, Grattan would not have wanted to keep even *them* in the forefront of his mind) were the Declaratory and Poyning's resolutions of April, and the Irish Mutiny Act of the summer of 1780.

Lecky's neglect to realize the importance of the Tenantry issue is more easily explained. He was writing in the days before the economic interpretation of history had appeared, and thus would not have been watching out for evidence of an economic nature: the modern historian thinks immediately of the economic motivation. Secondly, he did not consult newspapers, and so he knew little of parliamentary debates in Ireland before 1781 and even less of all those editorial comments, news reports, and letters in the newspapers which are the source of nearly all the information on this issue. Finally, there is scarcely anything beyond the merest formal references to the measure in the correspondence of statesmen.

On first consideration it would seem that Buckinghamshire's silence indicates that the Tenantry issue was of

little importance. This conclusion is ruled out simply because the evidence found in the newspapers makes it certain that it did have considerable importance. The fact
that Dublin Castle as a whole, excepting Beresford, supported the bill, and that a public meeting could thank
Buckinghamshire and Heron for their support, means
that the Lord-Lieutenant was well aware of what was happening and was at least favorably inclined. He had, however, a perfectly good reason for keeping quiet about it in
his correspondence: there were too many absentee owners
in England of Irish estates who might take a hostile view
of the Tenantry bill. It suited the Lord-Lieutenant's political purpose to let the Tenantry bill remain exclusively
an Irish affair and not risk making it an Anglo-Irish one
by any unnecessary mention of it in his letters to London.
This does not mean that the British Cabinet was unaware
of the bill—counsel had argued for and against it before
the English Privy Council—but it does mean that the
Lord-Lieutenant had good reason for keeping it *sub rosa*.
Hillsborough owned a great estate in Ireland and could
learn the full meaning of the bill from his land agents
without having to trouble the Lord-Lieutenant with
queries. Presumably, he did not attempt to attack it, since
according to Hussey Burgh, the absentee owners had not
opposed it. Buckinghamshire had learned in May that a
successful maneuver (Foster's amendment to Bushe's
Mutiny heads) could be made more easily if London were
not told too much, and the lesson seems to have been
remembered.

III

The Tenantry and Combinations measures had thus led
to the weakening of radicalism and to a deeper division
in the ranks of the Patriots. The result was a recovery of

strength and confidence in both the Government and the landlord classes. The revival of the independence (of extra-parliamentary pressures) of the latter enabled the Administration to regain its control of the House of Commons. In 1780 the Patriots had concentrated their attack on the British constitutional control of Ireland and, apart from attempts in the Commons to frighten the "venal" members into abandoning the Administration on specific issues, did not mount any assault on the owners of parliamentary boroughs. Outside parliament, however, various radical groups and many of the Volunteers did make efforts, piecemeal rather than systematic, to challenge aristocratic political domination. It is now proposed to describe this struggle which took the form of an attack on the borough-owning aristocracy.

The movement for Free Trade had united all sections and classes of the nation behind a demand that all could understand however much some members of parliament may have doubted its immediate relevance to Irish distress. Even if many were unwilling to vote against the Government, they were left little choice by the flood tide which was sweeping all before it. The holding of county meetings on a national scale, the non-importation movement. and the organization of politically conscious Volunteer corps drew into active politics large numbers of the middle classes. To this movement, this groundswell of political consciousness, the violence of Grattan's speeches gave vigorous encouragement. His denunciations of the Irish House of Commons as a "corrupt Senate" ruled by a "contemptible aristocracy," his calling on three millions of people to direct the conduct of three hundred, and his demand that members obey the instructions of their constituents, produced a widespread feeling of discontent with the legislature and, thus, with aristocratic domination.

During 1780 there were many letters and editorial statements in the press demanding the election to parliament of trustworthy members only or reform of the electorate in, or disfranchisement of, boroughs controlled by the aristocracy. In previous years there had been grumblings about "courtiers" and pro-government majorities, but nothing so explicit, acute, or sustained as in the twelve months that followed the Free Trade agitation. In the *Dublin Evening Post* of May 30, 1780, one of these correspondents called for a secret ballot as one of the ways in which landlord and governmental interference at elections could be abolished. Another called for an increase in the number of freeholders by proposing that each landowner be compelled to create a new freeholder for each £100 of landed property possessed. This writer wanted to see all election expenses defrayed by the electors. Yet another sought the removal of placemen and pensioners and the establishment of "full and equal representation of the people." The injustice of allowing each rotten borough the same representation as the city of Dublin was pointed out by "An Independent Irish Freeholder" who warned that electioneering jobbers and pro-government lords and bishops, as well as avaricious landlords, could be guarded against only by the people and the Volunteers. The middle and lower classes were "the safer objects of our confidence." [28]

Nevertheless, there was no organized attempt in 1780 to bring about a reform of parliament. Grattan's assaults were intended to coerce the "venal" members of the Commons into supporting or, at least, not opposing the demand for Free Trade and legislative independence; he was not seeking parliamentary reform as such, though his speeches could only have the effect of turning public opinion in that direction. His most important extra-parliamentary statement on this issue came at the end of the

session of 1780, when on August 30 he replied to a con-
gratulatory address from the radical Independent Dublin
corps of Volunteers. This was one of the three corps which
had just participated in the resolution condemned by the
Parliament as seditious. Grattan's declaration was a care-
fully worded comment on the contemporary situation and
an announcement of policy for the future:

[Ireland's situation is improved but] the conclusion of this
session has not been worthy of its commencement. I see with
concern an unnatural and idle contest instituted between
Parliament and its best friends; a contest, the fruit of the
two unfortunate measures that marked the close of the session: and having opposed both those measures, which seem
to have sunk in the public estimation the dignity of Parliament, it shall be my care to raise her credit by proposing, the
next session to limit the duration of the mutiny bill, and to
secure to the House of Commons her best and dearest privilege—the confidence of the nation; and also put an end to
a disgusting conflict, where Administration first incenses the
people, by forcing upon them an unconstitutional law, and
hopes to punish them afterward by impotent prosecutions.
. . . There is no mischief that may not be removed by the
constitutional interposition of the Free and Independent Electors of this kingdom.[29]

On the subject of parliamentary reform this statement
was vague and ambiguous and no doubt deliberately so.
Grattan's equivocation makes it clear that he was not excluding such an aim from his policy, but it is equally obvious that he was not committing himself to it.

The grant of pensions and offices by the government
was of course an important means of managing parliament, but aristocratic domination of boroughs and controlling influence in counties were the major impediments

to reform. In February, 1780, Buckinghamshire listed nearly 100 members of the Commons as under the influence or control of twenty-three individuals [30] (the latter consisted of ten peers, four prelates and nine commoners); and the list was not exhaustive since it omitted Lord Charlemont (who had nominated Grattan to his borough of Charlemont) and several other leading aristocrats such as Lords Aldborough, Granard, Clifden, and Donegall, all of whom owned boroughs. In 1780 a strong attack was launched against the leadership of the two principal borough-owners, the Duke of Leinster and the Earl of Shannon.

Both were owners of great estates, the former in Kildare and the latter in Cork. Buckinghamshire, in his communication to London in February, 1780, lists them as the patrons of the largest number of members of the Irish House of Commons, Shannon having eighteen and Leinster ten. Both had great mansions in Dublin (Leinster House with additions is today the Irish Parliament). While the duke was patron of fewer members than Shannon, he more than made up for it in prestige since he was the head of the Irish nobility and the scion of the illustrious Norman-Irish family of Fitzgerald. Both had taken leading parts in the formation of Volunteer corps, and in these bodies the protest against their leadership developed.

The hostility to the great borough-owners was not necessarily limited to the middle classes. It is easy to understand that aristocrats and gentry whose parliamentary influence bore no relation to the size of their estates must have felt ready to condone or even support an attack on those landlords who were patrons of many members of parliament. Shannon owned five boroughs, four of them in Co. Cork, and thus nominated ten representatives. This parliamentary strength won him powerful government favor and patronage with which he was able to procure the support of other landlords who owned boroughs or had influence in the county. The 18 members of parliament of whom he was the patron included Richard Townsend, one of the County representatives, and the Jephson and St. Leger (Lord Doneraile) families who controlled the boroughs of Mallow and Doneraile respectively. Another great landlord in Co. Cork was the Earl of Kingston, the ambition of whose son, Lord Kingsborough, was to represent Cork County. Yet he counted politically for little in Co. Cork since he had to sit for his family borough of Boyle, Co. Roscommon. It was small wonder that Kingsborough should have been a leader of the movement for parliamentary reform.

Similarly, the Duke of Leinster owned three boroughs, all in Co. Kildare, and thus nominated six members to the Commons. According to the Viceroy's report he was the patron of ten. These included the two representatives for Kildare County. How galling this must have been for other large landlords in the same county who found themselves virtually excluded from parliamentary representation!

In Co. Down there were three great landed families, the Hills (Earls of Hillsborough), the Wards (Earls of Bangor), and the Stewarts (later Marquises of Londonderry and Viscounts Castlereagh). The Stewarts owned no borough; and, as a result of an alliance between the Hill and Ward families in the 1783 election, Robert Stewart, one of the members for the County of Down, lost his seat. Small wonder then, that Stewart should have been a protagonist of parliamentary reform. As against the political "poverty" of this aristocratic family, many families who were merely gentry but who owned a borough could obtain seats in the Commons. For example the Pennefathers of Newpark (or Ballyowen), Co. Tipperary, owned the borough of Cashel and nominated two of themselves to parliament.

It is reasonably sure that such men as Kingsborough, Robert Stewart, and Charlemont saw the attack on the borough-owners in 1780 with at least a measure of approval, and may well have lent it some support. They all took a prominent part later on in the campaign for parliamentary reform, but their aims in this respect must not be confused with those of the middle classes. The divergence between the middle and the upper classes becomes clearer in 1783.

Shannon had been a consistent supporter of the Administration and in the late summer of 1779 tried to implement a plan approved by Buckinghamshire for bringing the Volunteers under some sort of state control. Leinster and Conolly gave the proposal their support. The method decided on was the giving of commissions by the Government to certain officers.[31] Shannon's efforts failed as "an alarm . . . respecting it had been rapidly and successfully spread the moment it transpired that such a scheme was in agitation . . . [and it] seemed to be condemned by almost all, before it had been well explained to any." [32] The hostility to him took active form towards the end of 1779 when some of the Volunteers under his command seceded and formed a new corps, the Cork Union. The *Dublin Evening Post* hailed the event:

Lords and great men never look farther than to establish a *pitiful aristocracy*. . . . What gives the Congress of America power? Being joined by, and joining themselves to *The People*. What now gives efficacy to the Parliament of this kingdom [Ireland]? Being strengthened by associations of their masters, *The People*.[33]

On January 10, 1780, a correspondent in the Cork news-paper, the *Hibernian Chronicle,* called for action to en-sure that parliamentary representatives would in future carry out the wishes of their constituents and not sustain English tyranny. He then proceeded to make an implied attack on Shannon by asking that since "the emancipation of this kingdom from foreign usurpation is on the eve of being completed, so let the emancipation of this county [Cork] from domestic tyranny, on the same moment be accomplished." Another writer congratulated the Cork Union Volunteers on the secession and suggested that officers who were placemen and untrustworthy should be expelled.[34] Shortly afterwards, a correspondent again at-tacked Shannon, and called for the abolition of the "political rottenness" recently exhibited in parliament.[35] A more revealing letter was published on January 20, 1780, asserting that Shannon's opposition to the Town-shend administration of ten years previously [when the power of the "undertakers" had been destroyed] had been miscalled patriotism. Much better is the present system in which

Every independent Gentleman now feels his own conse-quence, and if he hath business to transact with Government, he is respectfully attended to by the Viceregent. We are no longer obliged to humble ourselves to the supercilious ar-rogance of aristocracy, or are our complaints and requests debased by passing through the medium of a Lord Justice [Shannon].

On March 14, a writer called on the Volunteers of Belfast to imitate Cork by expelling all officers who would not support the movement for constitutional freedom.

But Shannon was not without his defenders, and the attempt to unhorse him failed. On January 20 there appeared a letter in the *Hibernian Chronicle* from the "General Committee of the Independent Volunteers of Cork," representing five corps of the city, which contradicted the report that "the Armed Societies of Cork, had withdrawn themselves from the command of the Right Hon. the Earl of Shannon . . . such assertion being absolutely false." This denial referred to a statement in the *Freeman's Journal* of December 24, 1779, that the Cork Volunteers had expelled Shannon and "two of his lumber troop" for having voted against Irish interests in parliament. The report concerning secession was not entirely false, since seceders from Shannon's following formed a separate corps, the Cork Union, and had Sir Edward Newenham review them the following September. The other corps remained under Shannon's general leadership. In June 1780, he reviewed these corps, one of which, the Culloden Society, had in the previous month sent their congratulations to Grattan for his Patriot activities.[36] This fact was a proof in itself that Shannon's leadership had not been seriously shaken, but it also proved that some of the Volunteers being reviewed by him had no intention of accepting his directions on their political conduct. His success in handling the review gave much satisfaction to Buckinghamshire.[37]

Many other letters were written in Shannon's favor. One attacked the Patriots and condemned the "great deal of mean spite and illiberal abuse, levelled at that illustrious Personage [Shannon]." [38] Much of this defense appealed to religious sentiment by praising Shannon for his stand against "Catholic increase" and the extension to Catholics of the franchise. This connection with Protestant interests provoked an interesting letter calling on Volunteers to conciliate Catholics and not be influenced by Shannon. The writer adds:

We daily, gentlemen, hear the sons of corruption vaunting, that in case the Volunteers of Ireland were forced to ascertain their country's rights by force of arms, that an abandoned M–y [Ministry] have nothing more to do than to turn the Roman Catholics loose on them as they did the Indians in America. . . . America has shown us a glorious example: there every Religion is on an equal footing; yet we see unanimity prevail. . . .[39]

In March a correspondent issued the warning that if Britain was driven to desperation by Irish demands, she might retaliate by calling on the Catholics as allies against the Protestants.[40]

The Duke of Leinster had until 1780 filled the role of Patriot, and as a consequence was held high in public esteem. In December, 1779, he and his wife had appeared at a Dublin theater, and the event was described by Beresford:

On Friday he went with his Duchess to the play-house, in royal pomp, being escorted by a company of volunteer grenadiers, two of whom stood sentry on his box; they came in as king and queen; she first, he at some distance of time. She was received by a most violent clapping of hands, &c., and the music played up a blackguard tune, called "Success to the Duchess wherever she goes." He then appeared, and was not only clapped, but also huzzaed for several minutes without ceasing. They bowed to the people several times, and seemed perfectly happy with their new dignity.[41]

But Leinster was tired of radicalism and satisfied with the grant of Free Trade. Henceforth, he was a champion of the constitutional *status quo*. The first public demonstration of this took place on March 2, 1780, when he sponsored the Lords' address of gratitude to the king on

the passing of the Plantations Act. He was reported as
having said in the debate:

I have been the people's servant as long as I thought them
right: all they can in reason ask is granted, but they want
more. Many neglect their business to attend meetings to
instruct their representatives on constitutional questions,
which I do not think expedient now to enter on: and when
they shall be agitated in this House, *I will oppose them.*[42]

The succeeding six months witnessed a vigorous campaign against him in press correspondence and editorials.
He was taunted for his support of the Government on the
embargo and in the early days of the agitation for an
extension of trade in 1778; and for having sacrificed public
esteem by becoming a "courtier." But like Shannon (one
of the writers bracketed the two together), Leinster had
his defenders. Several letters appeared stressing his patriotic conduct and moderation in the true interests of
Ireland. One correspondent maintained that until recently
it had been thought that Free Trade would be sufficient,
but now it was considered mere slavery not to want more;
another sympathized with him now that he was the object
of abuse, and praised him for his support of the Catholic
Relief Act.

Again, as in Shannon's case, the attack concentrated on
the duke's position in the Volunteers and this time with
greater success. As soon as the first assault was made, his
own corps, the Dublin Volunteers, came to his rescue with
an address praising him for

asserting the national rights; zealous to cherish the Volunteer
associations, and active to promote that parliamentary unanimity, which, supported by the spirit of the people, has so
eminently contributed to our success.[43]

One of the members of the corps, the very radical Napper Tandy, later attempted to have them pass a vote congratulating Grattan on his Declaratory resolution of April 19 and also motioned to have Leinster expelled. He failed in both and then he himself was expelled.[44] The outcome was that some fifty of the corps seceded to form a new body called the Independent Dublin Volunteers. This new group induced Grattan to be their colonel, having declared that it was "inexpedient to continue any longer under the command of his Grace the Duke of Leinster." [45] While he remained in command of his corps, the duke did not fare as well as Shannon, since the duke's men showed an even stronger disposition to go their own political way. On June 9 he was compelled to condone a resolution stating that the King, Lords, and Commons of Ireland were alone competent to make laws for Ireland, and that his corps would obey no other.[46] This declaration was directly opposed to his publicly stated policy and it was only his moderating influence which deterred them from making their resolution more radical.[47] In August his corps again passed the same resolution, and again he was in the chair and had to condone it.[48] Greater humiliation was to follow when the various Dublin corps chose Charlemont to act as reviewing general for their parade on November 4, King William's birthday. Twelve corps voted on the choice, seven for Charlemont, three for Leinster, and two for Luke Gardiner.[49] Nor did the humiliation pass unnoticed in the press. Times had changed since November of the previous year. The insult was all the greater since Charlemont was quite unsuitable as a Volunteer general in any but a political sense, since he had no military knowledge and suffered from serious ill-health.[50]

Leinster's uncle-in-law, Thomas Conolly, who was the

patron of five members of the Commons according to Buckinghamshire's list, also suffered from his support of the Government. He owned large estates in Co. Londonderry, where he was one of the county representatives, and busied himself there organizing Volunteer corps.[51] His exertions were so effective that he was thought likely in 1779 to become commander-in-chief of the Volunteers in the North,[52] but his pro-government activities in 1780 caused him the loss of this honor which went instead to Lord Charlemont.[53] And his defeat was advertised in two very abusive letters to the press.[54]

The two leading Patriots in addition to Charlemont who happened to be wealthy landed aristocrats were Denis Daly and William Brownlow; they were members of parliament for their respective counties, Galway and Armagh. They showed very definite signs of moderation in 1780. As already described, Brownlow had objected in November, 1779, to Grattan's radical statements about members having a duty to obey their constituents. Daly was also considered moderate in that month, and by moving the address on the passing of the Plantations Act, he showed that he was scarcely any longer in the Patriot camp. In fact, he came in for a mild form of the abuse which was heaped on Shannon and Leinster.[55] Brownlow supported Daly's address on the Plantations Act. It can be said that by the summer of 1780 both had broken if not entirely with the Patriots, at least with radicalism. George Ogle, a landlord and M.P. for County Wexford, had been a fire-eating Patriot until 1780 when he too supported the address on the Plantations Act. Though formerly the willing servant of his constituents, he refused to obey their instructions on the Tenantry Bill and, instead, remained neutral.

One of the very few large landowners who remained a

Patriot all through 1780 was Lord Charlemont, and he got his reward in becoming the acknowledged leader of the Volunteers. This revolt against the borough-owning landed aristocracy was understood by some to involve what today we would call class consciousness. A letter to the *Dublin Evening Post* stated that of recent years the democratic part of the state had grown too great for the "other part," particularly the aristocratic which, in spite of numerous peerage creations, was but a "feather in the scale when weighed against the Commons." The tenantry would strengthen the Commons by adding a yeomanry which would "swallow up the other two estates, and overturn the fabric of the constitution."[56] Another writer lamented the trend of events when "To be at war with nobility, is it not, now, deemed honourable; to wage hostilities against worth, if it happen to be titled. . . . [is it not] now looked upon as patriotic?" and he goes on to warn that "democratical enthusiasm leads to deception." [57]

The protest against the political domination of the landed aristocracy was as yet unorganized and only in its initial stages. In the Volunteers the movement possessed a most powerful weapon, but since there was division on the issue among the Patriots, and since Grattan had not yet decided to enter the lists, it lacked the leadership necessary for success. The Tenantry Act had the effect of cooling the ardor of radicalism and further dividing the Patriots. Shortly after the new viceroy, the Earl of Carlisle, had arrived in Dublin, he reported to Hillsborough on the Irish situation. His comments shows that it was now clearly realized in governing circles that an internal struggle for political power had begun, and that its outcome was far from certain:

. . . in this moment there does appear among a variety of men of the greatest weight and consequence in this kingdom, otherwise differently inclined and differently connected, a conviction that the Aristocratic part of the Government has lost its balance; that there is an evident necessity of regaining from the people that power, which, if suffered to continue in their hands, must end in the general ruin of the whole; that for their own security and happiness, English Government must be supported, that the wild notions of Republicanism become every day more the objects of contempt and derision, that, in short, the national fever is subsiding, unless unfortunately again called forth, in which case the return of the disorder may be too strong for the best endeavours of the well intentioned. These . . . are the sentiments of many of the first characters in this country . . . there are few of that number who have not [expressed] . . . cordial and unequivocal offers of support.[58]

William Eden, Carlisle's Chief Secretary, was more explicit:

We have been received in general here with a disposition in the leading men of talents and of property and Followings to give a decided and zealous support to His Majesty's Government . . . for the truth is that the toe of the peasant has lately pressed unpleasantly on the Kibe [ulcerated chilblain] of the aristocracy and gentry and there is a general wish in the higher class to resume the old energy of good Government, at the same time that the Mercantile body are good-humored in consequence of the late concessions and desirous to join with Administration in carrying those concessions to the full effect. . . .[59]

Later in his letter he referred to the "critical circumstance of a large armed body governed only by their own discretion." It is obvious that Eden in his use of the word peasant was not referring to the smaller farmers which was the meaning usually attached to the term then as now. Those classes were not in the Volunteers and were not menacing the traditional ruling elements. He was clearly using the term in contradistinction to "aristocracy and gentry" and was describing those rural strata below the rank of gentry but substantial enough to cause political concern to the upper classes.

Eden's and, to some extent, Carlisle's observations point to the new importance of the middle classes and to the fact that these hitherto quiescent strata had now become alive to the possibility of seizing a share in political power.

NOTES FOR CHAPTER X

1 This account of combinations is based on my article, "Class Conflict in a Pre-Industrial Society: Dublin in 1780," in the *Duquesne Review,* Fall, 1963.

2 See above pp. 188–90 for an account of the political aspects of these riots.

3 For suggesting this comparison I am indebted to Professor Val. R. Lorwin of the University of Oregon, author of *The French Labor Movement* (Harvard University Press, 1954).

4 I am indebted to Mr. Ashley Powell of the Irish Bar for much valuable information and advice on this form of land tenure.

5 DEP, July 19, 1783.

6 Scott to Robinson, April 13, 1779, *Beresford Corr.,* I, 39–40.

7 19 & 20 Geo. III (Ire.), c. 30: T. T. Mercredy, *The Law of Fee Farm Grants,* (Dublin, 1877), p. 11; William Ridgeway, *Reports of Cases . . . in the High Court of Parliament in Ireland . . .* (Dublin, 1795), I, 187, 418, 488; James Lyne, *A Treatise on Leases for Lives, Renewable for ever* (Dublin, 1838), p. 145 *et seq.*

8 Irish Commons, February 29, 1780, IPD.

9 Irish Commons, May 15, 1780, IPD.

10 The above debates are taken almost entirely from the IPD. In the *Grattan Memoirs* (II, 81–84) Grattan is quoted in a way that gives the impression that the bill originated with him. Unquestionably, it was Scott who launched the measure.

11 *Irish Commons Journal,* X, 153, 155, 160.

12 HJ, June 15, 1780; FJ, June 15, 1780; *Irish Commons Journal,* X, 167.

13 FJ, June 6, 17, 22, 24, 29, 1780.

14 DEP, July 1, 1780.

15 DEP, July 20, 1780.

16 FDJ, July 25, 1780.

17 FJ, July 25, 1780. In his reply Gardiner said he had supported the measure in the Commons, and he added: "I am no way surprised that my words on that subject have been, as usual, absolutely misstated in some of the public papers, but as I am certain you will always judge of both my words and actions with candour, such misrepresentations give me no concern."

18 DEP, July 25, August 1, 5, 12, September 5, 1780; FJ, August 1, 1780.

19 The list of voters on the critical division on the Tenantry Bill on August 11 is published in the *Hibernian Chronicle* of August 21, 1780.

20 DEP, August 12, 1780.

21 DEP, August 17, 1780.

22 SP 63/463, ff. 55–58.

23 Irish Commons, August 11, 1780, IPD.

24 This information is contained in a letter in the *Dublin Evening Post* of September 5, 1780.

25 *Irish Lords Journal*, V, 216–217.

26 *Hibernian Chronicle* (Cork), August 17, 1780. This newspaper devoted special attention to Roche's speech.

27 FDJ, August 26, 1780.

28 DEP, May 30, June 10, September 21, November 7, 1780.

29 DEP, September 5, 1780.

30 This is the list (SP 63/468, ff. 210–220) to which reference has been made in previous chapters.

31 Buckinghamshire to Weymouth, July 23, 1779; Weymouth to Buckinghamshire, July 31, 1779; Heron to Porten, August 30, 1779, SP 63/465, ff. 437, 459, 63/466, ff.130–31; North to Pery, August 3, 1779, HMC, Emly Papers, I, 201–202; Buckinghamshire to Heron, August 15, 1779. Heron Papers.

32 Shannon to Buckinghamshire, September 16, 1779, HMC, Lothian Papers, p. 356.

33 DEP, December 24, 1779.

34 HC, February 3, 1780.

35 HC, February 10, 1780.

36 HC, June 1, 1780.

37 Buckinghamshire to Hillsborough, July 13, 1780, *Grattan Memoirs*, II, 122.

38 HC, January 13, 1780.

39 February 28, 1780.

40 HC, March 30, 1780.

41 Beresford to Robinson, December 13, 1779, *Beresford Corr.*, I, 112–118.

42 DEP, March 7, 1780.

43 DEP, March 14, 1780.

44 DEP, April 25, 28, 1780; Buckinghamshire to Hillsborough, April 24, 1780, SP 63/469, f. 120.

45 HJ, April 28, 1780; DEP, April 28, May 2, 1780.

46 FJ, June 10, 1780.

47 Heron to Porten, June 10, 1780, *Grattan Memoirs*, II, 102.

48 DEP, August 31, 1780.

49 DEP, October 19, 1780.

50 His correspondence shows that ill-health prevented him from taking any active part in Volunteer activities through the summer and autumn of 1779 (HMC, Charlemont Papers, I, 350 *et seq.*). In March, 1780, he was assured by his friend, Francis Dobbs, that his lack of knowledge of military matters need not deter him from reviewing the Volunteers (*Ibid.*, 371–72).

51 Buckinghamshire to Germain, October 24, 1779, HMC, Lothian Papers, pp. 357–58.

52 FJ, November 13, 1779.

53 DEP, May 30, 1780.

54 HC, September 7, 1780; DEP, September 14, 1780.

55 Beresford to Robinson, November 18, 1779, *Beresford Corr.*, I, 77–81; DEP, April 8, 25, 1780, June 29, 1780, July 1, 1780, December 21, 1780.

56 DEP, August 24, 1780.

57 FJ September 30, 1780.

58 January 9, 1781 (the letter was endorsed on the 7th), SP 63/474, ff. 20–21.

59 Eden to Charles Jenkinson, January 29, 1781, Add. Mss., 34417, ff. 306–309.

XI

Carlisle's Quiet Year

During the comparative quiet that followed the hectic spring and summer of 1780, the new viceroy arrived to take over from the exhausted Buckinghamshire. He was Frederick (Howard), fifth Earl of Carlisle, a member of the wealthiest English aristocracy. His home in Yorkshire, Castle Howard, was a Vanbrugh masterpiece and one of the greatest residences in England. The new lord-lieutenant had all the prestige of the higher *noblesse*.

Dublin loved a wealthy viceroy prepared to provide lavish entertainment and spectacle. Carlisle's reputation for generous spending had preceded him; it was reported in the press (erroneously) over a month before his arrival that the furnishings of Dublin Castle were to be renewed with those of Irish manufacture.[1] His early months seemed to fulfill expectations as his *levees* were considered "the most splendid and brilliant that for many years have been seen at the Castle." At one of his balls the "dresses of their Excellencies . . . are all of Irish manufacture and

cost upwards of five hundred pounds. A noble example!" [2]
Though he did entertain on a larger scale than Buckinghamshire, Carlisle was not so rich as he had been. When a
young man, he was a gambling friend of Charles James
Fox, and the experience had placed a strain on his financial
resources. In those days he had been a dandy, and one of
his more florid affectations was the wearing of red shoes,
for which he now suffered some teasing in the Irish newspapers. By the time he decided to enter politics, he had
developed a more serious turn of mind.

Unlike his predecessor he did not make the mistake of
bringing over as chief secretary a man of little account
like Heron. Instead, he appointed William Eden, the
younger son of an aristocratic family and a schoolfellow
of Fox and himself at Eton. An able barrister before
entering politics, Eden was widely regarded as a clever
negotiator and moved on intimate terms with influential
figures in England.

The Viceroy was considered very civil, but rigid and
taciturn to an extent that gave offence. Beresford wrote:
"Lord Carlisle is thought stiff and distant; Eden, they say,
does not drink enough." [3] Conolly found him well bred
and easy in his manner though "very slack in conversation." [4] The press compared his "formal and distant civil-
ity . . . to all the great people of the kingdom" with the
more diplomatic attitude of his three predecessors. [5] On
the alarm of an invasion in the following September, a
great many Volunteer corps offered their services; one
group felt annoyed when asked to sit down, but "not with
the ease that might be expected from a nobleman who the
world was taught to believe is the perfect model of a finished gentleman." [6] A correspondent in the *Dublin Evening Post* in March attacked Carlisle for being so secretive
that even his closest advisers did not know what he or his

Chief Secretary had in mind.[7] The same newspaper stated in July that since it is considered necessary for the Lord-Lieutenant to meet the approaching session of the Parliament "with a smile, it is whispered, that . . . [he] has been practising for some time past, to unbend the rigidity of his muscles. If he succeeds, we may truly exclaim 'Ars Praestantior Natura'." [8] That there was more than a little truth in these comments was virtually admitted by the Lord-Lieutenant in a humorous letter to his father-in-law, Lord Gower: "When the word reserve is made use of as applicable to my conduct, it commonly means I have not disclosed some secret which I should have real cause to repent of all my life. . . ." [9]

Carlisle's reputation for harboring secret thoughts was mild in comparison with that of his Chief Secretary. William Eden was considered a poor orator but adept at making parliamentary "arrangements." William Knox considered that he "possessed a most insinuating, gentle manner, which cover'd a deeply intriguing and ambitious spirit." [10] William Wraxall thought him handsome and polite, but having in his "physiognomy, even in his manner and deportment, something which did not convey the impression of plain dealing, or inspire confidence." [11] In January, 1781, the *Dublin Evening Post* summed up the opinion of both men with the statement that Carlisle's aloofness was atoned for by Eden with "one hundred and two smiles, fifty-six broad grins, twenty-one sallies of wit, and fourteen anecdotes." [12]

Arriving in a country which had just been the scene of so many political difficulties, the Viceroy and Chief Secretary were under no illusions as to the trials that lay ahead. They were relieved to find, however, that the upper classes had been rendered uneasy by the disposition to radicalism, and were now ready to support strong government. Their statements on this aspect of Irish affairs have been quoted in the previous chapter. Their views, which coincide in essentials, place too much stress on the members of parliament and, despite the lessons of the previous year, not enough on the position outside the legislature. In February Eden informed his friend, Lord Loughborough:

Our public situation here continues as prosperous and as promising as the general state of the Empire can possibly admit. The Kingdom in general is well disposed towards us so far as we have hitherto been conversant among the principal people, and so far as we can judge from the public prints, the most violent of which now venture to give as fair an attention to Government as can in reason be desired.

In the same letter Eden expressed his entire satisfaction with the conduct of Carlisle, who was "more active, more punctual, and more discreet than any man of rank that I have ever known." [13] He was scarcely making due allowance for the fact that when a new administration entered office, the newspapers usually held their peace until they had taken the measure of the new policies. A few weeks later he referred to "our still-water system of politics" and added that "we are all quiet in this kingdom, and apparently well disposed to continue so." [14] In July he considered that unless constitutional issues should provoke excitement, it seemed as if the coming session of parliament would quietly concern itself with "the extension of commerce and the improvement of police." [15] Carlisle informed Lord Gower, in the letter of June 30 (to which reference has already been made) that matters continued quietly, though his words show that he was not as complacent as Eden in regard to possible difficulties which might arise when the Parliament would meet in October.

Beresford was satisfied with the political outlook, praising the ability and firmness of the Administration which was winning back many waverers to a steady support.[16] The Attorney-General, Scott, enjoyed the close friendship of both Carlisle and Eden.[17]

Beresford and Scott, as was shown in 1779, were not the best judges of political situations. They were still too much inclined to see "management" as the way to govern Ireland, and too little able to appreciate the strength of the forces outside parliament as well as the effect of the war. Consequently, it is not surprising that a Viceroy and Chief Secretary with whom Scott was so closely linked should have thought too much in traditional terms. They were not as fully aware of the precarious state of affairs as Buckinghamshire had been when he warned Hillsborough in the previous year: "No retrospective knowledge of Ireland can enable any man to form a judgment of the present situation." [18]

Much bitterness was expressed over the weakness of the Parliament in the summer of 1780, and energetic action was deemed necessary if it were to again play the "patriotic" role of the days of the Free Trade crisis. From the end of 1780 till late in 1781 the editorial and correspondence columns of the press paid great attention to the need to instruct parliamentary representatives at elections. Along with this went demands for a reform of the electoral system and the abolition of "rotten" boroughs. Admittedly, these expressions of discontent were more a matter of public opinion than practical attempts at reform. There had been discussion of this kind in previous years, but then it was harmless; in the more dynamic atmosphere of Ireland after the Free Trade agitation, criticism of the political system had an explosive potential.

A more substantial reason why Carlisle and Eden and

their advisers should have been less complacent was the growth in strength of the Volunteers. Though the numbers reported as taking part in the widespread manoeuvres of 1781 were probably exaggerated, the newspapers stressed their belief that they greatly exceeded those present at parades in previous years.[19] Beresford's satisfaction with the course of political events was all the more surprising since he witnessed this growth:

The spirit of volunteering is increasing every day and has now forced almost every gentleman to take a part, you may see by the newspapers that they avow themselves, the great Reformers of our Political Constitution, and in consequence of their intermeddling in politics, every man is attempting to turn them to his purposes, in the several counties, citys and boroughs, this drives us all to become Volunteers, and very much increases their numbers.[20]

As part of the increasing importance of the Volunteer movement in 1781, there was a remarkable rise in the number of Catholics. In January, for example, a corps was raised in Clonmel who were "mostly Catholics." [21] This increase in their numbers was shown up by two resolutions objecting to their recruitment: one in July by a county meeting in Meath, and the other in October by a gathering of the commanding-officers of several corps in Co. Wexford convened by George Ogle, their commander-in-chief.[22] The Meath resolution led to a series of protests in the newspapers. The *Dublin Evening Post* suspected it as a deliberate attempt to stir up enmity within the Volunteers; a writer in the same paper detected ministerial corruption, and added that in Munster and Connaught two thirds of the men were Catholics.[23] The *Freeman's Journal* reported that an alarm had gone abroad that an effort was being made to sow hostility between Catholic and Pro-

testant corps.[24] In November a correspondent in the same
newspaper attacked the Wexford Volunteer officers for
having stated that the existence of Catholic corps gave
rise to jealousies and disputes. He argued that corps composed of Catholics had been incorporated in most parts of
the country.[25] In December this paper praised the loyalty
of the members of that religion "who compose a great part
of our Volunteer army." [26] In the journalistic polemics of
the time, one must allow for a substantial amount of
exaggeration. The statement that two thirds of the Volunteers in Munster and Connaught were Catholics can be
written off to a vivid imagination. Had such borne a
resemblance to the truth, an "alarm" certainly *would*
have gone abroad.

A diversion occurred in early September, 1781, when a
large combined fleet of French and Spanish ships had been
sighted off the Scilly Isles and was believed to be making
for the Irish coast in the neighbourhood of Cork. The
country was alerted and dozens of Volunteer corps offered
their services to the Government. Carlisle gave a very
guarded reply, taking care not to give any formal recognition to the Volunteers, but merely thanking them as individuals. This refusal of recognition was heartily approved by London,[27] but provoked indignation in the
Irish press.[28] Carlisle's plan to employ the Volunteers in
the event of invasion is worthy of quotation:

At present it is my intention . . . to employ the Volunteer
corps both in detached services and in the protection of those
parts of the kingdom from which the military shall have
been withdrawn, which might otherwise be left exposed to
the ravages of the lower class of the people, too liable at all
times, and more especially in a time of confusion, to be
tempted to acts of violence and plunder.[29]

As the threatened invasion did not materialize, the Viceroy's plan was not put to the test.

The first major trial for the Government came with the opening of parliament in October, 1781. Carlisle sent a long letter to London mentioning issues likely to be raised, how he regarded them, and asking for instructions.[30] He believed he could divert any strictly constitutional questions, though he added the qualification, based on the experience of his predecessors, that the "pursuit of popular applause will occasionally lead individuals of this country beyond their better judgment and cooler professions." In order to combat a declaratory resolution he felt that policy must be adapted to circumstances since instructions sent beforehand by London might not be suitable. He saw no difficulty in defeating any attempted repeal of the perpetual Irish Mutiny Act, but was not so sure about the complicated matter of a repeal of Poyning's Law. He saw little point in opposing bills for Habeas Corpus and the appointment of judges on good behavior, since the administration of justice, in practice, recognized both. The duty on the import of refined sugars would again be raised, because in England the position had changed.

In reply, Hillsborough directed Carlisle to oppose in one way or another all constitutional questions, particularly any attempt to pass a declaratory resolution. Similarly, a repeal of the Irish Mutiny Act or of Poyning's Law would be inadmissible. The appointment of judges on good behavior should not be countenanced, since the Irish Commons on a previous occasion did not agree to a suspending clause. He enclosed North's opinion that Ireland should be allowed to adjust its sugar duties so as to bring them into line with the new arrangements in Britain.[31]

In his letter of September 15 the Lord-Lieutenant maintained that it was almost certain that the Parliament would applaud the Volunteers. Therefore, he considered it wise that the Government should praise their meritorious conduct on the recent alarm of invasion. "However unconstitutional and dangerous so large an armed force not raised under the King's authority may be," they existed in great numbers and possessed arms given them by the state.[32] In a second letter he again pleaded for this step so that the Administration might not lose their good opinion:

So long as those corps are commanded by noblemen and gentlemen of known attachment to Government, they cannot furnish subjects of apprehension; and so long as their loyalty is cherished and kept warm, the lower ranks will not withdraw themselves from commanders of a like disposition.[33]

Carlisle's pleas were in vain. The British Cabinet decided that no recognition whatever be accorded.[34]

On the whole the parliamentary session proceeded fairly quietly. The Speech from the Throne and the customary addresses passed without much difficulty. Grattan protested that the Speech thanking the Volunteers for their offers of help in September made no reference to them other than as private persons, and extended no recognition to them as Volunteers.[35] As in 1779 each House passed a vote of thanks to that force. Carlisle let it be known that the Administration would not oppose the vote. He felt that this gesture had been useful and was pleased with the opening of the session.[36]

The Patriots were interested in five measures: Habeas Corpus, the appointment of judges on good behaviour, the repeal of the Irish Mutiny Act and Poyning's Law, and a declaratory resolution designed to undo the British

Declaratory Act of 1719. Only the first, a habeas corpus act, was passed during the viceroyalty of Carlisle. It was introduced by Bradstreet, who accepted Eden's proposal to give a suspending power to Dublin Castle in times of emergency.[37] In this form it was acceptable to all, and received the royal assent on February 12, 1782.[38] This was one of those measures sought by the Patriots as a constitutional symbol, rather than for its practical value, since it was already part of the custom of the country; neither radical newspaper nor Patriot ever suggested otherwise.

The measure that had caused the greatest indignation in 1780 was the perpetual Mutiny Act and its repeal was eagerly sought. On November 13, 1781, Grattan moved for leave to have it amended, but after a very long debate he was voted down by 133 to 77. The discussion was not of any great interest, but Grattan's speech showed the extent to which his political outlook had changed since the days he so bitterly opposed the Catholic Relief Bill in 1778:

The new world had overturned the prejudices of the old; and the modern philosophy had made men look upon another as Brethren—not as Enemies—The Protestant of Ireland was the child of the Revolution [of 1688], and the Presbyterian the Father. The Roman Catholics . . . as loyal as any body of men in the British Dominions.[39]

Yelverton had arranged to move for the partial repeal of Poyning's Law but deferred action when news arrived of the surrender at Yorktown. Instead, on December 4, he moved for an address of loyalty and support in the struggle against the enemies of the British Empire. The motion was passed by the enormous majority of 167 to 37, and on the following day was adopted by both Houses. His motion was opposed by Grattan, Ogle, Brownlow,

Flood, Robert Stewart, and John Forbes. Their main objection was that the address was framed in a manner likely to encourage the war against the colonists. Yelverton replied that he had always reprobated that war and that the address had no such implication.[40] On reading it, one is inclined to agree with him.

Needless to say, Dublin Castle was jubilant over the success of Yelverton's address. Eden wrote:

[Yelverton] is a well meaning man, of strong understanding and generous feelings; personal[ly] kind towards me; but decidedly opposed in his general system to every possible administration. The rest of the Opposition were absurd enough to attack him on this occasion, and this made curious schism. My new associates Messrs. Daly, Bushe, Fitzgibbon, G. Ponsonby etc. all supported. . . . The division with Government was the greatest known on our Journals.[41]

Carlisle expressed his delight:

Yesterday was a day of singular triumph to administration, not resulting from any temporary ministerial expedient, but from a prudent improvement of public spirit, and unaffected zeal, which sprung up in a soil beyond the pale of ministerial interference, at least of any interference, but that which required the most delicate and nice management.[42]

On December 18 Yelverton moved his postponed motion for the better transmission of heads of bills to England. This meant depriving the viceroy and the Irish privy Council of the right to alter or veto these heads. Yelverton explained that the power was derived from an act of the reign of Philip and Mary and not from that of Henry VII. Flood opposed him on the ground that no such right existed. Hussey Burgh and David Walshe supported Flood, but the motion was committed without a division.[43]

In asking for instructions from London when transmitting the heads, Carlisle said he would be able to defeat the measure, but felt it was a just one.[44] London was not impressed, and as a consequence Scott had the measure defeated by procuring its committal to April 8 when the Commons would be in recess for the Spring Assizes.[45] Probably because of this hostility on the part of the government, Yelverton reintroduced the subject on March 2, but in a manner relating directly to Poyning's Law.[46] He was probably influenced by the excitement generated by the great Volunteer meeting at Dungannon in the middle of February. Permission to enter the motion was granted. In May, after the change to the Whig administration, Yelverton withdrew this measure for the purpose of framing an entirely new one.

The sugar duties, which had caused so much difficulty in 1780, required alteration because of a change in the British customs concerning that commodity. Again, they produced much hostility and anxiety, and provided Flood with an opportunity for a bitter attack on the British Government. Nevertheless, they were passed by a comfortable majority.[47]

On February 22, 1782, Grattan moved a declaratory resolution similar to that of 1780 but with even less success. His speech was described by the Lord-Lieutenant as lasting two hours and "calculated to excite popular heat and resentment." [48] As in 1780 the supporters of the Administration based their case on the inexpediency of the motion, but again stated that Ireland was not bound by British acts. The exception was the hardy Scott who made the very indiscreet assertion that "power is right." [49] In the ensuing months the Volunteers did not allow him to forget it. The debate did not reach the heights attained by that of 1780, and it aroused little public attention. This was not surprising since it was obviously intended as a gesture: the safe government majorities made any hope of success illusory. Grattan had been supported by Brownlow, Hussey Burgh, Forbes, Ogle, Flood, Yelverton, and the moderate Sir Lucius O'Brien. By early 1782 Carlisle was no longer fooled by purely parliamentary victories and expressed his pessimism to Hillsborough:

The principle of Ireland not being bound by the Laws of another Legislature is universally insisted upon with that enthusiasm and steady determination, which leave no reason to imagine it will be abandoned. It has been spread with such industry that every rank and order . . . are possessed of it. . . . The position is serious.[50]

It was high time that Carlisle should have arrived at the decision that his parliamentary victories were fast becoming paper ones, if not actual liabilities, since they advertised the gulf existing between legislature and opinion at large. Judging by the political situation in the latter half of 1780, and by his and Eden's assessment of it after their arrival in Dublin, it was obvious that they would be likely to procure large majorities in parliament. They knew of the disturbed state of public opinion, the menace of the Volunteers, and the danger of a situation in which members of parliament could be unduly influenced by a desire for popularity. Yet, their optimism during 1781 suggests that they had not taken these considerations fully to heart.

From the start of the session in October 1781, they applied themselves to winning over members to the support of government. On November 10 the Lord-Lieutenant informed London that efforts to establish a long-term system of support had succeeded beyond his fondest expectations: Daly, Fitzgibbon, Bushe, the Ponsonby interest, and the Earl of Donegall's following, excepting Yelverton, had been won over. Even Hussey Burgh was adopting a conciliatory attitude.[51] Brownlow, who had shown a leaning towards Dublin Castle in 1780, was considered by Hillsborough in March, 1781, as "well inclined to support Government." [52] Eden was equally satisfied with the Government's growing power, which he considered extended even beyond parliament. He regretted that their policy "exposes His Excellency and me to a large list of claims and pretensions. God knows how we are to satisfy them." [53]

In January Carlisle had pleased Conolly by appointing Dean Woodward of Clogher to the bishopric of Cloyne, a promotion recommended by Buckinghamshire. The late viceroy had also recommended a protégé of the Duke of Leinster for the likely vacancy in the deanery of Clogher, and Carlisle procured this favor. He obtained the bishopric of Killala for the brother of Speaker Pery. Consequently, he felt, and with reason, that all three would give his administration every support.[54]

Shortly before the end of 1780, the previous Administration had bought the rather uncertain support of the radically antigovernment *Freeman's Journal* with a secret service pension of £50.[55] Eden regretted that almost the entire secret service fund was allocated to other (and impersonal) objects. He thought that the Administration could be considerably strengthened by a reasonable supply of money for secret purposes, and had a plan whereby this amount might be obtained.[56] The outstanding newspaper of these years was the *Dublin Evening Post*, the property of the very able John Magee. From its inception in 1778 it was the most interesting of the journals, with the best news coverage and largest format. In January,

1781, it claimed that its circulation of 3,000 was the biggest in the country, and the claim was not contested. Its owner being a Protestant, it opposed the Catholic Relief Act of 1778 but later changed to the support of Catholic demands. The most surprising aspects of journalism in this period is the freedom which it enjoyed in its criticism —sometimes scurrilous abuse—of the Government and its members. The *Dublin Evening Post* suggested on one occasion that George III and Lord North were illegitimately related, and one could scarcely indulge the "freedom of the press" to a greater extent than that.[57]

In other ways the reader is puzzled by the press of those days. Bawdy descriptions of crime are sometimes published in the same column as denunciations that combine outraged decency with extreme prudery. The outstanding example of this kind of condemnation occurs in the *Hibernian Journal* of May 16, 1781:

An elegant Writer speaking of the Licentiousness of the Manners of France and Italy, gives us for a capital instance of Obscenity that at a Picture-shop in Verona, he was ushered into a ninner Apartment to view naked Figures painted from Life, which were actually exhibited there for Sale. Were the above Gentleman transported for a Moment within the Pale of this Metropolis, infinitely would he allow it to excell all others in every vicious Impropriety and Indecorum. The Species of Obscenity particularly, which he exposes with such just Abhorrence; who can deny that we have not amended and refined upon. While *our* Print-shops are publickly displaying the human Form of either Sex represented in the most bare-faced and inflammatory Attitudes, do not our very Streets make daily Expositions of the NAKED LIFE ITSELF!— The Quays, the most beautiful and populous Avenues of this City, are, (to the inveterate dishonour of her Guardians) infested continuously on each returning Summer Season with

stark naked Fellows of *all Ages*, who are suffered to strip and
bathe under our very Eyes, a circumstance, surely, which cannot fail of being recited, and heard with Disgust abroad, and
which must, at home, be high Treason to Delacacy and
Modesty, if either can exist where the Odious Practice has
so long met with Tolerance.

The most striking event of 1781 was the public and
unequivocal return of Henry Flood to the ranks of the
Patriots and his consequent dismissal from his office as
a Vice-Treasurer. In the summer Carlisle wrote that Flood
resented being expected to behave like a true servant of
the Crown.[58] In fact, he was treated with studied coolness
by the Lord-Lieutenant and Chief Secretary, the latter
even expressing the opinion that he should have been
dismissed by Buckinghamshire.[59] In November Flood
"threw away the scabbard completely," entering belligerently into every important parliamentary debate and sub-
jecting the Government to the most slashing attacks. Carlisle gladly recommended his removal and the appointment of Lord Shannon in his place. North and the King
readily agreed, the latter even suggesting that he also be
removed from the Irish Privy Council.[60]

Henry Flood was a man who stood alone in the political
Ireland of his day. Proud, imperious, truculent, and impatient, this ambitious man had undergone the chagrin
of seeing his reputation decline during his sojourn in
office since 1775. On critical occasions, as in the Free
Trade debates in 1779, he had been anything but a loyal
servant of the Crown, and it was only the desperate condition of the Administration which prevented his dismissal. Of independent means, he could afford to resign
whenever he chose, and the autumn of 1781 was a suitable
time to provoke the Administration into ejecting him.

The Parliament lay docile, so that his support was not needed and his hostility not feared. The country was full of smouldering discontent, and the Volunteers were organized to an extent not known before. It was a golden opportunity for a rabble-rouser to enter the fray and Flood was just the man. While Grattan spoke in classical phrases and a style so deliberate and polished as sometimes to err on the artificial, Flood's oratory was direct, clipped, and delivered when he wished, with the most bare-faced insolence. A parliamentary audience might be swayed by Grattan but just as easily alienated by Flood; he spoke too often and too bluntly, but his style was exactly what would appeal to the discontented outside parliament. These included Volunteer officers and delegates, mostly educated men, but unaccustomed to great oratory. In their indignation they would hope for fireworks, and Flood could give them all they wanted.

The radical newspapers accepted Flood back into favor as soon as they were convinced that he was the enemy of the Administration. Charlemont was delighted with his return to the Patriot fold, and, in consequence, summed up the political situation:

. . . a strong people—a weak minority—weak, I mean, in numbers, but in abilities transcendent—weak in proportion to the promise of last session, but very strong in comparison with former minorities. . . . Flood, whose incomparable conduct stands unrivalled . . . more able than ever.[61]

A few weeks later Charlemont wrote:

Our sun [Flood] has broke out from the clouds with redoubled lustre. His unparalleled conduct would scarcely be believed but by us who know the man . . . Yet Grattan still shines with unabated brightness.[62]

Two men of great ability were now competing for the popular leadership—Grattan and Flood. It was unlikely that the two could be friends since they were so different in character and temperament—Grattan younger and more sensitive, Flood imperious and blunt. The former had won his laurels through an undeviating loyalty to the Patriots' cause, the latter had abandoned this same cause. His motives in crossing to the Government's side in 1775 had been free from anything obviously base though undoubtedly influenced by impatience and ambition. Whatever his reasons, his action had stained his political record, so that he would always be vulnerable to abusive attack. Charlemont saw his return to the "minority" as a great increase in strength, but failed to realize that it might mean a clash with Grattan, and thus a rift in the Patriot movement.

NOTES FOR CHAPTER XI

1 DEP, November 9, 1780.

2 FJ, January 23, 1781; FJ, February 20, 1781.

3 Beresford to Allan, January 26, 1781, *Beresford Corr.*, I, 155–56.

4 Conolly to Buckinghamshire, January 13, 1781, HMC, Lothian Papers, pp. 380–81.

5 DEP, January 23, 1781.

6 DEP, September 15, 1781.

7 DEP, March 27, 1781.

8 DEP, July 17, 1781.

9 June 30, 1781, HMC, Carlisle Papers, pp. 509–511.

10 HMC, Knox Papers, pp. 265–66.

11 Quoted in G.E.C., *The Complete Peerage* (London, 1910), I, 334.

12 DEP, January 25, 1781.

13 Eden to Loughborough, February 24, 1781, Add Mss. 34418, ff. 333–34.

14 Eden to Germain, March 10, 1781, HMC, Stopford-Sackville Papers, I, 278–79.

15 Eden to Loughborough, July 11, 1781, Add. Mss. ff. 377–78.

16 Beresford to Jenkinson, July 15, 1781, Add. Mss. 38216, ff. 279–80.

17 Eden to Knox, March 11, 1781, HMC, Misc. 6, p. 239; Carlisle to Gower, June 30, 1781, HMC, Carlisle Papers, pp. 509–511.

18 Buckinghamshire to Hillsborough, February 9, 1780, SP 63/468, ff. 205–208.

19 In a letter to Buckinghamshire on the manoeuvres in Phoenix Park, Dublin, Lt.-Col. Vyse estimated the number as about half of that stated by the newspapers but described them as "well appointed and armed," (June 6, 1781, HMC, Lothian Papers, pp. 389–99).

20 Beresford to Jenkinson, July 15, 1781, Add Mss. 38216, ff. 279–80.

21 Basil M. O'Connell, "The Nagles of Garnavilla," *The Irish Genealogist* (July, 1956), p. 3.

22 DEP, July 5, 1781; DEP, October 23, 1781.

23 DEP, July 7, 17, 1781.

24 FJ, July 10, 1781.

25 FJ, November 22, 1781.

26 FJ, December 1, 1781.

27 Hillsborough to Carlisle, September 15, 1781, SP 63/476, ff. 71–72.

28 DEP, September 15, 1781.

29 Carlisle to Hillsborough, September 8, 1781, SP 63/476, ff. 61–62.

30 Carlisle to Hillsborough, September 15, 1781, Add. Mss. 34418, ff. 103–106.

31 Hillsborough to Carlisle, September 29, 1781, SP 63/476, ff. 180–83; North to Hillsborough, September 28, 1781, SP 63/476, ff. 185–86.

32 Carlisle to Hillsborough, September 15, 1781, Add. Mss. 34418, ff. 103–106.

33 Carlisle to Hillsborough, September 24, 1781, SP 63/476, ff. 174–75.

34 Hillsborough to Carlisle, September 29, 1781, SP 63/476, ff. 187–88.

35 HJ, October 10, 1781.

36 Carlisle to Hillsborough, October 10, 1781, SP 63/476, ff. 227–28.

37 HJ, November 5, 1781.

38 Carlisle to Hillsborough, December 29, 1781, SP 63/480 f. 8; Hillsborough to Carlisle, January 24, 1782, SP 63/480, ff. 84–89.

39 HJ, November 14, 1781.

40 HJ, December 5, 7, 1781.

41 Eden to Loughborough, December 5, 1781, Add. Mss. 34418, f. 203.

42 Carlisle to Hillsborough, December 5, 1781, SP 63/477, f. 159

43 HJ, December 19, 1781.

44 Carlisle to Hillsborough, December 29, 1781, SP 63/480, ff. 14–15, 16.

45 HJ, March 1, 1781.

46 HJ, March 4, 1781.

47 HJ, November 26, 1781; Eden to Loughborough, November 23, 24, 1781, Add. Mss. 34418, ff. 184, 187.

48 Carlisle to Hillsborough, February 23, 1782, SP 63/480, ff. 247–48.

49 HJ, February 25, 1782; Carlisle to Hillsborough, February 23, 1782, SP 63/480, ff. 247–48.

50 Carlisle to Hillsborough, February 23, 1782, SP 63/480, ff. 247–48, 249–50.

51 Carlisle to Hillsborough, SP 63/477, ff. 76–77.

52 Hillsborough to Eden, March 21, 1781, Add. Mss. 34417, ff. 325–26.

53 Eden to North, November 23, 1781, Add. Mss. 34418, ff. 182–83.

54 Carlisle to Hillsborough, January 7 (two letters), SP 63/474, ff. 18–19, 22: Hillsborough to Carlisle, January 20, 1781 (two letters), ff. 28, 30.

55 Heron to Eden, January 9, 1781, Add. Mss. 34417, f. 293.

56 Eden to Hillsborough, July 15, 1781, SP 63/475, ff. 98–99.

57 DEP, June 26, 1779.

58 Carlisle to Lord Gower, June 30, 1781, HMC, Carlisle Papers, pp. 509–511.

59 Edward Tighe to Buckinghamshire, July 31, 1781, HMC, Lothian Papers, pp. 390–91.

60 Carlisle to Hillsborough, November 2, SP 63/477, ff. 37–39; North to George III, November 10, 1781, ed. J. Fortescue, Corr. of Geo. III, V, 298; George III to North, November 10, 1781, ed. J. Fortescue, *Corr. of Geo.* III, V, 299.

61 Charlemont to Edmund Malone, December 17, 1781, HMC, Charlemont Papers, I, 390–91.

62 To Malone, January 2, 1782, HMC, Charlemont Papers, I, 378–79. The publication erroneously dates the letter 1781.

XII

The Revolution of 1782

The Government and the Parliament had failed to take sufficiently into account the significance of the intense activity of the Volunteers in 1781. Their manoeuvres could scarcely fail to stir up radical feeling and indignation with a legislature which continually gave sweeping majorities to unpopular measures. The chickens were coming home to roost, and the "system" built up by Carlisle and Eden at such expense was now about to turn to ashes in their hands.

The fuse for the great explosion was lit at Armagh on December 28, 1781, when the delegates of eleven corps comprising the Southern Battalion of the First Ulster Regiment agreed unanimously:

That with the utmost concern, we behold the little attention paid to the constitutional rights of this Kingdom, by the majority of those whose duty it is to establish and preserve the same.

319

That to avert the impending danger from the nation, and to restore the Constitution to its original purity, the most vigorous and effectual methods must be pursued, to root corruption and Court Influence from the Legislative Body.

The meeting decided that every Volunteer corps in Ulster be invited to send delegates to a provincial meeting in Dungannon on February 15 to consider the alarming state of affairs.[1]

Nothing so radical had been heard from any Volunteer body since the fiery resolutions passed by the three Dublin corps in August, 1780. Those now agreed upon at Armagh were more deliberate, more moderate, less open to the charge of sedition, and, therefore, more dangerous.

The Armagh meeting was not seen by the Administration as anything more than just another difficulty to be surmounted. Eden informed Hillsborough who, to his credit, took a more serious view;[2] his estate lay in Co. Down, and consequently he probably had a better understanding of the north of Ireland than most officials in Dublin Castle. Even as late as early February Eden considered "the Dungannon Business seems to give alarm in England: it will I believe take a very useful turn: I have some most respectable and weighty friends' attention to check it."[3] It is but to do justice to Carlisle and Eden, however, to remember that Charlemont failed to realize the radical nature of what was happening. He was commander of the very group in Armagh who had passed these resolutions, and should have been fully cognizant of their feeling and intentions; yet his correspondence shows that his early information on the proposed Dungannon meeting was incomplete, and that he did not anticipate its extraordinary importance.[4]

Francis Dobbs, a member of parliament and an officer

in the Battalion which had met at Armagh, came south to Dublin to confer with Charlemont. Suggestions for an agenda for the meeting at Dungannon were discussed at a conference which was also attended by Grattan, Flood, and James Stewart, M.P. for Co. Tyrone. It was decided to suggest several resolutions on constitutional matters and one praising the Patriots for their conduct in parliament. In addition, Grattan arranged that a motion applauding Catholic relief be included.[5]

On February 15 the great meeting was held. It concerned itself primarily with constitutional issues. The assembly resolved that the perpetual Irish Mutiny Act be repealed, that legislative independence be obtained, and that judges be appointed on good behaviour. With eleven dissentients it was agreed that support at election be given only to candidates willing to promote these measures. The meeting also resolved that Volunteers had the right to debate political affairs. In regard to Catholic relief, it was agreed that "we hold the right of private judgment in matters of Religion to be equally sacred in others as in ourselves," and "as men and as Irishmen, as Christians and as Protestants, we rejoice in the relaxation of the Penal Laws against our Roman Catholic fellow-subjects."

One of the most prominent Presbyterian ministers in Ulster, the Rev. Robert Black, stated:

I rejoice to hear a motion . . . in favor of our Roman Catholic brethren; Sir, I am proud to second it as a Protestant Dissenting clergyman; . . . as an Irish Independent Volunteer. . . . The Roman Catholics of Ireland have eradicated . . . those bigoted and superstitious notions.

The delegates then elected a committee of 32 from their number to act for the province of Ulster; this com-

mittee was instructed to elect nine of its members to combine with nine from each of the other provinces to form
a central body in Dublin.[6]

Carlisle forwarded to Hillsborough a description of the
meeting by one of the delegates present, Roger Bristow,
the Port Surveyor at Newry. He had tried to prevent his
corps from sending any representative to Dungannon but
failed, and was then himself nominated (it was quite characteristic of the Volunteers to send a delegate who was
privately opposed to the very purposes which he was
expected to pursue—the rank and file had not yet
achieved the experience and self-confidence for leadership). He stated that Dobbs had opened the assembly with
"a very artful speech" and proposed at least nine resolutions. Bristow had denied the right of Volunteers to talk
on political matters but found to his astonishment that he
was in a minority of one. His account tallies with that of
Dobbs and the official insertion in the press, even though
he had to leave before the end. He concluded that the
meeting would not produce any alarming result because
no definite plan had been adopted for implementing the
resolutions.[7] Time was to show how mistaken he was.

Charlemont was delighted with the turn which affairs
had taken. He considered that the resolutions had been
"so proper, and have met with such universal applause,
that . . . they will be universally acceded to. . . . Their
influence and their adoption are . . . already spread far
and wide."[8] The Bishop of Cloyne, Dr. Woodward, was
alarmed and sent his friend, Buckinghamshire, the press
account of the meeting:

The few I have heard mention it [the account] think it calm
and moderate. For myself, I like it the less for that reason.
If it had more of violence and passion, I should fear it less.

It partakes the coolness of my late acquaintance, Dr. Franklin, and I am persuaded was not penned at Dungannon. The resolutions relative to Papists never originated there; but any allies are welcome to strengthen the party.[9]

Conolly was equally dismayed and informed Buckinghamshire that the extravagant dispensing of patronage by Carlisle's government "has not produced a better effect with the Nation, the Parliament, and the Volunteers than the more honourable and economical system adopted by yourself." [10]

By early March Carlisle had at long last come to see that parliamentary majorities were useless and even damaging to the prestige of government. On March 3 he wrote bluntly to Hillsborough:

I must beg now leave to draw your Lordship's attention beyond the mere consideration of a Parliamentary Triumph, which may indeed afford exulting matter for repeated dispatches, but which, if made the sole object of attention, may ultimately be productive of very serious and calamitous consequences.

He now saw the fool's paradise which the Government had been living in while the Volunteers had been gathering their strength:

The restless and reasoning disposition of the Volunteers . . . which undoubtedly do not fall short of thirty thousand men actually in arms, and in the practice of frequent meetings and distant correspondencies with each other.[11]

He referred in his letter to "the resentments excited by the uniform success of my government," and considered that further parliamentary victories would merely expose the supporters of the Government to loss of popularity and, more important, to the danger of being expelled from the Volunteers. Ironically, on the very day before this letter was penned, Irvine, the Commander-in-Chief of the army in Ireland, wrote from London to Eden:

The King, the Ministers, and indeed all the World give you full credit for your management of the Publick affairs in Ireland, you by your ability and firmness have brought about, what they had lost even the shadow of till you went amongst them, I mean an Established Government upon English principles.[12]

And then, following immediately on the Dungannon assembly, there occurred that bursting into flame of months of smouldering anger and its spread throughout the country like a forest blaze. It was one of those explosions which can be explained by hindsight, but not fully foreseen because emotion and timing are of its essence.

In the succeeding two months innumerable Volunteer corps, counties, towns, and grand juries held meetings in support of some or all of the Dungannon Resolutions. Their insertions crowded the columns of the press, particularly the *Dublin Evening Post*. Many of these meetings entered fully into the decisions of Dungannon, but others limited themselves to a demand for legislative independence or, at least, omitted the more radical topics. Some went even further and bluntly maintained that members of parliament were the representatives of, and derived their sole power from, the people. The radical meetings were different from those merely forced by public indignation into going with the tide. Their concurrence was a proof of the success of Dungannon. When the locally omnipotent Beresford family was unable to prevent the Grand Jury of Co. Waterford and the county meeting from passing (admittedly moderate) resolutions, the game was up so far as Dublin Castle was concerned. Humiliation was complete when Lord Tyrone, the head of the Beresfords, allowed his own Volunteer corps, the Curraghmore Rangers, to join the merry throng. Carlisle informed Hillsborough that the failure of the Beresfords was the final proof of the enormous strength of the demand for legislative independence.[13]

In the middle of March Eden spoke as plainly to London as Carlisle had done two weeks previously:

The whole is a dispute about words, for as to real power in the English Parliament over this country, the idea is as idle as it wd. be to carry the [River] Liffey over the Wicklow hills. . . . Nothing can happen to discompose me, because I always ride at present in a check rein; but I could be angry.[14]

By this time the London Government had become conscious of the dangerous state of Ireland, and Hillsborough exhibited its anxiety:

Your cursed Volunteers, and Patriots have alarmed us here very much and the more so, as I fear Yelverton's [partial repeal of Poyning's Law] bill can not be returned for . . . [the Cabinet] would expose themselves to criminal imputation if they were to pass it without an act of Parliament here to authorize them. . . . That infamous Franklin by his agents is certainly attempting mischief in Ireland.[15]

The situation was entirely changed by the fall of Lord North's Government on March 20 and its replacement by a Whig ministry. During the first eight days of March, attempts had been made to form a coalition with the Whigs but to still preserve the Tory aspect of the Admin-

istration, and it was not until March 14 that the idea of a
coalition was abandoned. Finally, on March 20 the King
was induced to appoint a Whig government, and North
resigned.[16] This Irish "Revolution of 1782"[17] seems to
have originated in purely Irish circumstances but its development owed a great deal to the major change in the
British political situation.

The Whigs came into power under the premiership of
the Marquis of Rockingham as First Lord of the Treasury. Lord Shelburne joined the Cabinet as Secretary of
State for Home and Colonial Affairs, and thus the minister responsible for Ireland. Charles James Fox became
Secretary for Foreign Affairs. At the beginning of April
the Duke of Portland, head of one of the great Whig
families, was appointed to succeed Carlisle. The successor
to Eden as Chief Secretary was Richard Fitzpatrick, a
brother of the Irish absentee landlord, the Earl of Upper
Ossory. Portland was instructed by the new Whig Cabinet
to obtain an adjournment of the Irish Parliament until a
policy on the constitutional problems could be worked
out.[18] The new incumbents rushed across the Irish Sea
in order to anticipate the reopening of the legislature
scheduled for April 16.

The new Viceroy found the country much more disturbed than he had expected, and realized there was no
hope of procuring an adjournment. He then tried to have
Grattan postpone his declaratory resolution which had
been announced for the first day of the session. The Irish
leader would agree only if the Administration would give
explicit guarantees that the various constitutional aims of
the Patriots would be conceded. To such an all-embrac-
ing demand Portland could naturally not agree, and he
just had to let matters take their course. Miserably, he
commented on the "absolute submission which is paid to

them [the Volunteers] by every rank and order of men,"
and described Grattan as their spokesman.[19] The Whigs
were now to pay the price of using Irish grievances as a
stick with which to beat Lord North.

On the reopening of the session on April 16, Portland
presented the Speech from the Throne which amounted
to an admission that the British Government intended to
make concessions. It asked the legislature to take into
account the "discontents and jealousies prevailing" in
Ireland in order to obtain a "final adjustment as may give
mutual satisfaction" to both kingdoms. An address of
thanks was immediately moved by a supporter of the
Administration, to which Grattan added by way of amendment a declaration of rights and grievances which passed
nem. con. In his speech he compared Ireland with the
Colonies: "For acknowledging American liberty, England
has the plea of necessity; for acknowledging the liberties
of Ireland she has the plea of justice." He listed the major
constitutional aims of the Patriots as the repeal of the
1719 Declaratory Act, the repeal of Poyning's Law and of
the (perpetual) Irish Mutiny Act of 1780. In addition, he
demanded that the Irish House of Lords be recognized as
the final judicature for Ireland. In regard to Poyning's
Law he denounced the "unconstitutional power of the
Irish or English Privy Council." [20]

The part of Grattan's oration best remembered by later
generations exemplifies his rather artificial style and something of the vanity which often influenced his thinking.
One can realize how galling these words must have been
to the ambitious Henry Flood:

I found Ireland on her knees, I watched over her with an
eternal solicitude; I have traced her progress from injuries
to arms, and from arms to liberty. Spirit of Swift! spirit of

Molyneux! your genius has prevailed! Ireland is now a nation! in that new character I hail her! and bowing to her august presence, I say, *Esto perpetua!*

Continuing, he heaped praise on the national unity which had procured victory, but his words betrayed a subtle attempt to emphasize factors other than the Volunteers:

What was the cause [of our victory]? for it was not the word of the Volunteer, nor his muster, nor his spirit, nor his promptitude to put down . . . public disorder, nor his own unblamed and distinguished deportment. This was much; but there was more than this: the upper orders, the property, and the abilities of the country, formed with the Volunteer; and the Volunteer had sense enough to obey them. This united the Protestant with the Catholic, and the landed proprietor with the people.

Then came the parliamentarian's fear of the existence of any strong military body not under legal control. To a eulogy of their services he added a most diplomatic request that they disband:

And now, having given a parliament to the people, the Volunteers will, I doubt not, leave the people to Parliament, and thus close, specifically and majestically, a great work, which will place them above censure and above panegyric. These great associations . . . will perish: they perish with the occasion that gave them being, and the gratitude of their country will write their epitaph.[21]

There was no question of a debate because no member dared oppose Grattan. With the whole country roused, and with the knowledge that the British Cabinet intended making concessions, it would have been madness for supporters of Dublin Castle to do anything but acquiesce.

Enraged by the paralysis of government in Ireland, and chagrined by the obvious consideration that the British Whigs had strengthened the Patriots in Dublin, Fitzpatrick commented bitterly:

Debate indeed it can hardly be called, since that implies a free discussion. . . . Grattan's speech was splendid in point of eloquence, all declamation, very little, and what there was weak in argument, his manner I think, though certainly very animated, disgusting to the last degree from affectation.

He went on to express his anger with Lord Shelburne for "recommending to us to support the authority of England [while he declares] in the [British] house of Lords that the Claims of Ireland *must* be acceded to." [22] Portland was more restrained: "The People will not be inclined to recede from any of their demands. Lord Shelburne's speech has conveyed to them a belief that all is to be granted." [23] A week later, he directly informed Shelburne of the unhappy effect in Ireland of his speech in the British Lords. He pointed to the galling consideration that the Irish thought that the concessions were due solely to their own endeavours and owed nothing to the Whig victory in England. He added the very significant passage:

Let me entreat your Lordship therefore to be assured that it is no longer the Parliament of Ireland that is to be managed or attended to. It is the whole of this country, it is the Church, the Law, the Army, I fear, when I consider how it is composed, the merchant, the tradesman, the manufacturer, the Farmer, the labourer, the Catholick, the Dissenter, the Protestant; all sects, all sorts and descriptions of men. . . .[24]

And now there took place the "change in men and measures" (that happy eighteenth-century expression) which placated the bulk of the Patriots. Scott was removed from the position of attorney-general and replaced by Barry Yelverton; James Browne, Lord Westport's brother, who had succeeded Hussey Burgh as Prime Serjeant, was dismissed and Hussey Burgh restored; John Forbes was offered, but declined, the post of solicitor-general; and Peter Metge was made a judge. Charlemont, Grattan, and Ogle were consulted as friends of the new Administration. Flood was offered restoration to the Privy Council, but declined the honor. Unfortunately for their reputation, the first Irish appointment by the Whigs was that of Sir George Yonge to the lucrative position of one of the Vice-treasurers. He had been one of the most determined English opponents of Free Trade, and the Irish press was not slow to express its indignation.[25] Further dismissals were obviously in mind, and men like Beresford and Denis Daly feared for their offices.[26] But all calculations were upset, and politics came to a standstill with the death of the Marquis of Rockingham on July 1. Now the unity of the English Whigs tended to crumble and their great victory over George III and Lord North lost much of its importance.

Upon Rockingham's death the government resigned and a new cabinet was formed under Lord Shelburne. Thomas Townshend (later Lord Sydney) was appointed Home Secretary, thereby becoming the Cabinet minister responsible for Irish affairs. Fox refused to join the new government. As viceroy and chief secretary of Ireland, Portland and Fitzpatrick were replaced by Lord Temple and his brother, William Wyndham Grenville. Temple did not arrive in Dublin to take over his duties till the middle of September.

Under Rockingham's ministry the constitutional measures, which the Patriots had so long sought, were con-

ceded. The 1719 Declaratory Act was repealed, Poyning's
Law was altered, and the perpetual Irish Mutiny Act
made temporary and framed on the English model. These,
and a measure to appoint judges on good behaviour, had
become law by the end of July. Henceforth, the practice
of passing "heads" of bills was ended, and the power of
alter or veto bills taken away from the viceroy and Irish
Privy Council: only the English Privy Council which
meant, of course, the British Cabinet, would in future
be entitled to veto, but not to alter, bills passed by the
Irish Parliament. Furthermore, the summoning of parliament in Ireland would merely require a license from
the king.

While all this legislation was on its way through parliament, Newenham introduced the heads of a bill to deprive of the franchise all Revenue officers with salaries of
less than £200. His purpose was to reduce the influence
of the government in elections. The Chief Secretary, Fitzpatrick, said he had supported a similar bill in the British
House of Commons and approved in principle of Newenham's measure. He added that he would abide by the decision of the Irish Parliament and neither support nor oppose the measure.[27] This was just another example of the
dilemma in which the English Whigs found themselves
when they took over the administration of Ireland. Eventually, for fear of being thought hostile to it, Dublin Castle did give its support.[28] The measure was passed by the
Commons and approved by London, but on its return to
Ireland as a bill, it was rejected by the Irish House of
Lords. Beresford expressed his satisfaction and took credit
for helping to procure its defeat.[29]

Grattan was the hero of the hour. Volunteer corps all
over the country congratulated him and filled the newspapers with their insertions. A meeting of the Bar (the

advocates in the legal profession) decided to erect a monument to the Rights of Ireland with a special commemoration for Grattan: he had declined their offer to raise a statue to him.[30] The Irish Parliament voted him an honorarium of £50,000 which enabled him to buy a country home. In the high spirits of the time he stated (in reply to an address from a Volunteer corps in Co. Galway):

When we shall have obtained [legislative] freedom, . . . [Europe] will behold the same nation raising her Government above the necessity of corruption, by an emulation of independent support.[31]

Nearly a month later, on May 20, Newenham and his Liberty Volunteers, a radical politician and a radical corps, applauded Grattan. They saw in the achievement of the constitutional objectives the rooting out of corruption and the gaining of parliamentary reform.[32] Several other corps were equally optimistic about the implications of legislative independence, but most of the addresses did not go beyond constitutional matters.

On May 28 the Ulster and Connaught committees of Volunteer delegates jointly thanked Charlemont and Grattan and suggested that the latter be presented with a residence, just as the famous Duke of Marlborough had been rewarded with Blenheim Palace.[33] It was probably this address which prompted the *Hibernian Journal* to describe Blenheim as "that stupendous monument of bad taste," [34] but there was no implied hostility in this remark to Grattan. Even today many would agree with this expression of architectural taste.

On June 3, 1782, a great review of Volunteers took place in the Phoenix Park, at which Charlemont took the salute attended by Grattan and other leading Patriots. Portland was present in an unofficial capacity.[35] The crowd of onlookers was so large that the *Freeman's Journal* saw the empty city of Dublin as resembling Goldsmith's "Deserted Village," and added:

If we were allowed poetical expressions, we could say that every tree in the Park was *loaded with animated fruit;* for every branch afforded a support to some adventurous and inquisitive spectator who had courage to run the risk, and curiosity to see.[36]

Despite all the rejoicing and the national applause for Grattan, peace and content were not to last long. The apple of discord was thrown into the political arena by Henry Flood, the former Patriot leader whose glory had been tarnished by his years as a vice-treasurer. In the Irish Commons on May 27, he had stated that the repeal of the Declaratory Act might not be enough; the English had not given up the power of legislating externally for Ireland.[37] On succeeding days he made carping comments on the constitutional concessions, and finally on June 11 he openly attacked "simple repeal," and demanded a positive declaration by the British Parliament that it would renounce for ever any right to legislate for Ireland.[38] In the Commons on June 7, he had exchanged angry words with Grattan and Yelverton, the newly appointed Attorney-General. The reaction of the press was one of dismay; the *Dublin Evening Post* described it as a "little altercation," and the *Hibernian Journal* thought it should be "pillowed in oblivion."[39]

Initial reaction to Flood's demand for a Renunciation Act by the British Parliament was unfavorable, and Grattan's satisfaction with "simple repeal" was shared. On

June 19 the delegates of the Leinster Volunteers, with Charlemont as chairman, declared themselves satisfied. In addition, they passed a resolution of gratitude to the King, which must have been anything but welcome since it contained a reference to

. . . the late changes which your Majesty has been pleased to adopt in your Councils and Ministers; and for the measures tending to public economy, and diminution of undue influence, which we have been taught to hope are to be extended to this kingdom; and we trust the day is approaching, when corruption will be no more.[40]

It was a symptom of the strength of the Volunteers and of the weakness of the Irish Government that Portland should have transmitted this insulting address to London, and implored Shelburne to have some official assurance given that it had been presented to the King.[41]

In Dublin on June 18, the National Committee of the Volunteers, under the chairmanship of Lord Kingsborough, decided that "simple repeal" was sufficient and that there was no necessity for "renunciation." [42] On the previous day a meeting in Dungannon of the Ulster corps delegates voted an address to the King in which they stated their satisfaction with simple repeal. They nominated a deputation, including Francis Dobbs, to go to London to present their address.[43] Six months previously, such an action would have been treated by government in both Dublin and London as a gross impertinence, but, now the Volunteers were riding high. Portland begged Shelburne to see that the emmissiaries were graciously received and, if possible, to have them given some sort of royal favor. George III, who realized the importance of dispensing royal courtesies, received the Dungannon representatives in person. In addition, he took official notice of the address sent by the National Committee in Dublin.[44]

In the struggle over renunciation, Grattan had won the first round. His position was weakened by ill-health which necessitated his departure for a spa in Germany as soon as the parliamentary session closed towards the end of July, 1782. He did not return to Ireland until the middle of October. It is possible that his policy of peace might have withstood the oratorical onslaughts of Flood, but the dice were loaded in the latter's favor by a whole series of events.

In the British Commons on May 17, Fox had supported the concessions with a speech that was unlikely to placate Irish sentiment. He maintained that even though he had not been "an enemy to the Declaratory Act . . . relative to America," he had always made "a distinction between the internal and external legislation." Lest his words should fail to make an unpleasing effect on Ireland, Fox became more exact:

He was clear that the latter [the right of legislating externally] was, in reason and policy, annexed to the British Legislature; this right . . . would never have given umbrage to any part of the British empire, had it been used solely for the general good of the empire. . . . Ireland had the same reason [as had America] to spurn this power of external legislation, because it had been hitherto employed for the purpose only of oppressing. . . . Had Ireland never been made to feel this power as a curse . . . she never would have complained of it.[45]

In the succeeding months Fox came in for much hostile comment from Irish newspapers. His speech enabled Flood, as already described, to state in the Irish Commons on May 27 that Britain had not given up the power of legislating externally for Ireland. Much worse was to follow.

On July 5 the Earl of Abingdon asked for leave in the British House of Lords to introduce a bill vesting in the British Parliament the right to legislate externally for the whole empire including Ireland.[46] Since he got no one to second his request, it lapsed. His action was that of an eccentric but its effect on Irish sentiment was dynamic. The newspapers saw it as a potential menace, and it aided Flood in working up dissatisfaction with "simple repeal." In order to neutralize its effect, Fitzpatrick wrote a public letter to Hely Hutchinson, the Provost, stating that Abingdon's motion was of no consequence and had been misunderstood.[47]

By early July opinion, as shown by press correspondence and resolutions of several Volunteer corps, was beginning to turn to the support of Flood in his demand that the British Parliament pass a bill of renunciation. Fox's speech and Lord Abingdon's motion had been grist to his mill, and his powerful oratory must have played no small part in winning over much of the country to his side. At the end of July he went to Belfast and reviewed the Belfast Volunteer Company who elected him their delegate.[48] Before the end of June he had won the support of the *Dublin Evening Post,* the most important of the Irish newspapers, but was opposed by the equally radical *Hibernian Journal.* The *Freeman's Journal,* whose allegiance had been bought over by 1781 to a mild support of the Government, was ambivalent at first but finally declared itself for Grattan. The bitterness of the rift between the two leaders could be seen in the *Hibernian Journal's* editorial on Flood's visit to Belfast:

The Business of Mr. Flood to the North, must originate from the most patriotic motives . . . he finds an honest people . . .

enjoying the most perfect satisfaction; but he goes to convince them that . . . they should substitute his construction of *Constitution* for *industry*, and throw by the Labours of the Loom to follow this Don Quixote in his expedition against a Windmill.[49]

Grattan came in for a quantity of abuse for having accepted the parliamentary gift of £50,000. Shortly after departing for the Continental spa, the *Dublin Evening Post* described him as thanking his country "for enabling him to spend abroad fifty thousand pounds."[50]

On July 20 the Lawyers' corps of Volunteers appointed a committee to consider whether the repeal of the Declaratory Act was a total renunciation by the British Parliament of the claim to bind Ireland.[51] The very fact that this enquiry was instituted was a moral victory for Flood. The committee reported in November in favor of his contention with the statement that the British legislature

have not done any Act whatsoever, whereby they must or can be deemed to have fully, finally, and irrevocably, or in any adequate manner acknowledged the sole and exclusive right of the Irish Parliament to legislate for this Country in all cases as well external as internal.[52]

Grattan's position was further undermined by Portland's decision to organize a militia or, as it was called, Fencible regiments. The Viceroy's intention was enthusiastically supported, if not prompted, by "Gentleman Johnny" Burgoyne, the new commander-in-Chief in Ireland. Burgoyne thought that the Volunteers, not being under military discipline, could do little in battle against an invading force. Both men believed —and this was probably their principal aim—that the raising of Fencibles would be a means of "restoring the power of the sword to the Crown."[53] However, in a letter to Thomas

Townshend, the new Home Secretary in Shelburne's cabinet, Portland stated his belief that the Volunteers were of loyal disposition.[54] The proposal met with the approval of London [55] and it was agreed to raise six regiments, two in each of the provinces of Ulster and Munster, and one each in Leinster and Connaught. Portland nominated the officers who were to recruit the new force: Mervyn Archdall and Thomas Dawson in Ulster; Lord Inchiquin and Arthur Blennerhassett in Munster; Richard Talbot in Leinster; and William P. K. Trench in Connaught.[56] Archdall, Dawson, Blennerhassett, and Trench were members of parliament for the counties of Fermanagh, Armagh, Kerry, and Galway, respectively, and thus men of considerable following. Richard Talbot (of Malahide Castle, Co. Dublin) had served in the Austrian Army before becoming a Protestant and was a prominent landlord, while Inchiquin was a landed aristocrat in Co. Cork.

The raising of the Fencibles provoked fury throughout the country, especially among the Volunteers who naturally saw the new force as both a rival and a menace to themselves. The fact that all six officers were leading members of the Volunteers only added to the indignation. Throughout the autumn and winter of 1782 the radical press exhibited the hostility to Fencibles in editorials, correspondence, and the publication of addresses by Volunteer corps. Charlemont and most of the Patriots added their denunciations, but Grattan, after his return from the Continent in October, refrained from joining the popular cry. It was no help to him that one of the leading protagonists of "simple repeal," Francis Dobbs, took a commission in the Fencibles and was publicly condemned by the Committee of the Ulster Volunteers.[57] In his memoirs Charlemont described the establishment of the Fencibles as an "insidious measure" and saw it as the decisive factor in bringing the country over to the support of Flood and "renunciation." [58]

In the autumn two events further strengthened Flood's position. The first was a pamphlet written by Lord Beauchamp, the English Tory, who now played the former Whig game of embarrassing English government by stirring up trouble in Ireland. He addressed the pamphlet to the Volunteers of Ulster warning them to beware of "simple repeal" and to demand further security for Ireland's constitutional rights.[59] More important, was a judgment by Lord Mansfield in the English Court of Appeal on a Writ of Error from the Irish courts. The case had been entered in England before the repeal of the Declaratory Act had been effected, so that Mansfield may well have been legally correct in sitting on the case. Politically, however, it was disastrous for Grattan, since it was interpreted in Ireland as a proof that the English judges did not recognize the newly gained judicial supremacy of the Irish House of Lords.

On his return to Ireland Grattan was faced with a country of which he was no longer the national hero. The Royal Tralee corps of Volunteers, of whom he was an honorary member, asked him in November to support "renunciation" and oppose the raising of the Fencibles. In a cold reply he said he had already stated his view on "renunciation" and expressed the opinion that the coming of peace would solve the problem of the Fencibles. He added that he regarded the "attack" on Ireland's judicial supremacy (Mansfield's judgment) as an important new issue but was sure Great Britain would redress that grievance.[60] At the end of November he was asked by his own corps, the Independent Dublin, to support "renunciation." He replied that the Irish Parliament had asserted its "legislative independency" which had been fully acknowledged by the British legislature. He made an implied thrust at the dominating position of the Volunteers when he ended his reply with the words: "There is a final justice in public opinion on which I do not fear to stand." In this answer he grasped at a vague reference in the corps' address as a reason for introducing the subject of Catholic relief. He condemned the Penal Laws and expressed the view that they were tied up with British domination.[61] Since this topic was scarcely relevant, one can only conclude that Grattan was making a desperate effort to wean Catholics away from the anti-Catholic Flood. For this manoeuvre he was attacked in the press, one correspondent in the *Dublin Evening Post* writing: "I do not wonder, Sir, at your attempt to conciliate the favour of the Roman Catholics, since you were conscious you had lost the estimation of the Protestants in general." [62] On December 10 he was re-elected colonel by his corps but only by a small majority. As a result, the corps split and some of its members seceded to form a new corps, the Dublin Union, in opposition to Grattan.[63]

Charlemont was distressed by Flood's policy and wrote to him accordingly:

Some there are still discontented, and I am sorry for it; but how could it be otherwise, when they have the sanction and impression of your opinion—of your eloquence? O, my dear Flood, what are you about?[64]

In his memoirs Charlemont saw Flood's action as primarily due to chagrin at seeing Grattan the national leader.[65] In 1782 he agreed wholeheartedly with Grattan and felt bitter about the manner in which he was being abused:

I know him [Grattan] thoroughly, I know the bottom of his soul, and there is not a speck in it, and his wicked and consequently foolish detractors will find to their cost, that, in endeavouring to bespatter him, they will only dirty and blacken themselves.[66]

In 1783, Charlemont and Grattan quarreled over a comparatively trifling matter that seems to have been caused by extreme sensitivity on the former's part. Perhaps because of the blighted friendship, Charlemont was more critical of Grattan when writing his memoirs, because he then saw vanity as "perhaps the ruling passion of his nature." Also, in these later years, he felt that Grattan had stood by "simple repeal" partly from conviction, and partly out of hatred of Flood and friendship for the English Whigs, so that he became, in a sense, "a party man." [67]

When Portland's viceroyalty came to an end on the arrival of his successor, Lord Temple, on September 15, 1782, the storm over the Fencibles had just begun. The new Lord-Lieutenant felt indignant, as well he might, over Beauchamp's provocative pamphlet which he described as "that *execrable* and *iniquitous publication*." [68] At first he was opposed to the British Parliament's conceding a renunciation act, but Mansfield's judgment caused him to take an entirely different view. In early December he informed Shelburne that the court's action had "totally changed the appearance of things." [69] A few days later he advised the Prime Minister that

if the acknowledgement is not made clearly and irrevocably of the *Rights* claimed by Ireland, and now impeached by Lord Mansfield's *Decree*, there is not a man in that kingdom [Ireland] whom any consideration will induce to assist his Excy. in the King's Government.[70]

Even Charlemont, who had been so strongly opposed to the movement for "renunciation," now admitted in a letter apparently to Flood that he had been forced to change his opinion because of "Lord Mansfield's abominable conduct." [71]

By the middle of December the British Cabinet had decided to put a renunciation bill through the British Parliament.[72] In January, 1783, the bill was introduced and rapidly enacted. Its passage was a great victory for Flood and assured him the ascendancy over Grattan in the national leadership for more than a year to come. His following was particularly strong among the more radical elements, especially in the Volunteers.

Charlemont and Grattan had of course been delighted with the advent of the English Whigs to power in April, 1782, and naturally found favor with Portland's Administration. They had no intention, however, of accepting any official position in government.[73] In the autumn Lord Temple entered into an arrangement with Lord Charlemont's "Party" in order to prevent their supporting Flood. Temple informed Shelburne of his Machiavellian purpose with a candor quite unusual in the polished correspondence of statesmen:

I have . . . engaged them *solemnly* to make their stand agt. this popular opinion [the demand for "renunciation"]; and the consequence is, they are hourly losing ground with those on whom alone their strength is built, the middling and lower class of Volunteers. . . . At all events, it foments that *Spirit* of *Disunion* among the Volunteers, upon which alone I found my hopes of forming a government; for, in the present hour, the shadow of it does not *exist*.[74]

London approved of Temple's action.[75] Towards the end of October the Viceroy reported that Grattan was determined to stand his ground against Flood and was confident of success provided Dublin Castle supported him.[76]

Nothing further is known of these arrangements, but Grattan remained on good terms with the Irish Administration at least until the end of 1783.

When the decision to grant the Irish legislative demands was made in the spring of 1782, the British Whig Government hoped that some sort of treaty could be made between the two countries defining their constitutional relationship. The principal aim was to ensure an end of all further claims by the Irish Parliament. On April 28, 1782, Fox wrote to Fitzpatrick, the new Chief Secretary in Dublin:

My opinion is clear for giving them all they ask, but for giving it them so as to secure us from further demands, and at the same time to have some clear understanding with respect to what we are to expect from Ireland in return for the protection and assistance which she receives from those fleets which cost us such enormous sums, & her nothing.[77]

Shelburne put the problem in a nutshell by referring to the "confusion which must arise in all cases of common concern from two Parliaments acting with distinct and equal powers and without any operating centre."[78] He was willing to grant Ireland liberal concessions, but warned Portland that in return the Irish Parliament must give "a superintending power to be reserved to this country [Great Britain] for all purposes of common concern whether in matters of state or general commerce."[79]

Even after his arrival in Ireland and his realization that the situation there was anything but favorable, Portland believed that the Irish would not reject such a treaty once the legislative demands had been satisfied.[80] On June 6 he considered that Grattan and his friends would support an Irish bill structured along the lines requested by Shelburne.[81] The Lord-Lieutenant's optimism was soon shown to be unjustified by the information which Fitzpatrick brought to London two weeks later.[82] By this time, June 22, Portland had found that the political suspicions and jealousies arising in Ireland rendered hopeless any attempt to negotiate a treaty between the two countries. He recommended that the subject be shelved.[83] Little more was heard of the matter; henceforth Dublin Castle was kept busy trying to stem the tide of renewed political discontent.

Questions that must occur to the student of this period in Irish history are: What was the value of legislative independence? Did constitutional freedom really mean anything when the executive was appointed, and the parliament was usually kept under control, by the British government? Were the Patriots chasing rainbows?

Of one thing the historian can be certain: the Patriots, the Volunteers, the radicals, and the leading British statesmen, viewed the Irish constitutional claims as a matter of the first magnitude. The fervor with which they were pursued, and the obstinacy with which they were resisted, leave that conclusion without need of further proof. More than a generation of Irish Protestants had been reared in the belief that to attain these objectives was a patriotic duty. Educated in the English tradition of representative and native government, in the principles of the Glorious Revolution, the Irish Protestants, like the American colonists, desired to possess all the "rights of Englishmen." There was even more to it than that: not only the Patriots but the perennial supporters of Dublin Castle were keenly aware of the dignity of their parliament. Even when the Commons was in its most docile mood, it was an accepted principle that a money bill could not be altered in England, but must take its rise in College Green. It was not merely a desire for self-government: it was also a matter of *amour-propre*. It is small wonder, then, that the constitutional aims were sought with an intensity that was as much emotional as intellectual.

It was widely felt that once legislative independence was achieved, other objectives could be pursued. Parliamentary reform was seen as the most important of these objectives. The victory of 1782 had shown that obstinately defended bulwarks could be surmounted, and the crusading spirit continued to flourish. In the future what might not be gained?

For us who know of the failure of the reform movement and of the Act of Union in 1800, it is all too easy to think that the "Revolution of 1782" achieved nothing. This conclusion is hasty because it overlooks at least two important considerations. The first is that in England, in 1782, reform seemed to be setting out on a triumphal career with the Whigs; even Pitt came into power in December, 1783, with a reform policy in mind. These changes, if effected in England, were likely to be imitated in Ireland though probably on a modest scale. More important, but impossible to foresee in 1782, was the French Revolution which had the effect of rendering suspect all ideas of change in England for more than a generation. In Ireland it shook the self-confidence of the Protestant community and helped to bring about the Rebellion of 1798; twenty years of conciliation between Catholic and Protestant ended in the dust heap. Demoralization was so complete that many of the surviving Patriots welcomed the Act of Union as a necessary evil. Even then, it was only with difficulty that the British Government succeeded in destroying the Irish Parliament. The "course of Irish history" after 1782 was frustrated and, ultimately, shattered by events which varied from the unlikely to the exceptional. Viewed in this light, the achievement of the Patriots was not a petty thing.

Notes for Chapter XII

1 Dobbs, *History*, pp. 46–49.

2 Hillsborough to Eden, January 24, 1782, Add. Mss. 34417, f. 300. The letter is erroneously dated 1781.

3 Eden to Hillsborough, February 7, 1782, SP 63/480, f. 169.

4 HMC, Charlemont Papers, I, 391–92, 392, 395–96.

5 Dobbs, *History*, pp. 51–52; *Grattan Memoirs*, II, 204–206.

6 DEP, February 19, 1782.

7 Roger Bristow to Col. Ross, February 17, 1782, SP 63/480, ff. 228–230.

8 HMC, Charlemont Papers, I, 399.

9 HMC, Lothian Papers, pp. 410–411.

10 *Ibid.*, pp. 412–413.

11 SP 63/480, ff. 296–300.

12 Add. Mss. 34418, ff. 338–39.

13 Carlisle to Hillsborough, March 26, 1782, HO 100/1, ff. 3–4.

14 Eden to Loughborough, March 16, 1782, Add. Mss. 34418, ff. 363–64.

15 Hillsborough to Eden, March 12, 1782, Add. Mss. 34418, f. 350.

16 Christie, *The End of North's Ministry*, pp. 339–40, 350, 368–69.

17 This expression was used in the contemporary newspapers.

18 Minute of Cabinet meeting, April 8, 1782, *Corr. of Geo. III*, ed. J. Fortescue, p. 448.

19 Portland to Shelburne, April 16, 1782, HO 100/1, ff. 74–81.

20 HJ, April 17, 19, 1782.

21 *Speeches of Henry Grattan*, I, 123–30. Grattan's declamation, "spirit of Molyneux!" was a reference to William Molyneux (1656–1698), philosopher and scientist, friend of John Locke, and M.P. for Dublin University. Early in 1698, Molyneux had published a spirited defense of the legislative independence of the Irish Parliament, thus becoming the "father" of the Patriots.

22 Richard Fitzpatrick to Fox, April 17, 1782, Add. Mss. 47580, ff. 83–88.

23 Portland to Thomas Pelham, April 18, 1782, Add. Mss. 33100, ff. 107–108.

24 Portland to Shelburne, April 24, 1782, HO 100/1, ff. 133–39.

25 DEP, June 18, 1782.

26 Cooke to Eden, June 4, 1782, Add. Mss. 34418, ff. 466–69; Beresford to Eden, June 7, 1782, Add. Mss. 34418, ff. 470–71.

27 HJ, May 31, 1782.

28 Fitzpatrick to John Hely Hutchinson, June 8, HMC, Donoughmore Papers, p. 303; Beresford to Eden, June 13, 1782, Add. Mss. 34418, ff. 472–73.

29 Berseford to Eden, July 23, 1782, Add. Mss. 34418, f. 512.

30 DEP, May 21, 1782.

31 DEP, May 2, 1782.

32 DEP, May 25, 1782.

33 DEP, May 30, 1782.

34 HJ, May 31, 1782.

35 DEP, June 4, 1782.

36 FJ, June 4, 1782.

37 HJ, May 29, 1782.

38 HJ, June 12, 1782; DEP, June 29, 1782.

39 DEP, June 8, 1782; HJ, June 10, 1782.

40 DEP, June 22, 1782.

41 Portland to Shelburne, June 25, 1782, HO 100/2, ff. 157–59.

42 DEP, June 18, 1782.

43 DEP, June 25, 1782.

44 Portland to Shelburne, June 25, 26, HO 100/2, ff. 157–59, 173; Shelburne to Portland, July 6, 1782, HO 100/2, f. 193.

45 Fox's speech, DEP, May 23, 1782.

46 FJ, July 13, 1782.

47 *Grattan Memoirs*, II, 351–52.

48 DEP, August 1, 1782.

49 HJ, August 5, 1782.

50 DEP, August 10, 1782.

51 DEP, July 25, 1782.

52 HJ, November 20, 1782.

53 Burgoyne to Portland, June 22, 1782, HO 100/2, ff. 162–63; Portland to Shelburne, June 22, 1782, HO 100/2, ff. 146–48.

54 Portland to Thomas Townshend, July 18, 1782, 100/2, ff. 236–40.

55 Townshend to Portland, August 1, 1782, HO 100/2, ff. 282–84.

56 Portland to Townshend, August 29, 1782, HO 100/3, ff. 65–66.

57 DEP, September 21, 1782.

58 HMC, Charlemont Papers, I, 70.

59 Beauchamp, Lord, *A Letter to the First Belfast Company of Volunteers in the Province of Ulster* (Dublin, 1782).

60 DEP, September 19, 1782.

61 FJ, December 10, 1782.

62 DEP, December 26, 1782.

63 DEP, December 17, 19, 1782.

64 Warden Flood, ed. *Memoirs of Henry Flood,* p. 175.

65 HMC, Charlemont Papers, I, 61–63.

66 Charlemont to Alexander Halliday, August 11, 1782, HMC, Charlemont Papers, I, 416–418.

67 HMC, Charlemont Papers, I, 110, 80.

68 Earl Temple to Shelburne, October 28, 1782, Add. Mss. 24138, ff. 102–103.

69 Temple to Shelburne December 2, 1782 (Abstract), Add. Mss. 24138, ff. 103–104.

70 Temple to Shelburne, December 6, 1782 (Abstract), Add. Mss. 24138, ff. 104–105.

71 Charlemont to [Flood ?], December 28, 1782, HMC, Charlemont Papers, I, 423–24.

72 Thomas Townshend to Temple, December, 1782, HO 100/3, ff. 369–70; DEP, December 21, 1782.

73 Charlemont to Halliday, June 6, 1782, HMC, Charlemont Papers, I, 406; Grattan to Fox, April 26, 1782, Add. Mss. 47580, ff. 101–106.

74 Temple to Shelburne, October 9, 1782, Add. Mss. 24138 (Abstract), ff. 101–102.

75 Thomas Townshend to Temple, October 26, 1782, HO 100/3, ff. 235–40.

76 Temple to Shelburne, October 28, 1782, Add. Mss. 24138 (Abstract), ff. 102–103.

77 Fox to Fitzpatrick, April 28, 1782, Add. Mss. 47580, ff. 95–100.

78 Shelburne to Portland, April 29, 1782, HO 100/1, ff. 142–45.

79 Shelburne to Portland, May 18, 1782, HO 100/1, ff. 213–222.

80 Portland to Fox, April 28, 1782, Add. Mss. 47561, ff. 31–32.

81 Portland to Shelburne, HO 100/2, ff. 34–35.

82 Shelburne to George III, June 22, 1782, *Corr. of Geo. III,* ed. J. Fortescue, VI, 63–64.

83 Portland to Shelburne, June 22, 1782, HO 100/2, ff. 146–48.

XIII

The Catholic Relief Acts of 1782

In addition to the constitutional issues, the year 1782 was noteworthy for the passing of two acts in favor of the Catholics. Again, as in 1778, the sponsor was Luke Gardiner; he was supported by John Dillon, of Lismullen, Navan, Co. Meath, a member of an illustrious Norman-Irish family. Though his own branch had been Protestants for some generations, many of his Dillon relatives had remained Catholic and he was no doubt anxious to protect their interests. In preparation for the general election of 1783, Gardiner tried to obtain the support of Dr. Robert Fowler, the Archbishop of Dublin. Dr. Fowler, refused to help because he believed that Gardiner was an opponent of the Established Church and the supporter of all other religious persuasions.[1]

On November 29, 1781, Gardiner announced in the Irish Commons that after the Christmas recess he would bring in heads of a bill for the further relief of Roman Catholics.[2] During December the subject was brought up again in the Commons and met with considerable support. Scott, the Attorney-General, Fitzgibbon, Daly, and Hussey Burgh expressed their approval, while only Sir Richard Johnston, one of the lesser Patriots, indicated hostility. Grattan spoke of the fact that Catholics no longer acted politically in accordance with their private religious principles; and as religious controversy was held in contempt, bigotry was despised. In connection with the threat of invasion, Free Trade, and the constitutional issues, the Catholics had not attempted to make a bargain for themselves. Conolly supported the heads as "founded in strict policy, sound judgment and true religion." [3]

After the recess opposition was more evident. Several members, but none of any importance with the exception of Fitzgibbon, raised objections. Legal difficulties in connection with the Act of Settlement concerning the ownership of land appear to have been the substance of his argument, but Gardiner said he had obtained legal advice which would put fears in this connection to rest.[4] On February 20 Flood said he loved Catholics and wanted to give them security of property but no political power. The major issue at first was whether they should be given the right to buy land in fee simple, and not merely allowed to take leases of up to 999 years which had been granted by the Act of 1778. Ogle, who usually opposed the Catholic claims, considered that the right to buy outright might just as well be granted provided it would not confer any power in the control of boroughs. David Walsh quoted Montesquieu in saying that granting favors made converts of people faster than penalizing them. Other parts of Gardiner's heads referred to repealing laws against clergy, marriages between Catholics and Protestants, and education.[5]

Grattan on February 20 made an important statement

on his change of front since 1778 when he had opposed relief:

Their conduct since that period has fully convinced me of their true attachment to this country. . . . The question is now, whether we shall grant Roman Catholics a power of enjoying estates,—whether we shall be *a Protestant settlement* or an IRISH NATION?[6]

He gave his consent to allowing Catholics buy estates in fee simple as "the most likely means of obtaining a victory over the *prejudices of Catholics, and over our own.*"

On the subject of admitting regular, as opposed to pastoral, clergy to the kingdom, Yelverton said he had no fear of "an inundation of inhabitants to this country, even though they should be *Regular* inhabitants." A week later, Yelverton described opponents of the measure as having tolerance "on their lips but not in their hearts." They acted with the "obstinate inveteracy" of the Lady to Dr. Fell:

> I do not like thee, Doctor Fell,
> The reason why, I will not tell;
> But this I know full well,
> I do not like thee, Doctor Fell.[7]

A letter in the *Freeman's Journal* of February 16, 1782, made an equally humorous observation:

If McGardiner [sic] introduced . . . a bill authorizing a Catholic to sleep with his wife . . . some would oppose it on the principle that it clashes with the laws to *prevent the growth of Popery*; others would move that they should not bed together until *that day two years;* and the garret scribblers would point out the fatal consequences of such connections; they would allege that those Papists would beget *a white boy*.

Like Grattan's outburst the previous week, came Yelverton's demand:

Will you give the Papists landed property or not? It was time for them [the members of parliament] to assume the dignity of a Nation, and not continue what they had hitherto been, an insignificant Colony.[8]

Even though on February 20 an attempt to have the measure postponed indefinitely was defeated by an overwhelming majority, Gardiner thought it better tactics to divide the measure into two separate heads, one for property and clergy, and the other for education and marriage. In a sparsely attended house on March 6, the former was passed and sent to the viceroy for transmission to London. The new heads in regard to mixed marriages were rejected, but the heads concerning permission for Catholics to teach provided they had a license from the local Protestant bishop were approved.[9] This measure was brought by Gardiner to Dublin Castle on March 14 and in due course sent to England.

In the discussion on education on March 1, Hely Hutchinson, the Provost of Dublin University, suggested that legislation should be passed allowing Catholic clergy and laity to enter the university and allowing them their own Professor of Divinity. The Penal laws were disgraceful in forbidding Catholics to have any education at all, but the establishment of Catholic colleges should be forbidden as "subjects of religious disputation that have long slept in oblivion would again awake, and awaken with them all the worst passions of the human mind."[10]

In the Irish Parliament the measures had encountered little hostility. As soon as it was made clear that Catholics would not be able to buy land in boroughs so as to influence the return of members to parliament, the more anxious defenders of the Protestant Establishment were satisfied. Carlisle was nervous at first for fear that the Presbyterians might object. He described the protagonists of the relief as "chiefly independent Gentlemen, tho' some are disposed to show a degree of deference to the sentiments of Government." [11] Hillsborough advised Dublin Castle "not to stir any questions relative to Religion." He reminded Carlisle of the Gordon Riots in London in 1780 which were a consequence of the English Catholic Relief Acts of 1778:

The same factious and violent spirit is kept alive still in several parts of Scotland, in Yorkshire, in this town [London], and other parts of England; and I fear . . . it will give an opportunity to the Independents and Disaffected of the North [of Ireland] to raise Disturbances . . . which may go further . . . than it is easy to foresee.[12]

Owing to fear of the riots and jealousies likely to be provoked, he suggested that the Irish Government should gently discourage, or at least try to postpone the Catholic relief measure. Hillsborough's anxiety was not mere personal timidity. The Gordon Riots had been successful to the extent that there was no hope of further relief being enacted in Britain for many years. As Eugene C. Black has stated in his *The Association,* these riots "showed how perilously thin was that veneer of culture and moderation, so often considered the hallmark of the age of reason. Emotional religion lay deep in the hearts of eighteenth-century Britons." [13]

Nor was that fear an idle one when one remembers that so mild and gentle a Protestant as John Wesley, the founder of Methodism, was a most determined opponent of Catholic relief. On a visit to Cork city in April, 1778, he praised the Volunteers there who "if they answer no other end, at least keep the Papists in order." [14] On February 15 and April 1 of 1780, he published letters in the Freeman's Journal. The former included a defense of the scurrilously anti-Catholic pamphlet, *An Appeal from the Protestant Association to the People of Great Britain*. Both letters were concerned with English rather than Irish Catholics, and were part of a controversy with Father Arthur O'Leary, the Franciscan, who poked fun at Wesley's accusations. They seem to have aroused little interest in Ireland, perhaps because the *Freeman's Journal* was very much a pro-Catholic paper and probably not read by Presbyterians in the North, while Anglicans were unlikely to pay too much attention to a Methodist. In his second letter he wrote: "I would not have the Roman Catholics persecuted at all. I would only have them hindered from doing hurt: I would not put it in their power to cut the throats of their quiet neighbours."

William Eden, the Chief Secretary, was more sympathetic and wished the measure success "morally and politically," desiring to see the Catholics "much raised from their present desperate state of dejection." Whatever be its fate he was sure that the Government ought not stand forth to resist it and thus offend "four fifths of the people of this kingdom, who at present are full of loyalty and attachment." [15] Edmund Burke, naturally, was pleased with the relief to be given and wrote to Eden: "Your reflections on the Popery Bill I am glad to find are exactly correspondent with mine. It was a wise measure & when carried through will give credit to Lord Carlisle's government." [16] Both bills were approved by the British Government without alteration on April 10.[17]

On January 1, 1782, Charlemont wrote to Flood:

The house seems to me to be running mad on the subject of popery. Gardiner's bill, which, as castrated, may, for aught I know, be rendered innocent in its operations, is however, in my opinion, extremely exceptionable [i.e. objectionable] in its mode.[18]

Though Henry Flood supported the relief measures, he was by no means so happy about the matter as his public action would lead one to believe. In his reply to Charlemont, he expressed his real sentiments:

I am frightened about the Popery business. It ought to be touched only by a master-hand. It is a chord of such wondrous potency that I dread the sound of it; and believe with you that the harmony would be better . . . if it were, at least for a time, inaudible.[19]

In the Irish House of Lords on May 2, Bellamont led the opposition and was supported by the Bishop of Ferns, Lord Ely, and several other peers. However, two prelates, Cloyne (Richard Woodward) and Waterford (William Newcombe), spoke strongly in favor of the bill. The former said he knew

an Ambassador from England, who had been sent twice to Popish countries, and instructed to ask for some Toleration in favour of Protestants, a short answer was given, he was referred to the Statute Books of Ireland.

The Bishop of Waterford considered the enactment would "redound to the Honour of the Irish Legislature, and be applauded by all Europe." Other supporters were the

Lord Chancellor, Lifford, and the Chief Justice of the
King's Bench, Annaly. Lord Desart thought it good for the
nation "when America held out her ports, her trade and
her liberties . . . the bill would prevent emigration." [20]
Opposition in the Lords might have been more formidable but for the fact that Dublin Castle let it be known
that it desired the measures to succeed.[21] They passed the
critical division by 46 to 29. In his congratulations on the
successful course of the measures, Shelburne asked Portland, Carlisle's successor as viceroy, to try to induce the

Bishops and Clergy of the Protestant Church to endeavour
by the Purity of their doctrine and the example of their lives,
to win over the minds & soften the prejudices of other sects;
that by degrees the difference of religious tenets may be
overcome, or at least rendered less violent & implacable. . . .
As in the English Constitution the Church & State have so
near an affinity to each other, they may & ought to give such
mutual support as may conduce to the more firm Establishment and security of each.[22]

The first of the two acts gave Catholics the right to buy
in fee simple, that is to buy outright, all property except
such as would give them the power to nominate members
to parliament for boroughs and manors. The act freed
registered clergy from all penalties, but forbade entry into
the country of regular clergy in the future; the wearing
of clerical garb in public was prohibited; and the erection
of steeples and bells in their chapels was declared illegal.
The other act allowed Catholics to teach, provided they
held a license from the local Protestant bishop, and then
could teach only Catholic students; but no Catholic university, college, or school could receive endowments. An
important family safeguard was that Catholics could in
future be guardians to Catholic children.[23]

The newspapers treated the measures calmly and gave them but a fraction of the attention accorded to the Relief Act of 1778. Little bitterness was expressed by correspondents, and as soon as the "Mutiny of Dungannon" had taken place in February, public opinion had little time for anything but the legislative issues.

Along with these concessions to the Catholics, two measures in favor of the Presbyterians were enacted. One permitted Dissenting Protestant ministers to celebrate legally valid marriages between Dissenters, while the other allowed a Dissenter to take an oath by holding up his hand instead of kissing the bible.[24] The marriage bill went through the Commons without difficulty but provoked strong hostility in the Lords. Despite support from the Government, it passed by only 35 votes to 23.[25] A protest was then entered in the Journal of the Lords by nine lay and twelve spiritual peers, including Cloyne and Waterford, the two bishops who had given strong support to Catholic relief.[26]

The ease with which the Catholic relief measures were enacted is easily explained. The act of 1778 had broken the ice. The Acts of 1782 involved a mere extension of that act in relation to property and little more than a legal recognition of the existing situation where education was concerned. But there was another reason for the calm which surrounded the enactments. The Patriots needed the entire support of all the major elements in the country if they were to press successfully for legislative independence. Grattan admitted to a change of attitude since 1778 towards the Catholic claims. His later life proves that his conversion was sincere, but it was doubtless prompted by the need to unite all the major groups in the country behind the constitutional demands. Charlemont stated that in order to achieve this union "Mr. Grattan took an active and effectual part in the Catholic question." [27] The Volunteers had been admitting Catholics to their ranks in many parts of the country throughout 1781, and in the spring of 1782 many corps publicly encouraged the extension of this practice. Finally, there were the measures in favor of the Presbyterians which doubtless discouraged them from objecting to the grant of concessions to the Catholics.

Thus, 1782 was the great year of conciliation between the three religious denominations—Anglicans, Catholics, and Presbyterians. Never before had they known such a rapid growth of peaceable relations and diminution of ancient rivalries. The year also saw the attainment of the long sought constitutional aims, though the rejoicing over this victory was shortly to be blighted by the bitterness of the renunciation issue. In September there arrived the most popular viceroy of the generation, Earl Temple, whose attack on administrative corruption and waste was widely applauded. It is now proposed to examine the sojourn in office of this remarkable man.

George (Nugent-Temple-Grenville), third Earl Temple, who succeeded Portland, was an exceptional viceroy. His wife was a Catholic, daughter and heiress of the wealthy Irish absentee, Earl Nugent, who had become a Protestant but reverted to Catholicism on his deathbed. Perhaps the richest peer in England, Temple indulged in a viceregal splendor which Dublin had never known before. The *Dublin Evening Post* foretold that his income of £40,000 would enable him to spend on a lavish scale, and the prophecy was fulfilled.[28]

The newspapers constantly referred to the new Lord-Lieutenant's entertainments. A dinner to the Lord Mayor and Aldermen "out-did in sumptuous elegance any thing of the kind ever given at Dublin Castle." [29] In donations to charity Temple and his wife outshone their predecessors. On one occasion, Lady Temple paid the debts of over sixty tradesmen in order to procure their release from prison.[30] Her departure, at the end of her husband's period in office, was described as a great loss to the poor of Dublin. Shortly before he left Ireland in May 1783, the Earl gave £200 to the manufacturing poor of Dublin; and he bought 1500 barrels of oatmeal for distribution among the needy in the counties of Antrim, Down, and Monaghan.[31] Like his forerunners in the office, Temple made it a point that guests at important balls and receptions should wear clothes of Irish manufacture.

There was a more solid reason for popularity—his determination to root out waste and corruption in government departments. The press is constant in its praise for his assiduous investigations of administrative shortcomings. A case in point was his enquiry into the "Department of the State Music." He found that it cost £1260 a year and that except for the "inferior musicians almost all the other persons reside in England, and appoint deputies to act for them for some very trifling consideration." By cutting down on the absentees and giving proper rank to the most capable of those officiating, he expected to reduce the cost of the State Band by more than a third.[32] In his memoirs Charlemont described him as "the man best fitted of any I ever knew for the conduct of Irish affairs. . . . His love of business was such that he seemed to have no other passion. He did everything himself, and consequently everything was well done." [33]

Usually known by his later title, Marquis of Buckingham (not to be confused with Earl of Buckingham*shire*), Temple was in some ways the most effective Lord-Lieutenant of his time. Haughty, imperious and impatient, but energetic in his application to the routine of business, he made no friends among the nobility, but he does seem to have impressed the middle and lower classes very favorably. People not in a position to mix socially or officially with viceroys would naturally have been scarcely aware of his arrogance. He seems to have dealt kindly with his domestic servants,[34] and the politically conscious population were obviously pleased with his attempt to prune corruption in government offices. He wrote to Cabinet ministers in London in peremptory tones, demanding early attention to his queries and not hesitating to admonish. At times of approaching crises in Ireland, such methods were probably best. Some of Buckinghamshire's difficulties at the time of the Free Trade agitation might have been avoided had he used the same tone in addressing the procrastinating government of Lord North.

Shelburne's government had never had a secure basis in parliament, and his negotiation of an unpopular peace with America precipitated his downfall. Towards the end of February, 1783, he resigned and for about six weeks England had no stable government. Temple tendered his own resignation on March 12 but it was not immediately accepted.[35] As soon as his impending departure became known, addresses of appreciation poured in from all over the country, from county meetings, grand juries, and Volunteer corps. Many of these bodies expressed the hope that he would change his mind and stay. The formation of the Fox-North coalition government in April, 1783, rendered Temple's removal a necessity in order to create a vacancy for the nominee of the new English government.

No previous viceroy had ever formally acknowledged the existence of the Volunteers, but without even asking London's permission, Temple accepted their formal participation in the ceremonies connected with the inauguration of the Order of St. Patrick, on March 17. Three days later the *Dublin Gazette,* the official organ of the Government, stated in its account of the proceeding that the Volunteers "lined the streets through which the Procession passed, and kept order in the Church." Some two weeks later he received an address from the Dublin Volunteers who were arrayed in full uniform. The radical and consistently anti-government *Dublin Evening Post* described his resignation as a disaster for the country.[36] On his leaving Dublin in early June, the streets were lined by 700 Volunteers who stood in the rain, and he was followed by a procession of carriages several miles long. Nothing like it was to be seen again until the departure of Lord Fitzwilliam in 1795.

The new lord-lieutenant was Robert (Henley), second Earl of Northington, the son of a former lord chancellor of England, but a man with neither the wealth nor the social prestige of his predecessor. A bachelor with the reputation of a *bon-vivant,* he was described by the *Freeman's Journal* as likely to obey the abstemious Duke of Portland in all things except living on vegetables and water.[37] Apart from the fact that he administered Ireland during the campaign for parliamentary reform (with which he dealt effectively), he made little impression on the country. His chief secretary at first was William Windham, who was succeeded some months later by Thomas Pelham.

Notes to Chapter XIII

1 HMC, Lothian Papers, pp. 417–418.

2 HJ, November 30, 1781.

3 HJ, December 14, 1781, February 1, 1782; HC, December 31, 1781.

4 HJ, February 18, 20, 1782.

5 HJ, February 22, 1782; HC, February 28, 1782.

6 *Speeches of Henry Grattan,* I, 101–103.

7 HJ, March 1, 1782.

8 HJ, March 1, 1782.

9 HJ, March 8, 1782.

10 HJ, March 1, 1782.

11 Carlisle to Hillsborough, December 29, 1781, SP 63/480, ff. 10–13

12 Hillsborough to Carlisle, January 24, 1782, SP 63/480, ff. 84–89.

13 Eugene C. Black, *The Association, British Extra parliamentary Political Organization 1769–1793* (Harvard University Press, 1963), p. 131.

14 *The Journal of the Rev. John Wesley,* IV, 115–116.

15 Eden to Loughborough, January 29, 1782, Add. Mss. 34418, f. 309.

16 Burke to Eden, April 5, 1782, Add. Mss. 34418, f. 410.

17 HO 100/1, ff. 42–43; Portland to Shelburne, April 27, 1782, HO 100/1, ff. 153–56.

18 Charlemont to Flood, January 1, 1782, HMC, Charlemont Papers, I, 147–48.

19 Flood to Charlemont, January 7, 1782, HMC, Charlemont Papers, I, 392.

20 HJ, May 3, 1782.

21 Portland to Shelburne, April 27, 1782, HO 100/1, ff. 153–56.

22 May 18, 1782, HO 100/1, ff. 225–29.

23 21 & 22 Geo. III (Ire.), c. 24 and c. 62.

24 21 & 22 Geo. III (Ire.), c. 25 and c. 57.

25 HJ, May 6, 1782.

26 *Irish Lords' Journal,* V, 320–321.

27 HMC, Charlemont Papers, I, 47.

28 DEP, September 7, 1782.

29 FJ, November 7, 1782.

30 FJ, December 21, 1782.

31 FJ, May 13, June 28, 1783.

32 Temple to the Lords of the Treasury, February 12, 1783, Add. Mss. 40177, ff. 41–42.

33 HMC, Charlemont Papers, I, 81–82.

34 FJ, November 21, 1782.

35 Temple to Lord Sydney (the former Thomas Townshend), March 12, 1783, HO 100/8, ff. 230–31.

36 DEP, March 22, 1783.

37 FJ, May 6, 1783.

XIV

Class Conflict and Parliamentary Reform

Once the renunciation issue had been settled and constitutional independence accepted by all, parliamentary reform became the major topic of political interest. It is an historical truism that the British House of Commons at this time was archaic and corrupt in its representative structure; the Irish House was altogether worse. It consisted of 300 members, of whom 64 sat for the thirty-two counties, two for Dublin University and the remainder represented 117 electoral districts all of which, for convenience, will be called boroughs. Each district sent two members to the House of Commons. These 117 included about 100 boroughs (properly so called), some ten cities, and about seven manors. There was no distinction, except in the narrowest legal sense, between manors and boroughs; and most of the "cities" were places of episcopal residence or ancient towns too small to be considered cities even by the standards of the eighteenth century. Perhaps only five or six towns were large and populous enough to merit the contemporary title of city if used in a social and general, as opposed to a merely legalistic, sense. For the sake of convenience, therefore, it seems reasonable to apply the term "borough" to all electoral districts other than Dublin University and the thirty-two counties. There were at most only about six "real" cities—Dublin, Cork, Limerick, Belfast, Waterford, and Londonderry. Of these, Limerick and Belfast had so few electors that they were virtually "rotten" boroughs; only the remaining four cities, and at most half-a-dozen other towns, had an electorate sufficiently numerous and independent to exercise the franchise freely.

As in England, a rotten or otherwise corrupt borough was one in which representation was controlled by intimidation or bribery or a combination of both on the part of its "patron," who was usually the principal landlord of that electoral district. Sometimes a man could be the patron but not the landlord as in the case of Newtownards, Co. Down where the representation was "owned" by the Ponsonby family, though the great landlord of this small town and surrounding country was Robert Stewart. There was a general belief that most of the counties were reasonably free from corruption and, consequently, their representatives had considerable prestige. In fact, however, the landed aristocrats dominated the election in the majority of counties.

There were many lists of the boroughs and counties with descriptions of the number and types of electors in each, and the names of the patrons or of those who exercised a controlling influence. The *Dublin Evening Post* of January 25, 1783 published one (along with an earnest plea for reform from its author, the anonymous "Molyneux"), and the Volunteers drew up another towards the end of the same year. It is published in the

Grattan Memoirs.[1] The two lists (and there are others) are agreed that over 200 members of the Commons were nominated by patrons. These estimates do not even take into account the fact that fully half the county members were returned by landed aristocrats, either by virtual nomination, or by receiving their support in the elections. In Kildare, Cork, Waterford, and Galway, for example, at least one, if not both members, were the nominees respectively of Leinster, Shannon, Tyrone and the Daly family. Louth was divided between John Foster and the Fortescue family so that no election was held for that county in either 1776 or 1783. Even when voters were free to vote according to their wishes, it is obvious that it would be to their economic and social interest to support the local great landlord as his patronage could secure benefits for his followers. In fact, one of the reasons why landed aristocrats exerted themselves in politics was to increase their local influence and prestige. An example of this concern for status was the request by Hillsborough of the Viceroy for the nomination of a hearth-money collector in the village of Hillsborough, Co. Down: in his letter Hillsborough mentioned the importance of such patronage in maintaining his influence in the county.[2]

The press, with some exaggeration, usually described most county members as representing the "independent interest." This statement meant that they represented a substantial number of landlords and, perhaps, some humbler constituents free to vote as they pleased. In parliament they normally acted in accordance with the sentiments of the landlords of their county. Their "independence" arose from the fact that they were free from the influence or control of particular aristocrats and, above all, were not wedded to the support of the government.

Dr. Patrick Rogers in his *The Irish Volunteers and*

Catholic Emancipation [3] has divided the 117 boroughs into four categories according to the type of franchise:

1. 53 "Corporation" boroughs, where the right of election was confined to the corporation, a non-representative body.
2. 46 "Freeman" boroughs, in which all freemen, nominally at least, had the vote. By 1783 they had in many cases by prescription lost the right to vote.
3. 11 "Inhabitant householder" or "Potwalloper" boroughs, where every (Protestant) male householder had the vote.
4. 7 "Manor" boroughs, where the freeholders of the manor voted.

As already indicated in Chapter X (the revolt within the Volunteers against Leinster and Shannon), the feeling against borough-owning aristocrats was not necessarily limited to the middle classes, but was likely to be shared by those of the aristocracy and gentry who lacked political influence. There were two goals in the campaign for parliamentary reform, one being the abolition of rotten boroughs, and the other the alteration of the franchise. In 1781 and again in 1783, much was written in the press concerning reform. In 1782, on the other hand, attention was focussed on obtaining legislative independence and the renunciation bill. An examination of the expressions of opinion during these three years yields much of importance and helps to clarify the difference in aim between middle and upper classes.

Public opinion in 1781 and 1783 concentrated on several points: reform of the franchise; abolition of the rotten boroughs; extension of the boundaries of boroughs so as to include many more voters; the grant of the franchise

to greater numbers; the "counteracting of borough influence" by adding to the number of representatives for
the counties; the adoption of a secret ballot in place of
open voting; and the prevention of unqualified men from
voting.

On one point there was virtual unanimity. This was
the belief that the franchise should not be extended to
all or nearly all men. "Molyneux," in publishing the list
of counties and boroughs in the *Dublin Evening Post* in
January 25, 1783, called for the abolition of rotten boroughs, but stated: "Extending the right of voting at Elections, to almost all descriptions of men, especially of the
lower orders, threatens . . . such unavoidable scenes . . .
as can never justify the innovation.

The establishment of an effective means of preventing
unqualified men from voting was an aim that all classes
could support. The opportunities for fraud were legion.
Men were often accepted as entitled to vote on their own
or another's oath. In many boroughs non-resident freemen
could vote, and it was often difficult to challenge the
right of strangers to vote when they appeared at the poll.
In counties the voting took place in the county town, so
that many electors came from places thirty or forty miles
distant; furthermore, the polls usually remained open for
two or three weeks. Thus, impersonation and other mal-
practices were common. After each general election, petitions protesting against fraud poured into the House of
Commons, and were investigated by committees which
often declared elections invalid. During the election for
Cork County in 1783, one man was heard to say he was
"tired polling."

Many writers expressed a desire to see some of the
boroughs suppressed, and an increased number of representatives allotted to the counties. Their arguments were

rebutted on the grounds that the voting in counties was usually influenced by the borough-owning aristocrats, so that increased county representation would be of limited effect. Reference has already been made to the Earl of Kingston whose son, Kingsborough, had been obliged to sit for the family borough of Boyle, Co. Roscommon, when he would have much preferred to represent the County of Cork. Placing himself at the head of the more radical Volunteers corps, he managed to defeat Townsend, the nominee of Shannon, in the general election of 1783. The other Co. Cork seat fell to James Bernard of Bandon, an aristocrat popular with radical opinion. In Cork city Richard Longfield, who had broken with Shannon, was elected along with Hely Hutchinson who was, of course, able to succeed by his own efforts.

The newspapers were delighted with the defeat of Shannon's nominees and hailed it as a victory for reform. The Bishop of Cloyne, Richard Woodward, wrote sorrowfully to Buckinghamshire:

Lord Shannon's general interest is nearly overset by the democratic spirit now prevailing. Longfield, who is monstrously ungrateful, has beat him in the City of Cork, and he is in great danger in the county . . . the dignity of the Shannon family is *shorn of its beams* by the loss of a general influence over so great a county.[4]

Naturally enough, the newspapers hailed the victory over Shannon as a gain for the "independent interest" and a defeat for parliamentary "venality." Their exuberance was all the greater because Shannon was the country's largest borough-owner. Nevertheless, he was defeated not so much by a popular movement as by an alliance between Kingsborough and the two commoners, Bernard and Longfield, both of whom owned such large estates as to merit the description of aristocrat. The *Dublin Evening Post* virtually admitted that the struggle lay between aristocratic factions rather than classes, when it stated that Longfield's rental was bigger than Shannon's, and that the "independent interest" was composed of landlords whose incomes totalled over £160,000.[5]

The belief was widely expressed that landlords often "created" freeholders in order to increase their own political strength in counties and in those boroughs in which freeholders could vote. A meeting of the "Independent Electors and Inhabitants" of Co. Galway resolved in February, 1783, that "in order to establish the future freedom of election, we strongly recommend to independent Gentlemen to increase the number of Freeholds on their respective estates."[6] "Dependent" gentlemen could obviously do likewise, but the advice was scarcely as naive as it might sound, since the amount of land owned by what might be termed politically "underprivileged" landlords would obviously have greatly exceeded that possessed by the comparatively few borough-owners, whether aristocrats or gentry. Thus, in a competition to create freeholders, the "independent interest" would clearly defeat their landlord rivals. The evidence in newspaper editorials and correspondence of the existence of this practice is overwhelming, but one never found any explicit description of how the freeholders were actually "created." A letter almost unique because of its candour is in the papers of the Jephson family of Mallow Castle, Co. Cork. It was written to Denham Jephson, M.P. for the manor borough of Mallow:

But I do not fear, however, for the success of Sir James [Cotter] and you, if ye are diligent, industrious and active and make votes. . . . You have as good a right to make Freeholders out of Scarteen as out of your Estate in Mallow or anywhere else; I never was upon Scarteen. If you have not, you *ought* to have a survey of every Field in it; to each field you may give a name now and inform your Stewart and others of the Christening without telling Thomas your reasons and from time to time their memories ought to be kept up. Out of each field, by its name, you may spring and form a Freeholder, taking care in the Lease to give the field its new name and also its old name, if any, it had; if not, the new name must be so as to form and prove a certainty on the face of the Lease—By such a measure, I conceive you may make a good many Votes not to be shaken in any place and the sooner you begin the better—I will support your right to grant Freeholders out of Scarteen; it *may* but *can't* be disputed, that you have a good legal right.[7]

Another important suggestion was an enlargement of the area of boroughs in order to bring in an increased number of voters. In this way, the power of borough-owners would be reduced. As in the case of adding to the number of county representatives, this change would tend to benefit the local landlords whose estates would be partly or wholly included within the newly drawn boundaries. Like all the other reforms described so far, this was one which "underprivileged" aristocrats and gentry could profitably support, or, as in the case of rendering fraud more difficult, could accept without loss to their own position. The middle classes could also enthuse about these improvements since they would lessen the political power of the borough-owners, and thus bring about a diminution of the British government's domination of the Irish Parliament. These reforms would be of little benefit to those sections of the community seeking to acquire a share in political influence at the expense of aristocracy and gentry.

To find the middle-class elements in the agitation for

parliamentary reform, and to see them as having an aim distinct from that of the landlords, it is necessary to examine other aspects of the movement. These pertain to the nature and exercise of the franchise, and were discussed in the press with a view to creating a large number of voters sufficiently independent of landlord bribery and intimidation to be able to vote as free men.

On August 7, 1781, a correspondent in the *Dublin Evening Post* saw reform in

strengthening the independent interest by increasing the number of voters; one for every £100 per annum [a substantial income], would cast the balance on the side of virtue, and teach county members, &c., a language many of them have long since forgotten.

An impressive writer in the (Cork) *Hibernian Chronicle* in February, 1781, referred to the "nonsensical distinction of *Freehold*" and suggested that the franchise be limited to men of £20 a year, the minimum, he considered, necessary to render a man independent. He demanded that forty-shilling freeholders of less income than £20 be disqualified from voting.[8] This writer had entered upon the subject a few weeks earlier with the proposal that

the Elections to be made by the men of property in the Counties and in the Cities. No man, even in the Corporations to be admitted to vote who cannot bring two Electors to swear that they believe him actually possessed of an annual income of £20 a year, and no Protestant to be rejected who has this qualification, be the nature of the tenure what it may. What a monstrous absurdity is it to call the poorest and most precarious of all tenures a freehold, and to refuse a man the privilege of voting who has a thousand a year by a lease of 999 years.[9]

Obviously, landlords would regard any attempt to dis-
franchise the tenants of small holdings as a threat to their
own political influence. Likewise, it would injure their
position if the vote were allowed only to tenants of substance. Such changes in the franchise would mean bringing a large part of the House of Commons under the influence of the middle classes.

Along with these radical suggestions went a direct attack
on political domination by landlords. In April, 1781, a
correspondent addressing the voters of Co. Tyrone denounced landlord tyranny at elections:

Well do I know a landlord, in the vanity of his little power,
glories to see a hundred vassals in his train. . . . Consider for
a moment, were you to unite firmly against their influence,
what could landlords do? Would they, at the expiration of
your leases, think of unpeopling a whole county? . . . Where
is the man whom self-interest will suffer to turn out the
tenants of his whole estate?[10]

In an address to electors in April, 1782, the Ulster Committee of the Volunteers advised them to "regard not the
threats of landlords or their agents." [11] An indignant con-
tributor to the *Dublin Evening Post* in March, 1783, considered that county representation needed reform because
landlords had established "great numbers of Forty-shilling
Freeholders for the avowed and shameful purpose of voting at elections, and bearing down the independent Freeholders." [12] A month later a correspondent addressed the
electors of Co. Down:

Let us enter into a subscription to reimburse such tenants
as may be injured by their landlords for giving their un-
biassed votes, and to prosecute such landlords as may use
undue influence with their tenants.[13]

The suggestion that a secret ballot would give freedom to voters was countered by the argument that the landlords would demand to see the voting paper. This writer demanded the abolition of *all* boroughs and the taking of an oath by successful candidates to conduct themselves honestly in parliament. In July, 1781, the *Dublin Evening Post* showed its dislike of leadership by landlords in observing that more merchants should be elected:

. . . When their love of liberty, virtue, disinterestedness, and adequate abilities are acknowledged, there are none from whom we can, with more probability expect political and commercial freedom.[14]

With the exception of Sir Edward Newenham, a radical with a touch of the eccentric, and Henry Flood, who took up the agitation only in 1783, none of the Patriots attempted to arouse interest in parliamentary reform. On Yelverton's motion on Poyning's Law in April, 1780, Newenham said that if peers were to have an influence in the return of borough members to parliament, 100 members should be added to the representation of the counties.[15] In 1782 he was the only political figure to link legislative independence with parliamentary reform. In April of that year, in an address to the Volunteers of Mohill (Co. Leitrim), where he had purchased property, he called for "a more equal representation in parliament" by adding to the numbers returned by counties and "annihilating (that source of corruption) the *rotten* Boroughs."[16] Under his chairmanship, his corps—the Liberty Volunteers—passed resolutions in May, 1782, one of which demanded "a more equal representation."[17] Three months later, the High Sheriff and Freeholders of Co. Dublin applauded his efforts for parliamentary reform.[18] In the weeks after the constitutional demands had been conceded, he introduced to the Commons two measures, one for the exclusion of placemen and pensioners, and the other, as already described, for disfranchising Revenue officers with salaries of less than £200. The purpose of these motions was to lessen the influence of Dublin Castle in the Commons.

It is significant that all of Newenham's statements and actions aimed at reforms which landlords could support without injury to their own political power. Even he, for several years the most radical of the Patriots, had no intention of sacrificing the power of landlords in order to give political influence to the middle classes. As already described, Grattan had been ambiguous on the subject of parliamentary reform in the late summer of 1780 when he addressed his indignant corps, the Independent Dublin. It was obvious that the middle classes must seek their political aims in themselves, in other words, in the Volunteers. And this they did.

In April, 1781, a correspondent in the *Dublin Evening Post* called on *all* voters, and not merely *gentlemen*, to attend a county meeting called for the nomination of candidates for a future election. He asked them, even those worth only forty shillings a year, to talk up with spirit since there now existed a golden opportunity, in that "the nation is a Camp of Soldiers armed in your cause." [19] This belief in the Volunteers as the instrument for obtaining concessions for both the Patriots and the more radical elements was widely expressed in letters and editorials in the newspapers. In June, 1781, the *Dublin Evening Post* stated:

The leaders of the friends of Ireland, sensible from repeated experience, how vain are their greatest and best endeavors in

Parliament, in opposition to the influence of corruption, have wisely determined to exert themselves for the future in a different and more effectual manner. To increase the already powerful army of Volunteers, and to inspire them with a patriotic ardour, and a noble cause of *true and unmutilated freedom*, will be the best security of their rights and privileges.[20]

A writer in the press in June, 1782, warned the public that since the forces of corruption could still conquer the parliament, an effective reform was necessary to confirm the constitutional gains. He added that the people must stick fast to the Volunteers since it was they who gave them their "power in the nation." [21] In July, 1782, a correspondent said: "the people, as freeholders, never yet had decisive influence; as Volunteers, they have." [22]

The campaign for parliamentary reform was initiated in March, 1783, by a call from the delegates of the Munster Volunteers for a reform of the rotten boroughs.[23] On July 1 the officers of 45 corps met at Lisburn, Co. Antrim, and suggested a meeting of the delegates of all the Ulster Volunteers.[24] Similar resolutions came later in July from officers meeting at reviews in Ulster at Belfast, Londonderry, and Broughshane.[25] As a result, the delegates of 278 corps met at Dungannon on September 8, 1783.[26] James Stewart, M.P. for Co. Tyrone, presided and among those present was the brilliant and eccentric Frederick Augustus (Hervey), fourth Earl of Bristol and Bishop of Derry, commonly known as the Earl-Bishop. It was decided to hold a national convention of Volunteer delegates on November 10 in Dublin for the purpose of considering parliamentary reform, which was seen as necessary to save the country from "an absolute monarchy, or, that still more odious government, a tyrannical aristocracy." In

October a meeting of delegates in each of the provinces, Leinster and Connaught, was held at which preparations were made for the national assembly in Dublin.[27]

The Volunteers had always been more numerous in Ulster than in the other provinces and because of the radical opinions of the Presbyterian population, it is not surprising that parliamentary reform should have found its most vigorous support in the northern counties. Having always retained the franchise and the legal right to sit in parliament, and since 1780 entitled to be members of borough corporations and to hold government office, it was not surprising that these Dissenters should now seek real political influence. The connections and sympathies with the American colonists had, no doubt, enlivened their desire to achieve some real equality with the Anglican ascendancy.

At the opening of the 1783–1784 session of the Parliament in October, the Administration proposed a vote of thanks to the Volunteers in order to forestall a similar motion by the Opposition.[28] This tactic was clearly part of the preparations which the Viceroy, Lord Northington, was making in order to frustrate any attempt to reform parliament. In a letter to the Home Secretary, Lord North, in September, Northington had said:

A Parliamentary Reform is the grand subject of discussion intended to be proposed by the Delegates of the Volunteer corps. They are not yet decided in what shape to introduce it. . . . The unconstitutional conduct of the advocates of this measure has given just cause for alarm, and has checked the zeal of many of its best friends.[29]

In reply, North made it clear that the British Government was determined to oppose any reform.[30] Fox, the other leading member of this coalition government, was equally firm:

Unless they [the Volunteers] dissolve in a reasonable time, Government, and even the name of it, must be at an end. . . . If they are treated as they ought to be—if you show firmness, and that firmness is seconded by the aristocracy and Parliament—I look to their dissolution as a certain and not very distant event; if otherwise, I reckon their [the Volunteers'] Government, or rather Anarchy, as firmly established as such a thing is capable of being. . . . Volunteers, and soon, possibly, Volunteers without property, will be the only Government in Ireland, unless they are faced this year in a manful manner. . . . All other points appear to me to be trifling in comparison of this great one of the Volunteers.[31]

The Bishop of Clogher, John Hotham, wrote to his former patron, Buckinghamshire, on the very alarming state of the country. He saw the legislature and "men of property" as menaced by the Volunteers, and feared an outbreak of violence.[32]

Though encouraged by Dublin Castle to take his place as one of the delegates elected by the Volunteers of Co. Londonderry, Thomas Conolly refused. When the Convention was nearing its last sittings, the Bishop of Cloyne wrote that Conolly was now applauded for his wisdom in remaining away: "Government strongly urged Mr. C[onolly] to attend. . . . He saw deeper, and obstinately refused. They now see he was right." [33] Though nominated by his corps, the Dublin Independent, Grattan also refused to attend the Convention (as the national meeting of the Volunteer delegates was known) and was expelled by the unanimous vote of the corps on December 2.[34] As a constitutionalist, Grattan disliked having the Volunteers attempt to bring pressure to bear on the Parliament on an *internal* problem. It was different, he explained in a letter to Charlemont, when the purpose of overawing the legislature was to strengthen a national protest against English domination. His attitude to the campaign was one of qualified and confused approval:

I do most extremely, as you know, approve of a parliamentary reform. . . . The boroughs are very numerous and exceptionable [i.e. objectionable], and yet by attempting to strike them off we may lose an increase of county members. . . . The repetitions of Dungannon meetings will alarm parliament, as if the delegates were coming in the place of the legislature . . . at the same time I acknowledge that the business of more equal representation might have little chance unless taken up by the people. . . . It is certainly the great object.[35]

In what he says it is clear that his idea of reform accorded with landlord rather than middle-class sentiments.

Charlemont's views were similar to Grattan's. In his memoirs he stated that in the earlier years he had approved of the Volunteers because they were pitted against English claims, but by 1783 he feared violence if they were hostile to their own legislature on an internal matter. In November, 1782, he had thought that England was likely to create in her own constitution "a more equal representation" and that Ireland would almost certainly follow her example, so that there was no need to "precipitate the business in the present disturbed state of men's minds." He considered that "requisitions of this nature ought in the first instance to proceed from the people, rather in their capacity of freeholders than in that of Volunteers." [36]

A highly cultivated person, whose appreciation of art had benefitted from a long residence in Italy, Charlemont was hardly suitable as the leader of a radical movement. Subject to chronic ill-health, handicapped by a nervous dislike of speaking in public, and never having served in the Army, he was chosen commander of the Volunteers because of his known integrity and independence of Dublin Castle. To these characteristics was added a loyal confidence in his friends and a capacity to appreciate their sincerity when they differed from him in politics, as in the case of Flood's taking office in 1775, an action which Charlemont saw with deep concern. Extremely sensitive, he could be selfrighteous and was very conscious of his virtue as a Patriot. His revealing memoirs show that he was singularly lacking in a sense of humor, a defect that led him to praise his own political principles and conduct with a candor bordering on the naive. A Christian and no deist, he shared the views on religious toleration of his rationalist age. Though opposed to giving political rights to Catholics because they might become a menace to the Protestant minority, he was not hostile to them from any theological principle. He was so friendly to the Presbyterians that one feels that his Protestantism was closer to nonconformity than to Anglicanism. He would have liked nothing better than to have been the Irish equivalent of a radical aristocratic English Whig, but this role was virtually impossible to play in Ireland because of religious and economic factors. Perhaps the best description of his personality and ambitions has been found in a marginal note in a contemporary book:

A most amiable accomplished man, learned in every branch of polite Literature, his Conversation the most lively and entertaining never seem exhausted. A true lover of his country in his publical Principles, an Enthusiast for the British Constitution, a most determined Revolution Whig. He was taken from this mortal stage in good time; the Union and Proceedings since that would have made him miserable beyond Conception. His Passion for the Parliament was extreme, it was indeed his foible; the loss of it would have broken his heart. I had the Honour to have some share in his Confidence and esteem and much and often do I feel the want of such a well-informed good naturly pleasing friend.[37]

At Lisburn, Co. Antrim, on July 1, 1783, the delegates of 45 corps of Volunteers met and appointed a committee of correspondence charged with the task of seeking advice on a reform of parliament from leading English radicals —Major John Cartwright, Lord Effingham, John Jebb, Rev. Richard Price, the Duke of Richmond, and Rev. Christopher Wyvill.[38]

The Lisburn committee addressed a letter to each of the six men. Having described some of the points which had been discussed and on which it was difficult to decide, the committee asked: Should rotten boroughs be abolished? Should county representatives be increased? Should suffrage be extended and, if so, to whom? Should there be a secret ballot? and shorter parliaments? What specific mode of reform would the recipient suggest? Should compensation be paid on the abolition of rotten boroughs?

Cartwright advised that the franchise be extended to all men, and the secret ballot be employed to enable them to cast their votes freely. He had seen the benefits of this system in South Carolina. Though he admired the new constitutions of the States of America, he could not agree with their limiting the vote to such as possessed a certain income. Since the income required was frequently so small, he regarded such a qualification as "the very nonsense of inveterate prejudice." Cartwright's reply was not very helpful.

Lord Effingham said that he would enfranchise almost everybody in the boroughs. A secret ballot could be circumvented by bribery as in Sweden. Increasing the county representation would merely admit additional aristocratic families to an influence in returning members to parliament.

Jebb advised against adding to the number of county members as it would tend to give government increased opportunities for bribery, and greater power to the aristocracy. He approved as expedient and just the paying of compensation to the owners of rotten boroughs when these were abolished. In a second letter he expressed the opinion that one-member constituencies would be excellent. Making property a qualification for voting only led to "perjuries and endless altercations."

Rev. Richard Price, the Unitarian, suggested that counties be divided up into one-member constituencies. "In America, where new forms of government are established, more liberal than any the world has yet seen, this right [the franchise] is limited to persons who pay taxes and possess property." He felt that perhaps in Ireland it might not be prudent to have so wide a suffrage, but he would suggest giving the vote to all holders of property of a certain value. Rotten boroughs should be abolished and compensation paid, not as a right but out of necessity.

The Duke of Richmond believed in universal suffrage and annual elections. Adding to the representation of counties would merely increase the power of a few great families so that the people's most essential concerns, "life, liberty and property" would continue to be controlled by the aristocracy. When he proposed reform in 1780, some feared that universal manhood suffrage would give new opportunities of bribing to aristocrats; others feared that this suffrage would produce the "confusion of a democratick republic." Each argument, he considered, nullified the other. Property and riches would always have an influence, and rich men who were popular would always obtain votes. Another objection voiced was that political equality would lead to equality in property. This argument was false since equality in political rights was compatible with "unequal shares of industry, labour, and genius" and because "the equality and inequality of men are both founded in nature." He wished to see the Crown as the Executive, the Lords the deliberative power, and the Commons as representing the people. He disapproved of secret balloting as leading to "concealment and deceit." Trivial circumstances of that kind tended to form the national character and "it is most consistent with that of a British, or an Irish freeman, that all his actions should be open and avowed." The owners of suppressed boroughs, he felt should be compensated as a matter of expediency but not of right.

The Rev. Christopher Wyvill wished to see the franchise extended to all fit classes of men, and "where the right of universal [manhood] suffrage has not been found actually inconsistent with the public safety, it ought not to be abridged." In Ireland he thought the franchise could be given safely only to "every class of men, who from the possession of property to some small amount, may be thought likely to exercise their franchise freely, and for the public good." In the American Republics, Wyvill continued,

property is more equally divided, and the manners of the people are more simple, orderly and incorrupt . . . and yet in them some qualifications of property have been thought necessary. . . . In Massachusetts, and some other American States, the landed qualification exceeds that of an English freeholder.

He disliked a secret ballot:

In places where no undue influence can be exerted, the concealment of the ballot is totally unnecessary. But where that influence is predominant, it ought to be resisted, not by a practice encouraging cowardly disingenuity and breach of promise, but by open and honourable means.

The duration of parliaments ought to be limited to less than eight years. Boroughs lacking population he continued, should be abolished and compensation paid to their owners, not because of strict justice, but out of a concern for equity and in order to lessen opposition. The seats thus suppressed should be distributed among the counties and the principal cities and towns.

In regard to the burning question of whether to extend the franchise to Catholics, Cartwright and Richmond expressed no opinion. Effingham considered it a matter to be judged only when the political inclinations of Catholics and the influence of their priests had been taken into account. Jebb, Price, and Wyvill gave emphatic support to the suggestion that Catholics be enfranchised. Wyvill, an Anglican clergyman with leanings towards Unitarianism, considered that "the established religion would be secure as it is at present, because Catholic voters could not elect Catholic legislators." Price was clearly very anxious to see Catholics in Ireland given the suffrage, though he admitted that there might be stronger objections to the grant than he was aware of.

With the exception of Cartwright (whose plea for universal manhood suffrage regardless of property rights was not very constructive), the replies were primarily concerned with giving the vote to a very large number of people with a small property qualification, and with reducing the power and influence of the aristocracy. There was no mention of the gentry. In Ireland, on the other hand, the aim of reformers among the middle classes was to take away most of the power of the borough-owners,

and to create a large number of middle-class voters of
sufficient property to be independent of their landlords,
aristocrats or gentry. The Irish reformers were clearly
more concerned with class distinctions than were their
English equivalents. No doubt this difference in attitude
reflected the comparative poverty and sparsity of the middle classes in Ireland, and the deeper cleavage between the
Irish landlord classes and their tenantry.

II

The Convention met in Dublin on November 10, 1783,
at the Rotunda, a large assembly hall.[39] The majority of
the delegates were landlords or members of landlord families.[40] Charlemont was elected chairman and procedure
was conducted with parliamentary decorum. On the first
day activities were limited to formalities, but on the second day a cat was thrown among the pigeons by George
Ogle, obviously acting at the suggestion of Dublin Castle.
Always an opponent of Catholic claims, Ogle said that
he had a letter written by a Catholic peer [Kenmare]
stating that Catholics were not making any request for the
right to exercise the franchise. The effect was very discouraging to many of the delegates who had intended supporting the grant of this right to the Catholics. As a result of
Ogle's statement, it was decided by a majority vote to
shelve further discussion of this topic.

The radical *Dublin Evening Post,* which had opposed
the Catholic Relief Act in 1778 but since then had favored
concession, praised the Catholics for having refrained from
requesting admission to the franchise.

There scarce exists a doubt now, that the Convention having
got rid of a matter, which was likely to embarrass them exceedingly, will concur in some general plan to emancipate

this country from the thraldom of two or three *little* great men, and give the people that share in the Constitution, of which they have been deprived for ages.[41]

But the Catholic Committee had no intention of allowing Lord Kenmare to suppress their demands, and on November 14 delivered a message to the Convention which was read by the Earl-Bishop. In his own defense Ogle said that he had not actually seen any letter, but had been informed by Sir Boyle Roche that such was the opinion of Lord Kenmare and his friends. A week later Kenmare issued a public denial that he had ever written such a letter. The manner in which he expressed himself, and some of the statements in his denial, suggest that Ogle and Boyle Roche did convey to the Convention the *substance* of Kenmare's opinion.

Northington remained unperturbed and did not share the alarm felt by Fox and the Bishop of Clogher. The reason for his calm is obvious: he knew the attitude of many of the delegates to the Convention who were members of parliament and opponents of radical reform. On November 17 he wrote to Fox:

It [the Convention] is composed of such an heterogeneous lot, their characters, principles and views so different, that its resolutions are not likely to be such, as will create material embarrassment or distress to Government.

He regretted the "court" which Lord Temple, as viceroy, had paid the Volunteers, and added that it would have been imprudent to have tried to prevent the holding of the Convention:

The next step was to try by means of our Friends in this Assembly [the Convention] to perplex its proceedings, and create confusion in their deliberations, in order if possible, to bring their meeting into contempt, and to create a necessity of its dissolving itself. These methods have had a considerable effect . . . many have returned to their homes disgusted. . . . Friends of all denominations new and old agree that no consequences are to [be] feared, and that it will end in confusion and contempt will attend its fall.[42]

Early in the proceedings of the Convention, a committee under the chairmanship of Flood was appointed to prepare a plan of parliamentary reform. In due course the committee made its report. Their plan, which was accepted by the Convention, can be substantially stated as follows:

1. Non-residents to be prohibited from voting in counties and boroughs unless possessed of a freehold or lease worth at least £20 a year.
2. All decayed [i.e. rotten] boroughs to have their boundaries extended in order to include neighboring parishes or baronies.
3. All boroughs to be deemed decayed if they do not have a certain number of voters over and above the status of "potwalloper."
4. All Protestant freeholders having a minimum of £10 a year to be given the franchise in boroughs.
5. All bylaws made by corporations in order to contract the right of franchise to be rendered void.
6. A general election to be held every three years.

The plan was obviously designed to reduce the power of the borough-owners by extending boundaries and by rendering void all bylaws designed to limit the number of voters. The emphasis on extending and limiting the franchise to men possessed of some substance, reflected the middle-class demand for a more independent type of elector. The middle classes and the politically "under-

privileged" landlords would welcome the plan in its attack
on the borough-owners, but only the middle classes could
approve of the alterations proposed in the franchise.

The plan was a moderate one if judged solely by its
concrete recommendations. Its radicalism lay in the two
principles it implied. One was the need for fundamental
change in the political structure. The other was the right
of an extra-constitutional body—the Volunteers—to prepare and present to the legislature a program for the
legislature's reform. The Irish House of Commons would
accept the plan only if the plan was supported by overwhelming force. Such was not the case. The British Government was determined to have the reform defeated, and
the Irish landlord classes were not likely to grant political
power to the middle classes without a struggle. The decision of the Convention to limit the benefit of the reform
to Protestants meant that all Catholic support was lost.
An extension of political power to the Protestant middle
classes could only mean that Protestant ascendancy would
be buttressed. Catholics had nothing to gain and much to
lose should this reform be enacted. The pro-Catholic
Freeman's Journal attacked the plan as a menace to the
economic welfare of Catholics.[43] The radical and Pro-
testant-owned *Dublin Evening Post* showed strong approval of the reform by continuing to eulogize Flood.[44]

As soon as the plan had been accepted by the Convention, Flood obtained approval for his presenting it at once
to the House of Commons. Charlemont's desire that it
first be sent down and placed before county meetings
was defeated. On November 29 Flood proposed the motion, seconded by William Brownlow, that "leave be given
to bring in a bill for the more equal representation of
the People in Parliament."

The motion met with a most hostile reception. The

Attorney-General, Yelverton, refused to discuss it because he considered it an insult to the House:

Shall we sit here to be dictated to by the point of the bayonet? I honour the Volunteers, they have eminently served their country; but when they turn into a debating society, to reform the Parliament and regulate the nation. . . . Is the Convention or the Parliament of Ireland to deliberate on the affairs of the nation?

Flood attacked those who had accepted the assistance of the Volunteers in the campaign for Free Trade and legislative independence, but now chastised them:

What has now transformed those men . . . into hydras, gorgons and chimeras? I'll tell you, it is borough interest . . . the bill . . . means to destroy the infamous traffic of boroughs, and preclude the honours of peerage from every ruffian who has borough interest.

The opponents of the motion echoed the Attorney-General's argument that the House would not accept dictation from any external body. The Patriot, Bushe, said: "I am against the bill, as it comes to us from an assembly where the sword is the writ." Several members, including Forbes, varied this argument with the qualification that they favored parliamentary reform and approved of the bill, but objected to its coming from an armed body. Lieut-General Cuninghame said: "I cannot think that either of the Gentlemen who brought in this bill serious or in earnest." Ogle, who had taken such a prominent part in the Convention, admitted "he was instructed by his county to support a National Reform," but showed his hostility to the motion by declaring that "he would not pledge himself to any specific measure the present bill contained." Grattan gave a straightforward but not very enthusiastic support to the motion. It was defeated by 157 votes to 77.[45]

The usual supporters of the government naturally opposed the measure, as did the owners of boroughs. Ogle, Forbes, and nearly all the other Patriots except Bushe voted in favor of the measure. Since Ogle and Forbes had expressed virtual hostility to the motion, one may conclude that the minority of 77 was not a very determined one. The three aristocratic victors over Shannon in the general election—Kingsborough, Longfield, and James Bernard—also voted for the motion.

Having failed to persuade the House of Commons to accept its plan, the Convention decided to send it down for consideration by county meetings. In the following March Flood again submitted the reform bill to the Commons, and this time it was supported by resolutions from nearly all the counties. Since the parliament had rejected the motion when it was backed by a Volunteer assembly, it was not now likely to listen to "peaceful" requests. The bill was treated with polite contempt, and the correspondence of the new viceroy, the Duke of Rutland, shows that parliamentary reform was no longer a vital issue in Irish politics. Several times during 1783, there had been muffled reports in the press that the Volunteers were decreasing in numbers. The Convention was their last great rally; during 1784 they gradually ceased to be an important force.

It has been shown that Charlemont and Grattan disliked seeing the Volunteers attempt to overawe the Parliament. Grattan's conduct was perfectly honest; the somewhat passive support he gave to the reform when presented to the Commons sincerely reflected his hesitant attitude to the subject. Charlemont on his own admission was opposed to having the Convention, and intrigued to have men of "rank and fortune" appointed as delegates so that the assembly could be steered along a moderate course. He saw its failure with relief.[46] His hostility to the principal aims of the Volunteers appears in his candid description of his attitude to the whole subject of parliamentary reform:

The true definition of a just and beneficial reform in the representation of the people is simply this, that property should be equally and fully represented. But change this into the allowance of suffrage to every indigent individual . . . and, instead of constitutional freedom, the alteration would be productive of anarchy, and of the worst of all possible democratic republics. As a true friend to liberty I abhor democracy, which may, in my opinion, be thus defined: that it is in effect no other than a fluctuating despotism.[47]

This opinion was written before the advent of the French Revolution so that his adamant opposition to "democracy" was not a reaction to revolutionary violence. He obviously believed that in attempting to lead the Convention into moderate courses, and away from the chief objectives of the Volunteers, he was performing a meritorious work. His self-righteousness and vanity blinded him to the fact that his conduct was deceitful. This can be shown by his justification of his action on the grounds that the radical reformers intended to give the vote to almost every man and to create a "democracy." Apart from one or two letters to the press, there is nothing in the resolutions of Volunteers, or in all the different press editorials and correspondence, to suggest that any segment of the community thought of giving the vote to all men or of setting up a "democracy." The radicals of the day were attempting to make the middle classes a serious influence in politics: that was the limit of their radicalism. It was perhaps an attempt to still the small voice of conscience (which may well have troubled him once the excitement of the times had given way to cooler reflection) that induced him to attribute unjustly an extreme radicalism to the more vigorous protagonists of reform.

Ogle had been in a precarious financial position for some time before the Convention sat. Obviously because of his depleted resources, a Wexford county meeting in June, 1782, had informed him that there would be no objection to his taking office now that Ireland was ruled by a benevolent administration. In July, 1783, he was appointed to the Irish Privy Council.[48] Northington attempted to obtain for him the post of Registrar of Deeds but without success.[49] In supporting the request, Northington described Ogle as having given

the most decided and cordial support upon all occasions to my Administration, and to the furtherance of the King's affairs in the House of Commons: his zeal likewise induced him to attend the convention, of which he was chosen a member, when he exerted his efforts constantly to check and control the mischievous tendency of measures proposed there, and to support what might be the wishes of Government.[50]

It is small wonder that the movement for parliamentary reform should have failed so completely. The Volunteers might not have faded from the scene in such good temper had they seen the letter which Northington wrote to Lord North:

I have great pleasure in observing the general satisfaction which the spirited proceedings of the two Houses of Parliament have given; which I am well informed has been expressed even by many of the Gentlemen who were members of the Convention, and who, led by too strong an attention to their country interests gave a degree of countenance to measures with which their private opinions did by no means concur.[51]

Historians have attributed various motives to Henry Flood for taking up a radical position in Irish politics after he had rejoined the ranks of the Patriots towards the end of 1781. Jealousy of Grattan and chagrin at seeing him the national leader, desire to be avenged on the government, restless ambition, a keen sense of reality in seeing that parliamentary reform was vital to the independence of the Irish Parliament, have all been ascribed to his conduct. No writer seems to have considered that Flood may have had little interest in reform. An examination of certain evidence raises this question. The renunciation issue had made Flood the national leader in place of Grattan. He appears to have had nothing to do with the initiation of the campaign for parliamentary reform. It was well under way before he became identified with it. Charlemont took the salute at the various Volunteer reviews in Ulster in the summer of 1783, and it was to him their delegates sent addresses on reform. At the great meeting of the representatives of 278 corps in Dungannon on September 8, 1783, Flood was unable to attend, supposedly because of an attack of gout.[52] A short while later he left for England where he was elected for the rotten borough of Winchester on the nomination of the Duke of Chandos. Opinion in Ireland, according to both the *Dublin Evening Post* and the *Freeman's Journal*, had been puzzled by his absence at Dungannon and his sudden departure for England.[53] On December 3, the day after the Convention ended its sessions, Flood left for London where he made his first speech in the British Commons. That he should have been absent in England in the autumn during the very middle of the campaign for parliamentary reform suggests a lack of earnestness in its pursuit. Suspicions of his sincerity are not lulled by the letter which Northington wrote to Fox on November 17:

Flood has shown much disinclination to attend these meetings [of the Convention] but has been frequently summoned. . . . He declared his reverence for the old constitution, that it could not be touched without infinite hazard, and if he had not been pressed, would have avoided giving any plan or assistance to them.[54]

On March 17, 1784, the day before Flood again introduced a motion for parliamentary reform in the Irish Commons, the Duke of Rutland, Northington's successor as viceroy, wrote:

I do not well know what credit I should give to an opinion, which is hinted to me, that Mr. Flood himself is more anxious now to have the Point *decided*, than for its *successful decision*. I shall not wonder if he returned speedily to England.[55]

The evidence suggests that Flood took up parliamentary reform because he was expected to do so, in his capacity as the radical national leader. He may not have believed it likely to succeed, but to refuse to give the requested leadership would have been fatal to his position in the country. Had he been enthusiastic or had he seen a reasonable chance of success ahead, he would probably have foregone his nomination to the seat at Winchester, and concentrated all his attention on the reform issue. His taking office in 1775 had shown that he was not a man to persevere in the pursuit of lost causes. Should this interpretation of his actions be true, there is all the more reason to see a tragedy in the great campaign for parliamentary reform.

III

The period of the American Revolutionary War was in many ways the most progressive era in eighteenth-century Ireland. From a position of impotence in 1775—so discouraging that Henry Flood saw no hope of effecting improvement except in the service of government—the Patriots grew in strength until, by 1782, they had achieved most of the aims sought for over a generation. The economic depression for which the war was largely responsible had produced a widespread indignation which Grattan and his colleagues knew how to exploit. By bringing into politics the middle classes, and with the powerful assistance of that primarily middle-class organization, the Volunteers, the Patriots were able to overawe the entrenched opposition of British government and people. There followed one gain after another—Free Trade, constitutional independence, legal equality for Presbyterians, and with the positive approval of the British Cabinet, the first installments of Catholic emancipation. With these victories the Patriots were reasonably satisfied, especially as developments in both countries were tending towards a degree of parliamentary reform.

When the middle classes demanded a share in political power the Patriots felt that reform was in danger of going too far. Their radicalism extended little beyond the distribution of political influence among landlords in proportion to their landed wealth, thereby destroying the dominance of the borough-owners and bringing the Parliament more effectively under the control of Irish opinion. Once denied the leadership of the Patriots, the middle classes had neither the experience nor the self-confidence to organize a campaign on their own. They fell back into political quiescence except for a small group of Presbyterians in the north who formed a connecting link with the era of the French Revolution.

The quarrel between Grattan and Flood has been regarded by historians as a tragedy, but it was hardly that important. No doubt, it encouraged division and bitterness within the Volunteers and middle classes, thus reducing their strength, but it made little difference to the Patriots since Flood stood alone. It is arguable that he was not an entirely sincere protagonist of the reform movement he led. Since his plan was limited exclusively to the benefit of Protestants, it would very probably have been opposed by the Catholics now becoming an influential section of the body politic. They had nothing to gain and much to lose from a reform that would buttress Protestant ascendancy. Where Grattan and most of his colleagues were looking ahead to an Ireland of mixed religions in which government would be predominantly, but not solely, Anglican, Flood looked back to Charles Lucas' ideal of a self-governing "Protestant nation."

The radicalism of both the Patriots and the middle classes was of a limited nature. It sought concrete settlements of particular grievances, and differed profoundly from the more fundamental principles of the United Irishmen a dozen years later.

It remains to consider the statement so frequently made by historians that the Volunteers and the more radical of the Patriots contemplated violence and separation from Great Britain. In support of this erroneous conclusion there is a mass of superficial evidence. One can point to the words of indignant Irish leaders; the resolutions of hot-tempered Volunteer corps; the correspondence of dispirited viceroys; the destructive arguments of the opposition in the British Parliament; the fears of British cabinet ministers; and the cries of the self-interested in both countries. Dr. Raymond J. Barrett has stated that the obvious similarity in regard to the British Parliament of Ireland and the American Colonies "may, perhaps, have exerted an undue fascination for historians." [56] It may likewise be said that this similarity has induced historians to accept alarmed and heated statements as the expressions of considered opinion. There is scarcely a vestige of reliable evidence to support the theory that any segment of the Volunteers or any influential or responsible Irish leaders seriously meditated either violence or a separation from England.

NOTES FOR CHAPTER XIV

1 *Grattan Memoirs*, III, 472–87.
2 Hillsborough to Buckinghamshire, March 4, 1779, HMC, Lothian Papers, p. 347.
3 Patrick Rogers, *The Irish Volunteers and Catholic Emancipation, 1778–1793* (London, 1934), p. 83.
4 Woodward to Buckinghamshire, September 21, 1783, HMC, Lothian Papers, pp. 419–20.
5 DEP, October 7, 1783.
6 DEP, February 27, 1783.
7 For permission to quote from this letter, I am indebted to Brigadier M. D. Jephson, C.B.E., of Mallow Castle, Co. Cork.
8 HC, February 26, 1781.
9 HC, February 8, 1781.
10 DEP, April 10, 1781.
11 DEP, April 9, 1782.
12 DEP, March 29, 1783.
13 DEP, April 10, 1783.
14 DEP, July 21, 1781.
15 HJ, April 28, 1780; DEP, April 28, 1780.
16 DEP, April 20, 1782.
17 DEP, May 25, 1782.
18 DEP, August 1, 1782.

19 DEP, April 10, 1781.

20 DEP, June 2, 1781.

21 DEP, June 15, 1782.

22 DEP, July 30, 1782.

23 FJ, March 11, 1783.

24 DEP, July 8, 1783.

25 DEP, July 22, 26, 29, 1783.

26 DEP, September 13, 1783.

27 DEP, October 9, 11, 1783.

28 Northington to North, October 14, 1783, HO 100/10, ff. 178–79.

29 Northington to North, September 23, 1783, HO 100/10, ff. 106–112.

30 North to Northington, October 7, 1783, HO 100/10, ff. 236–49.

31 Fox to Northington, November 1, 1783, *Grattan Memoirs*, III, 106–112.

32 Hotham to Buckinghamshire, November 7, 1783, HMC, Lothian Papers, pp. 421–24.

33 Woodward (Bishop of Cloyne) to Buckinghamshire, November 30, 1783, HMC, Lothian Papers, p. 426.

34 DEP, December 4, 1783.

35 Grattan to Charlemont, August 10, 1783, HMC, Charlemont Papers, I, 114–115.

36 HMC, Charlemont Papers, I, 114–115, 159–63.

37 This description is a marginal note signed, "E.S.S.," against the entry concerning Charlemont in *Long's Peerage of Ireland* (1789 ed. III, 157) in the Widener Collection, Widener Library, Harvard University. For this information I am indebted to Professor Holden Furber of the University of Pennsylvania.

38 The letters of Price, Wyvill, and Effingham are taken respectively from the *Dublin Evening Post* of September 25, 30 and October 11, 1783: Jebb's two letters (August 13, 14, 1783) are in *A Collection of the Letters . . . to the Volunteers of Ireland on . . . a Parliamentary Reform*, pp. 114–122, 73–79: Cartwright's two letters (August 26, 31, 1783) are respectively in *A Collection of the Letters . . . to the Volunteers . . . on . . . a Parliamentary Reform*, pp. 98–103, and the *Dublin Evening Post*, September 27, 1783: Richmond's letter appears in *Proceedings Relative to the Ulster Assembly . . . on . . . a More Equal Representation . . . in the Parliament of Ireland*, pp. 49–63.

39 The description of the proceedings of the Convention is based primarily on the excellent account in Dr. Patrick Rogers' *The Volunteers and Catholic Emancipation*, but has been checked against that of Charlemont (HMC, Charlemont Papers, I, 113–133), the

description in the *Dublin Evening Post* which was nominated by the Convention to make reports of the debates, and the pamphlet, *The History of the Proceedings and Debates of the Volunteer Delegates of Ireland on the Subject of Parliamentary Reform* (Dublin, 1784).

40 The list of delegates is published in the *Grattan Memoirs,* III, 467–71.

41 DEP, November 11, 1783.

42 Northington to Fox, November 17, 1783, Add. Mss. 47567, ff. 54–61. This letter is published with some slight errors in the *Grattan Memoirs,* III, 129–32.

43 FJ, December 6, 23, 1783.

44 DEP, December 23, 27, 1783.

45 DEP, November 29, December 2, 1783.

46 HMC, Charlemont Papers, I, 123–25.

47 *Ibid.,* 136.

48 Sackville Hamilton to Evan Nepean, July 31, 1783, HO 100/9, f. 283.

49 Northington to Fox, August 10, 1783, Add. Mss. 47567, ff. 16–18.

50 Northington to Lord Sydney, January 25, 1784, HO 100/12, ff. 64–65.

51 Northington to North, December 4, 1783, HO 100/10, ff. 350–51.

52 DEP, October 7, 1783.

53 DEP, October 7, 1783; FJ, October 11, 1783.

54 Northington to Fox, November 17, 1783, Add. Mss. 47567, ff. 54–61.

55 Rutland to Sydney, March 17, 1784, HO 100/12, ff. 192–96.

56 Raymond J. Barrett, *op. cit.,* pp. 23–26.

Net public income and expenditure of Ireland

Year to March 25	Total Net Income £	Total Expenditure £	Raised by creation of debt £	Applied to reduction of debt £
1769	771,000	825,000	—	30,700
1770	721,000	698,100	73,800	15,200
1771	708,000	808,500	46,200	26,500
1772	676,300	737,800	92,300	25,800
1773	718,500	807,100	92,300	2,600
1774	662,700	672,100	49,000	26,600
1775	721,100	911,500	195,700	1,800
1776	714,300	733,800	32,300	14,000
1777	877,000	1,006,800	129,200	200
1778	658,300	741,700	91,100	100
1779	592,200	873,300	339,100	200
1780	556,400	833,500	231,400	—
1781	739,900	1,015,300	322,500	4,600
1782	764,400	837,500	195,600	60,000
1783	1,106,500	1,313,700	387,600	128,100
1784	1,013,900	1,142,300	273,900	203,800

These figures are taken from the audited accounts of the Vice-Treasurer of Ireland as published in [Henry William Chisholm's] *Public Income and Expenditure of Great Britain and Ireland, 1688–1869,* (British House of Commons Papers, 366, 366–1: London, 1869, Vols. I-II), 438–39. The amounts are published in British currency (£12 British equalled £13 Irish) and, in this appendix, are given to the nearest £100.

APPENDIX B

The three resolutions concerning the grant of Free Trade to Ireland, introduced to the British House of Commons by Lord North on December 9, 1779, and passed on December 14, 1779:

1. That it is the opinion of this Committee that it is expedient to repeal so much of any of the laws passed in Great Britain, as prohibit the exportation from the Kingdom of Ireland, of all woolen manufactures whatsoever, or manufactures made up, or mixed with, Wool or Wool Flocks.

2. That it is the opinion of this Committee, that it is expedient to repeal so much of an Act, made in the nineteenth year of the reign of his late Majesty King George the Second, as relates to the exportation of Glass, Glass Bottles, or Glass of any denomination whatsoever, from the Kingdom of Ireland.

3. That it is the opinion of this Committee, that it is expedient to allow the trade between Ireland and the British Colonies in America, and the West Indies, and the British Settlements on the coast of Africa, to be carried on in like manner, and subject to the same regulations and restrictions, as it is now carried on between Great Britain and the said Colonies and Settlements; provided all goods and commodities of the growth, produce, or manufacture of such colonies and settlements, shall be made liable, by laws to be made in Ireland, to the same duties as the like goods are or may be liable to upon importation into Great Britain.

The above copy of the resolutions is published in the *British Commons Journal*, XXXVII, 509–510.

APPENDIX C

Invoice of goods shipped to Maurice O'Connell of Derry-nane, Co. Kerry, by Denis MacCrohan in Nantes, November 29, 1755.

Nantes anno 1755

INVOYCE of 6 hds: 1 anr: brandy 14 anrs: tea 2 aunes Cambrick 1 pair silk stockins 3 handkerchief 2 loafs Sugar 2 lb tea & 1 lb rap'e shiped on board the John Captn. fitzgerald bound for Ballinskilla for acct. & ordr: of Mr. Maurice Connell viz.

MOC 6 hds. Cong: 194 Vts. @ £76 per 29 Vts.
clear of charges as per Collins acct.   £ 508. 8. 3
1 anr: Do [Cong:] 13 pots @ 17s per pot Do
[clear of charges as per Collins acct.]   11. 1.
10 anrs: Bohea weigg:

75½	...........20½
76	21
81½	...........21½
81	22
77	21
80½	21
75	...........20½
76	22
76½	21
78½	...........21½

777½   212
212
—————
565½

per fit on the
wracking   17½
—————
548 Nt. at 86s.6d per lb   1000. 2.

4 anrs: green tea weigg. 67½............21

67 22

65 20

62½...........20½

262   ....83½

83½

178½

per fit on the

wracking   5½

173 Nt. @ 78s.3d per lb   676.17. 3

14 empty anrs. at 52s per pce. £36. 8.

Cordidge leading &c.   £14.14. 0   51. 2.

2 aunes Cambrick £16: 1 pair silk stockins

£12:1 lb rap'e   £4.10. 0   32.10.

3 handkerchief 2 @ 70s per pce. £7 & 1 @ 40s   9.

2 lb green tea £7.16: 2 loafs sugar weigg:

7½ @ 18s per lb   £6.15   14.11.

Stowidge of 6 hds. brandy at 10s per tun   15.

2304. 6. 6

Commission @ 2½ per o̅   57.12. 1

1755   Errors & ommissions excepted Nantes

29th 9^ber Denis MacCrohan   £2361.18. 7

Explanation of terms and abbreviations in the foregoing invoice as follows:

hds. — hogsheads   anr. — anker (cask or keg)

aune — ell   rap'e — rappee (snuff)

Maurice Connell — during the Penal Days Catholics considered it politically discreet to drop the "O" and, sometimes, even the "Mac" or "Mc" in their names.

Cong: — containing   Vts — Vats (a liquid measurement of varying sizes)

Bohea — type of tea   weigg. — weighing

75½............20½ indicates gross weight and weight of anker

Nt. — nett.   pce — piece

s. — shillings   d. — pence

Cordidge — cordage   Stowidge — stowage

tun — large vessel or container

9^{ber} — November   per $\overset{o}{o}$ — % (per cent.)

Bibliography

BIBLIOGRAPHICAL NOTE

The principal sources on which this book is based are newspapers and the correspondence of statesmen, published and in manuscript. The Dublin newspapers were published three times a week and the Cork *Hibernian Chronicle* twice. They each consisted of four pages, most of which was taken up with non-Irish matter transcribed from English journals and with advertisements. News items and editorial comments concerning Ireland received little space by modern standards. Nevertheless, the newspapers are the most important single source for the Irish history of the time. They contain five types of information which are, substantially speaking, not available elsewhere: Irish House of Commons debates (the *Irish Parliamentary Register* reports only the debates from 1781 onward); news items: editorial comments; letters to the press (often published later as pamphlets); and the inserted addresses and resolutions of associations and public meetings.

The most important manuscript correspondence is that of the British Cabinet minister responsible for Ireland (the Secretary of State for the Southern Department until March, 1782, and thereafter the Secretary of State for Home and Colonial Affairs) with the viceroy and chief secretary in Ireland. A quantity of additional correspondence has been published in the volumes of the Historical Manuscripts Commission.

404

Pamphlets have been studied only to a limited extent, since many were published in the newspapers before appearing in pamphlet form.

ABBREVIATIONS

Add. Mss.	Additional Manuscripts, British Museum
SP	State Papers, (London) Public Record Office
HO	Home Office Papers, (London) Public Record Office
DEJ	*DublinEvening Journal*
DEP	*Dublin Evening Post*
FDJ	*Faulkner's Dublin Journal*
FJ	*Freeman's Journal*
HC	*Hibernian Chronicle*
HJ	*Hibernian Journal*
HMC	Publications of the Historical Manuscripts Commission
IPD	Irish Parliamentary Debates (attributed to Sir Henry Cavendish, M.P.), Library of Congress.

CONTEMPORARY SOURCES

RECORDS

British House of Lords Journals
British House of Commons Journals
Irish House of Lords Journals
Irish House of Commons Journals
The Parliamentary History of England . . . (London, 1814)
The Parliamentary Register of the History of . . . *the House of Commons of Ireland,* (Dublin, 1784 *et seq.*), I *et seq.*
Irish Parliamentary Debates in manuscript (attributed to Sir Henry Cavendish, M.P.), Library of Congress. This

source has been examined for the years 1777 through 1779, and for the discussion of the Tenantry Bill in 1780. Lack of time prevented further investigation.

Dublin Gazette

[Henry W. Chisholm], *Public Income and Expenditure of Great Britain and Ireland, 1688–1869,* (British House of Commons Papers, 366, 366–I: London, 1869, Vols I–II).

MANUSCRIPT MATERIAL

SP 63/445–63/480, January, 1775, to March, 1782.

HO 100/1–100/12, March, 1782, to April, 1784.

Add. Mss. 24137–38, Shelburne Papers (Papers of William, second Earl of Shelburne).

Add. Mss. 33100, Pelham Papers (Papers of Rt. Hon. Thomas Pelham).

Add. Mss. 34417–19, Auckland Papers (Papers of William Eden).

Add. Mss. 37833–35, Robinson Papers (Papers of John Robinson).

Add. Mss. 38211–216, 38218, 38306–307, 38344, Liverpool Papers (Papers of Charles Jenkinson).

Add. Mss. 40177, Grenville Papers (Letter-Book of the first Marquis of Buckingham, formerly third Earl Temple).

Add. Mss. 47561, 47567, 47579–581, Fox Papers (Papers of Charles James Fox).

Book of Postings and Sales, Public Record Office, Dublin.

Barrett, Raymond J., "A Comparative Study of Imperial Constitutional Theory in Ireland and America in the Age of the American Revolution", Ph.D. Dissertation, Department of History and Political Science, Dublin University, 1958.

Heron Papers, National Library of Ireland (Papers of Sir Richard Heron).

Jephson Papers, Mallow Castle, Co. Cork, Ireland (Papers of Brigadier Maurice D. Jephson, C.B.E.).

MacGeehin, Maureen, see Wall, Maureen.

Wall, Maureen, "The Activities and Personnel of the General Committee of the Catholics of Ireland, 1767–84", M.A. major dissertation, Department of History, University College, Dublin, 1952.

NEWSPAPERS

Dublin Evening Journal
Dublin Evening Post
Faulkner's Dublin Journal
Freeman's Journal
Hibernian Chronicle
Hibernian Journal

PUBLISHED CONTEMPORARY MATERIAL

Publications of the Historical Manuscripts Commission:
Abergavenny, 10th Report, Appendix VI.
Carlisle, 15th Report, Appendix VI.
Charlemont, I, 12th Report, Appendix X.
Dartmouth, III, 15th Report, Appendix I.
Donoughmore, 12th Report, Appendix IX.
Emly I, 8th Report, Appendix I.
Emly II, 14th Report, Appendix IX.
Knox, Miscellaneous VI.
Lothian.
Rutland III, 14th Report, Appendix I.
T. J. Savile Foljambe, 15th Report, Appendix V.
Stopford-Sackville, I and II.

OTHER PUBLISHED CONTEMPORARY MATERIAL

Correspondence of John Beresford. ed. William Beresford. London, 1854, Vols. I–II.

Correspondence of Edmund Burke. eds. C. W. Earl Fitzwilliam, and R. Bourke. London, 1844, Vols. I–IV.

Correspondence of Edmund Burke. Vol. III, ed. George H. Guttridge. Cambridge University Press, 1961.

Correspondence of Edmund Burke. Vol. IV, ed. John A. Woods, Cambridge University Press, 1963.

Writings and Speeches of Edmund Burke. Boston, undated, Vols. I–XII.

Dobbs, Francis. *History of Ireland from 12th October, 1779 to 15th September, 1782,* Dublin, 1782.

Memoirs of Richard Lovell Edgeworth. Begun by himself and concluded by his daughter, Maria Edgeworth. London, 1821.

Original Letters . . . to Henry Flood. ed. Thomas Rodd. London, 1820.

Complete Works of Benjamin Franklin. ed. John Bigelow. New York 1887–1888, Vols. I–X.

Writings of Benjamin Franklin. ed. A. H. Smyth. New York, 1905–1907, Vols. I–X.

Correspondence of King George III. ed. Sir John Fortescue. London, 1927–28, Vols. I–VI.

Memoirs of the Life and Times of Henry Grattan. ed. Henry Grattan [the Younger]. London 1839–1846, Vols. I–V.

Speeches of Henry Grattan. ed. Henry Grattan the Younger. London, 1822, Vols. I–IV.

[Hely Hutchinson, John]. *The Commercial Restraints of Ireland . . .* Dublin, 1779.

Retrospections of Dorothea Herbert, 1770–1789. London, 1929.

The Inchiquin Manuscripts. ed. John Ainsworth. Dublin, 1961.

Extra Official State Papers. ed. [William Knox]. Dublin, 1789.

Correspondence of Emily, Duchess of Leinster. ed. B. Fitzgerald. Dublin, 1957, Vols. I–III.

Lewis, Richard. *The Dublin Guide.* Dublin, 1787.

Lyons, J. C. *The Grand Juries of the County of Westmeath, 1727–1853.* Ledestown, 1853, Vols. I–II.

"The Irish Free Trade Agitation of 1779." ed. George O'Brien. *English Historical Review,* October, 1923 and January, 1924.

O'Connell, M. J. *Last Colonel of the Irish Brigade.* London, 1892, Vols. I–II.

Writings of George Washington, 1745–1799. ed. J. C. Fitzpatrick. Washington, D.C., 1938, Vols. I–XXXIX.

Watkinson, John. *A Philosophical Survey of the South of Ireland.* Dublin, 1778.

The Journal of the Rev. John Wesley. London, 1827, Vols. I–IV.

Wraxall, Nathaniel W. *Historical Memoirs of my own Time.* London, 1818, Vols. I–III.

Young, Arthur. *Tour in Ireland, 1776–1779.* ed. A. W. Hutton. London, 1892, Vols. I–II.

PAMPHLETS

Anonymous. *A Sketch of the History of Two Acts of the Irish Parliament.* London, 1778.

Anonymous. *Humble Remonstrance for the Repeal of the Laws against the Roman Catholics. . . .* Dublin, 1778.

Anonymous. *A Roman Catholic's Address to Parliament. . . .* Dublin, 1778.

Beauchamp, Lord. *A Letter to the First Belfast Company of Volunteers in the Province of Ulster.* Dublin, 1782.

Caldwell, Sir James. *An Enquiry how far the Restrictions Laid upon the Trade of Ireland . . . are a Benefit or a Disadvantage . . . to England. . . .* Dublin, 1779.

[Hely Hutchinson, John]. *The Commercial Restraints of Ireland Considered. . . .* Dublin, 1779.

Historical Remarks on the Pope's Temporal and Deposing Power. . . . Dublin, 1778.

The History of the Proceedings and Debates of the Volun-

teer Delegates of Ireland on the Subject of a Parliamentary Reform. Dublin, 1784.

A Collection of the Letters which have been addressed to the Volunteers of Ireland on the subject of a Parliamentary Reform. London, 1783.

Proceedings Relative to the Ulster Assembly of Volunteer Delegates. . . . Letters from the Duke of Richmond, Dr. Price, Mr. Wyvill, and Others. Belfast, 1783.

A Volunteer's Queries in Spring, 1780. Dublin, 1780.

NEAR CONTEMPORARY

Barrington, Sir Jonah. *The Rise and Fall of the Irish Nation.* Dublin, 1863.

Curry, John. *An Historical and Critical Review of the Civil Wars in Ireland . . . With the State of the Irish Catholics . . . to 1778.* Dublin, 1793.

Flood, W. H. *Memoirs of the Life and Correspondence of . . . Henry Flood. . . .* Dublin, 1838.

Hardy, Francis. *Memoirs of . . . James Caulfield, Earl of Charlemont.* London, 1810.

An Old Juror. *Observations on the Grand Jury Law of Ireland. . . .* Cork, 1817.

Plowden, Francis. *An Historical Review of the State of Ireland, from . . . Henry II to its Union with Great Britain.* London, 1803, Vols. I–II.

Tyerman, Rev. L. *The Life and Times of Rev. John Wesley.* New York, 1872, Vol. III.

Wakefield, Edward. *An Account of Ireland, Statistical and Political.* London, 1812.

Wyse, Thomas. *Historical Sketch of the Late Catholic Association of Ireland.* London, 1829, Vols. I–II.

MORE MODERN

Ashton, T. S. *Economic Fluctuations in England 1700–1800.* London, 1959.

Beckett, J. C. *Protestant Dissent in Ireland, 1687–1780*. London, 1948.

Black, E. C. *The Association, British Extraparliamentary Political Organization 1769–1793*. Harvard University Press, 1963.

Briggs, Asa. "The Language of 'Class' in Early Nineteenth-Century England," *Essays in Labor History: In Memory of G. D. H. Cole*. Asa Briggs and John Saville, eds. New York, 1960.

Burns, R. E. "The Belfast Letters, the Irish Volunteers 1778–79 and the Catholics," *Review of Politics*, XXI (October, 1959).

Burns, R. E. "The Catholic Relief Act in Ireland, 1778," *Church History*, (June, 1963).

Butterfield, Herbert. *George III, Lord North and the People, 1779–1780*. London, 1949.

Christie, Ian R. *The End of North's Ministry, 1780–1782*. London, 1958.

Cogan, Anthony. *Diocese of Meath, Ancient and Modern*. Dublin, 1862–1870, Vols. I–III.

Coupland, R. *The American Revolution and the British Empire*. London, 1930.

de Moleyns, Thomas. *The Landowners and Agents Practical Guide*. Dublin, 1899.

Donaldson, A. G. *Some Comparative Aspects of Irish Law*. Duke University Press, 1957.

Dunaway, W. F. *The Scotch-Irish of Colonial Pennsylvania*. University of North Carolina Press, 1944.

Falkiner, C. L. *Essays Relating to Ireland*. London, 1909.

Fitzmaurice, Lord Edmond George. *Life of William, Earl of Shelburne, Afterwards First Marquis of Lansdowne*. . . . London, 1912, Vols. I–II.

Froude, J. A. *The English in Ireland in the Eighteenth Century*. New York, 1881, Vols. I–III.

Harlow, V. T. *The Founding of the Second British Empire, 1763–1793*. London, 1952, Vol. I (one volume only).

Inglis, Brian. *The Freedom of the Press in Ireland, 1784–1841*. London, 1954.

James, F. G. "Irish Smuggling in the Eighteenth Century," *Irish Historical Studies,* (September, 1961).

Johnston, Edith M. *Great Britain and Ireland, 1760–1800.* Edinburgh, 1963.

——— "The Career and Correspondence of Thomas Allan, c. 1725–1798," *Irish Historical Studies.* (March, 1957).

Lecky, W. E. H. *A History of Ireland in the Eighteenth Century.* London, 1892, Vols. I–V.

Lorwin, V. R. *The French Labor Movement.* Harvard University Press, 1954.

Lyne, James. *A Treatise on Leases for Lives, Renewable for ever.* Dublin, 1838.

McDowell, R. B. *Irish Public Opinion, 1750–1800.* London, 1944.

McDowell, R. B. "United Irish Plans of Parliamentary Reform," *Irish Historical Studies,* (March, 1942).

MacGeehin, Maureen, see Wall, Maureen.

MacNevin, Thomas. *The History of the Volunteers of 1782.* Dublin, undated.

Mahoney, T. H. D. *Edmund Burke and Ireland.* Oxford University Press, 1960.

Mercredy, T. T. *The Law of Fee Farm Grants.* Dublin, 1877.

Murray, Alice E. *A History of the Commercial and Financial Relations between England and Ireland from the Period of the Restoration.* London, 1903.

O'Brien, George. *The Economic History of Ireland in the Eighteenth Century.* Dublin, 1918.

O'Connell, Basil M. "The Nagles of Garnavilla," *The Irish Genealogist,* (July, 1956).

O'Connell, M. R. "Class conflict in a pre-industrial society: Dublin in 1780," *Duquesne Review,* (Fall, 1963).

O'Connor, T. M. "The Embargo on the export of Irish provisions 1776–1779," *Irish Historical Studies,* (March, 1940).

O'Sullivan, William. *The Economic History of Cork City*

from the Earliest Times to the Act of Union, (Cork University Press, 1937).

Ridgeway, William. *Reports of Cases . . . in the High Court of Parliament in Ireland. . . .* Dublin, 1795.

Rogers, Patrick. *The Irish Volunteers and Catholic Emancipation, 1778–1793.* London, 1934.

Simms, J. G. *The Williamite Confiscation in Ireland, 1690–1703.* London, 1956.

Wall, Maureen. "The Catholics of the Towns and the Quarterage Dispute in Eighteenth-Century Ireland," *Irish Historical Studies,* (September, 1952).

———— "The Catholic Merchants, Manufacturers and Traders of Dublin 1778–1782," *Reportium Novum,* II (1959–60).

———— *The Penal Laws, 1691–1760: Church and State from the Treaty of Limerick to the Accession of George III.* Dundalk, 1961.

Wall, Thomas. *The Sign of Doctor Hay's Head.* Dublin, 1958.

Watson, J. S. *The Reign of George III, 1760–1815.* Oxford University Press, 1960.

Wector, Dixon. "Benjamin Franklin and an Irish 'Enthusiast,' " *Huntingdon Library Quarterly,* (January, 1941).

Index

Abingdon, Willoughby (Bertie), 4th Earl of, 336

Administration, Irish, *see* Government, Irish

Africa, 52, 216

Agar, Charles, Protestant Archbishop of Cashel, 208–209, 276

Aldborough, John (Stratford), 1st Earl of, 285

Allan, Thomas, M.P., 53, 188

America, Americans, Patriots' attitude to, 25; comparisons with Ireland, 17, 27, 30–31, 146, 190, 335, 396; effect of smallpox on, 31; religion in, 31–32, 109, 290; concessions to, 53; Newry address hostile to, 69–70; soldiers in Ireland sent to, 71, 133; hostile to Catholics, 106, 124; Irish immigration, 29, 106, 131, 144, 152, 356; praise of, 116, 380, 382; lost to Britain, 120, 130–33; difficulty in moving troops from one province to another, 237; demand the "rights of Englishmen," 344; unpopular peace treaty with, 360; political structure, 380–82; suffrage in, 381; 44, 146, 191, 196–97, 216, 228, 290

American Revolution, Irish Parliament and, 25–27; Irish sympathy with, 31–35; effect on Irish economy, 38, 152; Catholic Bishop of Ossory on, 111; 146

American Revolutionary War, developments in Ireland during, 22, 394; Irish Parliament and, 27, 308–309; and economic depression in Ireland, 37, 50, 152, 156–57, 394; comparison with Irish situation, 146, 150; 190

Anglicans, legal position in Ireland, 16–17; sense of national identity, 20; sympathy with Americans, 28, 32, 124; emigration to America, 28, 31; attitude to American Revolution, 32–35; power of, 103; Shelburne's opinion of Anglican Church, 356; conciliation with Catholics and Presbyterians, 358; 121, 190, 209, 354, 376, 379; *see also* Protestants

Annaly, John (Gore), 1st Baron,

415

ment, 133, 144; decides to concede Free Trade, 137, 187, 189, 192; neglect of Ireland, 144, 146, 149, 157, 159, 189; negligence of, 157; suggests Union with Ireland, 161; refuses to alter policy on Free Trade, 173; seeks low sugar duty, 220, 248; on legislative independence, 227, 325, 339–340; on Irish Mutiny Bill, 235–36, 238–41; on Tenantry Bill, 281; many resolved to support, 295; against recognising the Volunteers, 305, 307; bitterly attacked by Flood, 310; realises the dangerous state of Ireland, 325; fall of North's Government, 325–26; instructs Portland to have Irish Parliament adjourned, 326; makes constitutional concession, 327–28; new ministry formed by Shelburne, 330; attitude to royal addresses from Volunteers, 334–35; approves of formation of Fencibles, 338; decides to enact Renunciation Bill, 342; hopes for constitutional treaty with Ireland, 343–44; usually able to control Irish Parliament, 344; opposes parliamentary reform, 376, 387; defeated by Patriots, 394; *passim*

Government, Irish, unable to organize a militia, 38, 63, 72–74, 85; facing ruin, 42; retrenchment, 42; arguments on embargo, 46–47; disappointed in Hussey Burgh, 48; fears effect on Ireland of rejection of trade concessions, 60; financial embarrassment of, 37–38, 62–

63, 71–74, 85, 87–88; withholds official recognition from Volunteers, 85–87, 307; on Catholic relief, 109–110, 113, 118, 123, 354–56; weakness of its position, 134, 160, 206, 220–21, 234–35, 238–39, 255–56, 295, 329, 334; recovery of, 232, 234–35, 247, 249, 250, 253–55, 258–59, 282, 311–312; called on to prosecute for seditious libel, 252; on Tenantry Bill, 277; merchants resolved to support, 295; newspapers well disposed to, 302; offered services by Volunteers on alarm of invasion, 305; jubilant over Commons' loyalty vote on news of Yorktown, 309; buys support of *Freeman's Journal* 312, 336; dismissal of Flood, 314; fails to realize growing strength of Volunteers in 1781, 319; does not realize importance of Armagh meeting, 320; Buckinghamshire's and Carlisle's administrations compared, 323; "change of men and measures", 329–330; attitude to royal address by Volunteers 334–35; forms Fencible regiments, 338; attempts to sow dissension among Volunteers, 342; arrangement with Charlemont 342–43; influence in Irish Commons, 374; gives official recognition to Volunteers, 360–61; thanks Volunteers, 376; and Presbyterian relief 122, 206, 357; *passim*

Gower, Granville (Leveson-Gower), 2nd Earl, 146, 301, 302